T0234052

Connecting Arduino to the Web

Front End Development Using JavaScript

Indira Knight

Apress®

Connecting Arduino to the Web: Front End Development Using JavaScript

Indira Knight
London, United Kingdom

ISBN-13 (pbk): 978-1-4842-3479-2   ISBN-13 (electronic): 978-1-4842-3480-8
https://doi.org/10.1007/978-1-4842-3480-8

Library of Congress Control Number: 2018946546

Copyright © 2018 by Indira Knight

This work is subject to copyright. All rights are reserved by the Publisher, whether the whole or part of the material is concerned, specifically the rights of translation, reprinting, reuse of illustrations, recitation, broadcasting, reproduction on microfilms or in any other physical way, and transmission or information storage and retrieval, electronic adaptation, computer software, or by similar or dissimilar methodology now known or hereafter developed.

Trademarked names, logos, and images may appear in this book. Rather than use a trademark symbol with every occurrence of a trademarked name, logo, or image we use the names, logos, and images only in an editorial fashion and to the benefit of the trademark owner, with no intention of infringement of the trademark.

The use in this publication of trade names, trademarks, service marks, and similar terms, even if they are not identified as such, is not to be taken as an expression of opinion as to whether or not they are subject to proprietary rights.

While the advice and information in this book are believed to be true and accurate at the date of publication, neither the authors nor the editors nor the publisher can accept any legal responsibility for any errors or omissions that may be made. The publisher makes no warranty, express or implied, with respect to the material contained herein.

Managing Director, Apress Media LLC: Welmoed Spahr
Acquisitions Editor: Natalie Pao
Development Editor: James Markham
Coordinating Editor: Jessica Vakili

Cover designed by eStudioCalamar

Cover image designed by Freepik (www.freepik.com)

Distributed to the book trade worldwide by Springer Science+Business Media New York, 233 Spring Street, 6th Floor, New York, NY 10013. Phone 1-800-SPRINGER, fax (201) 348-4505, e-mail orders-ny@springer-sbm.com, or visit www.springeronline.com. Apress Media, LLC is a California LLC and the sole member (owner) is Springer Science + Business Media Finance Inc (SSBM Finance Inc). SSBM Finance Inc is a **Delaware** corporation.

For information on translations, please e-mail rights@apress.com, or visit http://www.apress.com/rights-permissions.

Apress titles may be purchased in bulk for academic, corporate, or promotional use. eBook versions and licenses are also available for most titles. For more information, reference our Print and eBook Bulk Sales web page at http://www.apress.com/bulk-sales.

Any source code or other supplementary material referenced by the author in this book is available to readers on GitHub via the book's product page, located at www.apress.com/978-1-4842-3479-2. For more detailed information, please visit http://www.apress.com/source-code.

Printed on acid-free paper

Table of Contents

iii

About the Author

Indira Knight is an accomplished developer and motion designer who has expertise in computer programming and broadcast graphics. For the last eight years she has concentrated on web development and data visualizations. She is a Creative Technologist and has worked on prototypes and projects that have included connecting web interfaces with Arduino. She is also an active member in the development community and in 2017 started a meetup in London on WebXR.

Indira holds a master's degree in 3D Computer Animation from Bournemouth University and also a master's degree in Computer Science from Birkbeck, University of London. She has worked on web applications, interactive art installations, popular game titles, independent films, and for network television.

About the Technical Reviewer

Mark Furman, MBA is a systems engineer, author, teacher, and entrepreneur. For the last 18 years, he has worked in the Information Technology field with a focus on Linux based systems and programming in Python, working for a range of companies including Host Gator, Interland, Suntrust Bank, AT&T, and Winn-Dixie. Currently, he has been focusing his career on the maker movement and has launched Tech Forge (`techforge.org`). He holds a Master's degree in Business Administration from Ohio University with a focus on Business Intelligence. You can follow him on Twitter @mfurman.

Introduction

Being able to create physical interfaces for web pages opens up new areas for innovation and creativity. It allows you to think of your project in two different mediums. You can create interactive displays and games, set up IoT components, then collect and process your own data; you can express your ideas in new ways.

An Arduino is a great way to create physical interfaces. It was designed to be an easy-to-use electronics platform that allows you to attach electronic components that can send and receive data. The respected Arduino community can be very helpful and creative if you need assistance.

The electronic components can be inputs or outputs. I have seen Arduinos used to create music, light shows, ovens, robots, art, and so much more. There is such a wide range of components including buttons, motors, potentiometers, sensors, and buzzers that can be attached to an Arduino.

Arduinos can send and receive data from a web server. This means you can control elements on a web page with physical components and use physical components to display information from your web page or online data.

To do this you need an understanding of both electronics and programming. While this book is not an introduction to programming or electronics, it will give you the information you need to get an Arduino to interact with a web server.

You will be using two programming languages: JavaScript for the web programming; and the Arduino programming language, which is a set of C and C++ functions.

This book is a mixture of practical and theoretical. It tells you how and why things work, followed by exercises to build confidence and understanding. It gives you a taste of different programming language techniques, including how to make a web server, data visualization, and 3D animation. It will give you a grounding to understand the concepts involved and a starting point to creating your own projects.

If you are interested in exploring the boundless possibilities of the physical and digital, this book is for you. It will give you an understanding of how IoT and connected devices work and allow you to find new ways to interact with your audience. It covers the electronics and programming you need to get started to build physical interfaces for web pages.

In This Book

Chapter 1. Arduino, Circuits and Components covers the electronic basics you will need for the book including Arduino hardware and software; electricity in circuits; connecting components; and the four basic Arduino circuits: analog input, analog output, digital input, and digital output.

Chapter 2. Creating a Web Server will give you an understanding of web technologies and how to set up a Node.js server and send data to a web page using WebSockets.

Chapter 3. Arduino to Front End (Part I) joins together the knowledge from the first two chapters so you can start sending data from an Arduino to a web page.

Chapter 4. Introduction to Creating Web Content looks at how web pages are formed using HTML, CSS, SVG, and basic JavaScript.

Chapter 5. Front End to Arduino covers the techniques needed to send data from a Node.js server to an Arduino and ways to display the data with electronic components. You will use LEDs and LCDs to display data.

Chapter 6. Arduino to Front End (Part II) continues from Chapter 3 with a more in-depth look at how components can interact with elements on a web page. You will be displaying metrics collected by the Arduino.

Chapter 7. Visualizing Data is an introduction to the JavaScript library D3.js. D3.js allows you to create data visualizations on web pages. You will continue the exercise from Chapter 6 by adding a bar chart to the web page.

Chapter 8. Create a Web Dashboard first looks at the principle of data visualization and then uses sensors to gather data that is displayed on a web dashboard.

Chapter 9. Physical Data Visualization with Live Data is an introduction to web APIs and how they can be used to get data from an external web server. Earthquake data is used as an example and an LCD, LED, and Piezo are used to display the data.

Chapter 10. Creating a Game Controller gets you to create a simple game with the JavaScript library Three.js, which can be controlled with a physical game controller. It covers the basics of 3D on the Web and how you can control 3D objects with a joystick attached to an Arduino.

Getting Started

There are both software and hardware requirements for this book. On the whole I have tried to use electronic components that are included in the Arduino starter kit. There are a few chapters where this hasn't been possible, and in those cases I have tried to keep to components that are cheaper and commonly available. Appendix A lists some suppliers of Arduino Components.

You will be using a number of JavaScript libraries in this book, and these libraries are constantly updated. I have worked with the same version number of the libraries throughout the book and have listed the version number needed. Though these will not be the latest version for a library, they do all work together. As different people write the libraries, updates to one can break how it works with another.

You will need a code text editor to write your code, and there are a number available online that can be downloaded such as Sublime Text, Atom, and Visual Studio code. Different developers will prefer different editors, and some are geared more toward certain programming languages.

The exercises have been tested on a Mac and PC. They have been fully tested on MacOS Sierra version 10.12.5 and Windows 10 Home and should also work on Mac OS X version 10.8.5. They have also been tested on Chrome and Firefox web browsers. On the Mac they have been tested on Chrome 49.0.2623.112. On a PC they have been tested on Chrome version 63.0.3239.132. They should also work on Firefox 57.0.4 and Firefox 45.9.0.

In 2015 a version of JavaScript was released that included major changes to the language, including new functionality and changes to syntax. The version was called ECMAScript 6, or ES6, and later was called ES2015. This book is based on ES5 versions of JavaScript and does not include the new syntax or functions from ES6 or later. This is because not all browsers support the new versions of JavaScript in the same way, and further libraries would need to be used. This book will give you an understanding of the principles of JavaScript and how it works. In Appendix B there are some details of the functionality that was added in later versions of JavaScript.

It's now time to get started. Chapter 1 will introduce you to the Arduino and some of the basic circuits used throughout the book.

CHAPTER 1

Arduino, Circuits and Components

This chapter is an introduction to electronics for Arduino. It will explain how an Arduino is set up and how electricity flows through the circuits and the components. By the end of this chapter you will have used some basic components and created the four base circuits: analog input, analog output, digital input, and digital output.

Arduino

Arduino allows you to create your own electronics projects. It is a collection of open source hardware and software that allows you to attach and control other components to create an electrical circuit. Projects such as an automated plant watering system, a pizza oven, or a remote controlled toy car can be made with an Arduino. When you use an Arduino for a project you need to do the following:

- Connect components to it.

- Write a program to control the components.

- Verify that the program is written correctly.

- Upload the program to the Arduino.

© Indira Knight 2018
I. Knight, *Connecting Arduino to the Web*, https://doi.org/10.1007/978-1-4842-3480-8_1

The Arduino needs to be connected to a computer via a USB port to upload a program to it. Programs for Arduinos are called sketches. Once the sketch is uploaded, it is stored on the microcontroller and will stay there until another sketch is uploaded. Once a new sketch is uploaded the old sketch is no longer available.

Once the sketch is uploaded you can disconnect the Arduino from the computer, and if it is connected to another power source the program will still run.

Note   Once a sketch has been uploaded to an Arduino, it is not represented in the same way you wrote it. You cannot get the sketch back from the Arduino in a form that can be read as the original sketch, so make sure that you save your original code if you want to keep it.

Arduino Hardware

An Arduino board is made up of a number of components, including a microcontroller, digital and analog pins, power pins, resistors, a diode, a capacitor, and an LED. Figure 1-1 shows an Arduino Uno.

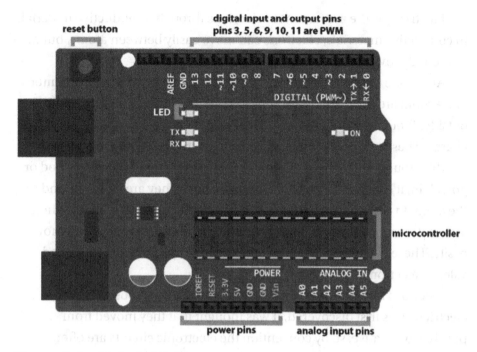

Figure 1-1. *An Arduino Uno*

A Microcontroller has a central processing unit (CPU); it stores the uploaded sketch and processes and directs the commands.

The digital and analog pins are used for sending and receiving digital and analog data.

The Arduino also has a serial interface that allows the Arduino to send data to a computer via the serial port; this is the way we will be sending data to and from a computer in this book.

Electricity

With an Arduino you create an electronic circuit that powers the components attached to it. Wires made of a conductive material connect the components that let electricity flow through them.

Electricity is the movement of electrons through a conductive material. In conductive materials, electrons can move easily between atoms, but in non-conductive materials they can't.

Atoms are made up of protons, neutrons, and electrons. In the center of the atom are the nucleus, protons and neutrons; electrons are on the outside. Protons have a positive charge and electrons have a negative charge. These two charges are attracted to each other. The electrons are in orbit around the nucleus. In non-conductive materials such as wood or porcelain, it is difficult for the electrons to move; they are tightly bound to the atom. In conductive materials such as copper and other metals, there are electrons that are quite loosely bound to the atoms, so they can move easily. These electrons are on the outer edge of the atom and are called valence electrons.

Electrons move around the circuit from negative to positive. When electricity was first discovered, it was thought that they moved from positive to negative, so by convention the electronic circuits are often drawn from positive to negative, positive to ground (GND). In the circuits in this book the electricity will be flowing in one direction; this is called a direct current (DC), and in an alternating current (AC) the direction changes a certain number of times a second.

To get the electrons in a conductive material to start moving they need a push, and this push is the voltage. Voltage is the difference between higher potential energy and lower potential energy in a circuit. The electrons want to flow from higher potential energy to lower potential energy, from the positive to the ground.

There are a number of ways that voltage is produced. In a battery, it is produced by a chemical reaction. A build-up of electrons is created at the negative end of the battery. When a connection is made to the positive end of the battery, the negative electrons are attracted to the positive, from the higher potential energy to the lower potential energy. This causes them to push the electrons on the wire; the electrons are shunted along the wire.

In Electricity current is the amount of electrons per second that passes a certain point. The current is measured in amps. Each component on the circuit uses up part of the electricity and turns it into another form of energy such as light or sound. The components on the circuit use all the energy in the circuit.

A circuit also has resistance. Resistance is how much the material the current is flowing through slows it down. Resistance is like an obstacle in the way of the current. Resistance is measured in ohms and uses the symbol Ω. Electricity will always choose the easiest way to flow, the path of least resistance. Figure 1-2 is an interpretation of the relationship between voltage, current, and resistance.

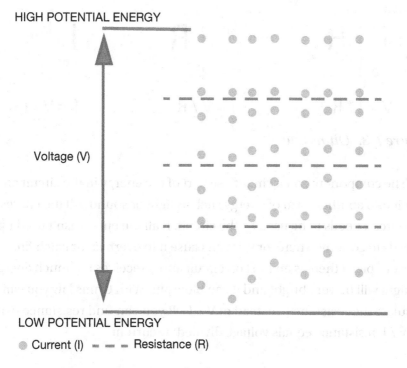

Figure 1-2. An interpretation of voltage, current, and resistance

Ohms Law

The physicist and mathematician Georg Simon Ohm discovered a relationship between voltage, current, and resistance; this relationship is called Ohms law. Ohms law says that voltage is equal to amps multiplied by resistance, and it is written as V = I * R where V is volts, I is current, and R is resistance. With this formula you can also find resistance R = V / I and to find current I = V / R, these can be seen in Figure 1-3.

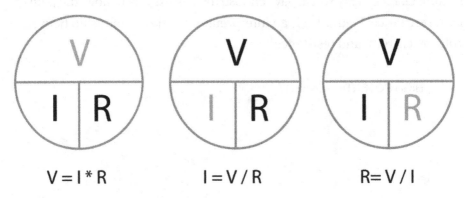

$$V = I * R \qquad I = V / R \qquad R = V / I$$

Figure 1-3. *Ohms law*

The components on a circuit use part of the energy in the circuit and turn it into another form of energy such as light or sound. All the energy on a circuit needs to be used by the circuit. If all the energy isn't used up it needs to go somewhere, or this can cause it to overheat or catch fire. For example, if there is an LED on circuit and it receives too much energy, the light will be very bright and it can blow out. With Ohms law you can calculate the resistance, instead of V = I * R you can find resistance using R = V / I, resistance equals voltage divided by current.

Resistors

Resistors are a crucial component for circuits as they limit the amount of current on the circuit. A resistor has a certain amount of resistance to the current flow. Every component has a maximum amount of current, measured in amps that it can safely use. For example, if a component can take a maximum of 0.023 amps, which is 23 milliamps, and your circuit is receiving 5V (volts), then a 220-ohm resistor will need to be added to the circuit to use the LED safely. The electrical components will use some of the power from the circuit; this is called a voltage drop so this can be taken into account when working out resistance. Figure 1-4 shows an example of how this is worked out with Ohms law, with different voltages and current.

$$resistance = \frac{voltage}{current}$$

resistance for a component that uses a maximum of 0.023 amps in a 5V circuit

$$resistance = \frac{5V}{0.023\ amps} = 217\ ohms$$

A 220 ohm resistor would be used, the closest resistor to 217

resistance for a component on a 5V circuit that uses a maximum of 0.02 amps and uses 2V (a 2V voltage drop)

$$resistance = \frac{5V - 2V}{0.02\ amps} = 150\ ohms$$

Figure 1-4. *The formulae to find the resistance needed for a circuit*

When you get a component, it should also have a data sheet, which may be online. This will give you information about the voltage drop and the maximum amps. This will allow you to work out what resistor you need for your circuit.

Resistors have a value measured in ohms; they have a color code to show that value. The value of the resistor tells you what amount of current it will dissipate.

Electronic Circuit Diagrams

Circuit diagrams visually describe a circuit. There are sets of icons that are used for showing components on electronic circuits. In this book I won't be using electronic circuit diagrams to show the circuits used in the projects but will use images of the Arduino and the components. Figure 1-5 gives you an idea of what a circuit diagram looks like. It is the circuit diagram for an LED.

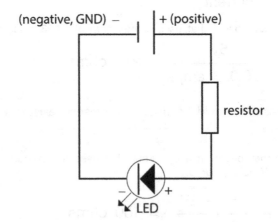

Figure 1-5. *A circuit diagram for an LED with a resistor*

Figure 1-6 shows some of the icons that can be used in a circuit diagram.

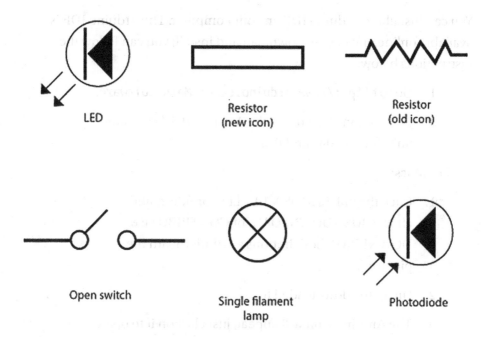

Figure 1-6. *Some circuit diagram icons*

Arduino Software

Arduino has its own programming language; it is a set of C and C++ functions. Arduino programs are called sketches, and they have a .ion extension. Arduino has its own integrated development environment (IDE) that has an editor and other tools to help you write and upload the code.

Downloading and Setting Up the Arduino IDE

You can install the Arduino IDE on your computer. The Arduino IDE is available online and easy to download and install; you can follow the instructions below:

1. Go to `https://www.arduino.cc/en/Main/Software`.

2. The section "Download the Arduino IDE" contains links for the Mac and PC.

For Macs:

1. Click the link Mac OS X 10.7 Lion or newer and choose JUST DOWNLOAD, or CONTRIBUTE & DOWNLOAD; both buttons are underneath the picture.

2. Unzip the downloaded file.

3. The Arduino icon will appear, just click on it to open the IDE.

For PC:

1. Click the link Windows Installer or Windows ZIP file for non-admin install depending on the Admin rights you have on your computer. Choose JUST DOWNLOAD, or CONTRIBUTE & DOWNLOAD.

2. Unzip the download file.

3. You should be able to open the IDE with the icon.

When you open the IDE a new sketch should open. Figure 1-7 is an example of an edit window.

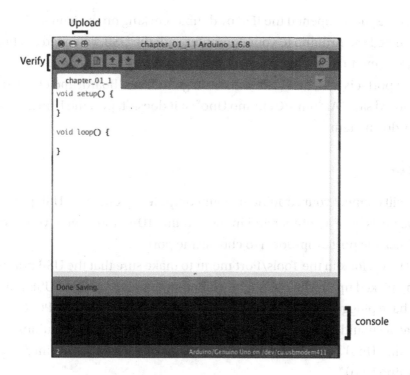

Figure 1-7. *An Arduino IDE edit window*

The sketch will contain two functions, setup and loop. There is a tick icon at the top of the page. This is pressed to verify that your code is written correctly. If there are any problems you will get a message in the console in red. The arrow icon is clicked when you want to upload the sketch to your Arduino. The console will show you messages connected to your sketch. It will show you any errors in your code and information when the sketch is verified and uploaded.

Connecting an Arduino to a Computer

You will need a USB 2.0 type B cable to connect an Arduino Uno to your computer. The USB will be used to send data to and from the Arduino as well as powering it. Different types of Arduinos will use different types of cable.

Once you've opened the IDE by double-clicking on the icon and connected the Arduino to your computer with the USB, you need to check the tools menu to see that the Arduino Uno is listed as the board and which port it is attached to. In the menu go to Tools/Board, and check that the board says "Arduino/Genuino Uno"; if it doesn't, pick the Uno from the drop-down menu.

Ports

You will connect your Arduino to your computer by one of its USB ports; these ports have a number and in the Arduino IDE's tool menu, you need to check the port drop-down to choose the port.

Have a look in the Tools/Port menu to make sure that the USB port is being picked up. It will look slightly different depending which USB port you have plugged the Arduino into and if you are on a Mac or a PC. On a Mac it should say something like "dev/cu.usbmodem621 (Arduino/ Genuino Uno)". On a PC it will say something like "COM4 (Arduino/ Genuino Uno)."

WRITE A SKETCH

An Arduino has a built-in LED so the easiest sketch to write is one that controls this and makes it blink. It is the first sketch most people will write and is so common that the Arduino you have might already have it installed when you get it.

The Arduino IDE has a number of example sketches and blink is one of them. In the IDE, if you go to File/Examples/01.Basics you will see the blink sketch. You can either open it from there or copy it from the code in Listing 1-1. You will need to save it before you upload it.

Listing 1-1. blink.ino

```
void setup() {
  pinMode(13, OUTPUT);
}
void loop() {
  digitalWrite(13, HIGH);
  delay(1000);
  digitalWrite(13, LOW);
  delay(1000);
}
```

The Code Explained

Whenever you open a new sketch you will always be given the setup and the loop functions. The setup function is called once when the program is first run. The loop function will keep looping and carrying out the commands in it while the Arduino has power. blink.ino is using the LED on the Arduino and controlling it. This LED is at digital pin 13 on the Arduino, so in the setup you use the pinMode function to say that pin 13 is being used as an output, and it will light up.

The loop has a digitalWrite function that tells pin 13 if it should be high or low (on or off). The delay function pauses the loop for a bit; otherwise it would just run onto the next line of code once it had finished the previous line. The delay is in milliseconds. Table 1-1 explains blink.ino in more detail.

Table 1-1. `blink.ino` *explained*

```void setup() { pinMode(13, OUTPUT); }```	setup is a function. Functions can return values, in this language you need to declare what it will return when you write the function. Both setup() and loop() don't return anything so the void keyword goes before them. A function is made up of the function name followed by parentheses. The parentheses can be empty or can contain arguments. The argument is passed to the function when the function is called. The curly braces enclose the code for the function.
```pinMode(13, OUTPUT);```	The Arduino library comes with a number of functions that you can use. pinMode is one of them and digitalWrite is another. When you use a function, it is called calling a function. To call a function you write the function name followed by parentheses. If the function is expecting arguments, they are put inside the parentheses. If it's not they are left empty. The call to the function is finished with a semicolon. The semicolon lets the program compiler know that it is the end of the call or the command.

You can verify the code to check that it is syntactically correct, then upload it to the Arduino. To verify it you press the tick arrow at the top of the code, and to upload it you click on the arrow icon. These are both shown in Figure 1-7.

Note   The Arduino IDE is very sensitive to syntax errors, if you forget a ";" at the end of a command, or write something in lower case when it should be in upper case you will get an error. The IDE is pretty good at letting you know where the error is and they are normally easy to fix.

The Breadboard

The breadboard is used in electronics for prototyping; it is a way to attach components to an Arduino without soldering. It is made of plastic and has a series of holes in it for the pins of the components and for wires. They commonly have two strips of holes down either side for power and ground. Inside the breadboard are strips of metal that are conductive. The wires and pins connect with these strips of metal to make a circuit. They can come in different sizes. Figure 1-8 shows a breadboard.

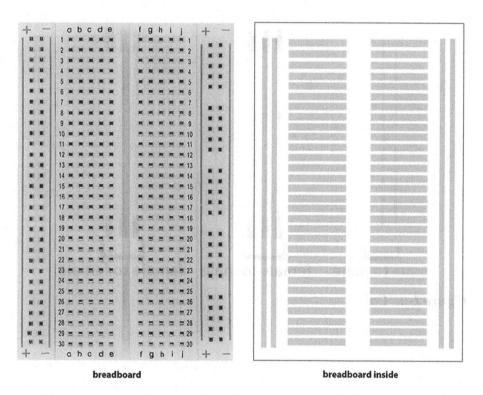

breadboard   breadboard inside

Figure 1-8. *A Breadboard*

Cables

The Arduino starter kit comes with a number of cables you can use in most of the projects to make a circuit between the Arduino and components using a breadboard. There are some components that have pins that are hard to fit into a breadboard. In Chapter 10 when you make a game controller, you may need to use cables with a different head. There three types of cables: male to male, female to male, and female to female. They are shown in Figure 1-9.

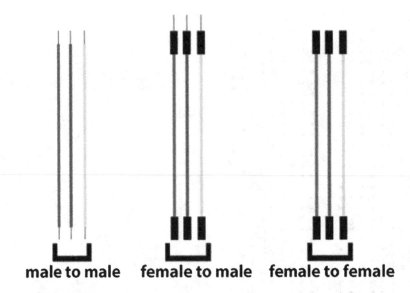

male to male   female to male   female to female

Figure 1-9. *Cables*

Digital and Analog

On an Arduino you can use digital input, digital output, analog input, and analog output. A digital input or output can have one of two states, on or off (high or low). The analog input or output can be between 0 and 1023 when 5V is being used. The following exercises in this chapter show examples of digital output and input, and analog input and output.

Caution   you must unplug your Arduino when you are connecting components. While it is connected to your computer, it has electricity running through it, which could cause an electric shock. If there is too much power for a component, it can pop or explode so you don't want to be too close if that happens.

DIGITAL OUTPUT

A component used for digital output receives a HIGH signal for on and a LOW signal for off. The code in Listing 1-1 uses digital output. In this exercise you will use the same code as in Listing 1-1, blink.ino, which is an LED attached to the Arduino. For this you will need:

- 1 x Arduino Uno

- 1 x LED

- 1 x 220 ohm resistor

The components are shown in Figure 1-10 and the setup of the components is shown in Figure 1-11. Make sure you have unplugged your Arduino from the computer or any power source before attaching the components. The long leg of the Arduino is positive, and the short leg is negative.

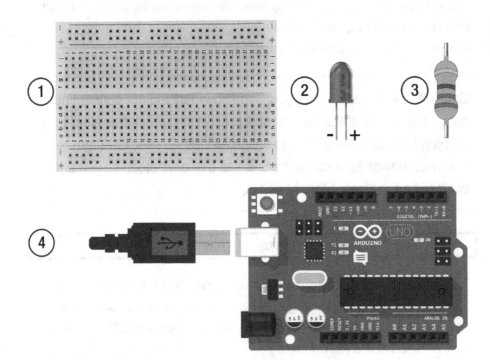

Figure 1-10. *Components for the digital output exercise:*
1. Breadboard, 2. LED, 3. 220 Ohm resistor, 4. Arduino Uno

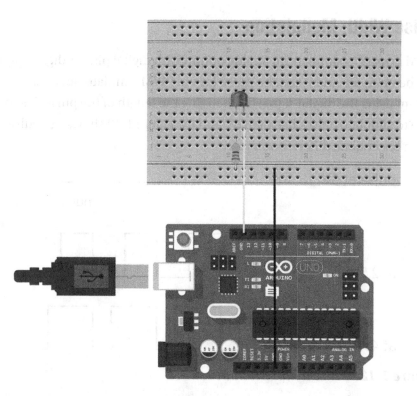

Figure 1-11. *Setup for the components for the digital output exercise*

Plug your Arduino back into your computer with the USB. If the last program you uploaded was the blink.ino, then you should see the LED blinking. If not, upload the blink.ino again.

Analog Output

Analog output and input produce a range of numbers that go up and down in sequence. On an Arduino some of the digital pins have a "~" symbol next to them. These pins are used for analog output and use PWM (pulse width modulation).

Pulse Width Modulation

PWM is used to simulate an analog output with digital pins. A digital signal can be on or off, and it sends a pulse for on. PWM simulates an analog system using the digital signal by changing the length of the pulse; it's "on" time to simulate pulses between 5V and 0V. Figure 1-12 shows the pulse width to simulate different voltages.

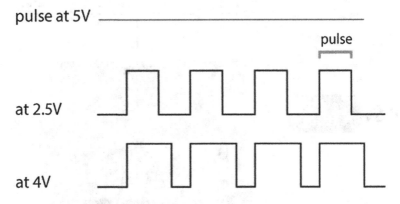

Figure 1-12. *Pulse width modulation*

ANALOG OUTPUT

As the analog signal can produce a range of numbers, you can do things gradually. In this exercise an LED will fade up slowly before turning off then fading up again. The components for this exercise are the same as Figure 1-10. Make sure the Arduino is unplugged, and then set up the components as shown in Figure 1-13. The LED is connected to digital pin 9, which has a ~ next to it. Create a new ino sketch, I called mine chapter_01_1.ino, and copy the code from Listing 1-2 into it.

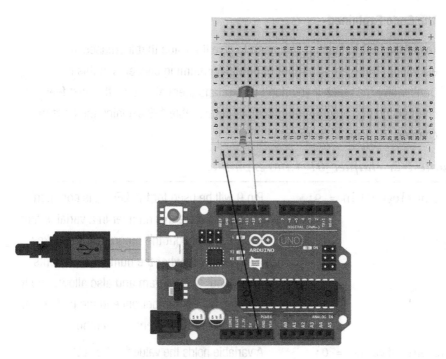

Figure 1-13. *Setup for analog output*

Listing 1-2. chapter_01_1.ino

```
int analogOutPin = 9;
int outputValue = 0;

void setup() {
  pinMode(analogOutPin, OUTPUT);
}

void loop() {
  if (outputValue >= 40){
    outputValue = 0;
  } else {
    outputValue = outputValue + 1;
  }
  analogWrite(analogOutPin, outputValue);
  delay(200);
}
```

21

The Code Explained

To get the LED to fade up, you need to give it a value that increases in each loop. There are a number of new programming concepts in this code. Don't worry too much if you don't understand them all yet, as the next few chapters go into programming in more detail. Table 1-2 explains the code in chapter_01_1.ino in more detail.

Table 1-2. *chapter_01_1.ino explained*

`int analogOutPin = 9;`	Pin 9 will be used for the LED; it is common practice to store this number in a variable that is used throughout the program. This makes it easier to see what the number represents throughout the program and also allows you to change the pin number once in the code if you decide to use a different pin number.
`int outputValue = 0;`	A variable holds the value for the LED.

`if (outputValue >= 40){`
`    outputValue = 0;`
`} else {`
`    outputValue = output`
`    Value + 1;`
`}`
	An if else statement checks if something is true; if it is it does one thing and if not it does another. In this case it checks if the value of the variable outPutValue is greater or equal to 40; if it is it makes the variable contain the value 0, which turns the LED off, and if not it increases it by 1, turning the brightness on the LED up.

`analogWrite(analogOutPin,` `outputValue);`	The analogWrite function has two arguments: the pin number and a value, and in this case the value in outputValue is sent to the component attached to pin 9. In this case it is an LED, and this will change the brightness of the LED.

Upload the sketch to the Arduino; you should see the LED increase in brightness then go off.

Digital Input

A good circuit to show a digital input is a switch button. The switch button is either up or down, and it is in one of two states, pressed or not pressed. It brings in another concept called Input Pullup.

There is a problem for an Arduino with a switch. When a switch is open, it does not complete a circuit, and there is no voltage so the Arduino doesn't know what the input is; it could be 0 or it could be 1. As it doesn't know you can get strange results, it creates noise as the input value is unknown and it tries to put something in. This problem is solved with pullup resistors; it sets a voltage when the switch is open.

Pullup resistors are built into the Arduino and can be accessed when using the pinMode() function by setting it to INPUT_PULLUP instead of just INPUT. The pin will read HIGH when the switch is open and LOW when it is pressed.

DIGITAL INPUT

For this exercise, you will use a button to switch on and off the LED on the Arduino. For it you will need:

- 1 x Arduino Uno

- 1 x switch button

Remember to disconnect the Arduino from your computer when you are changing components. The switch is attached to the breadboard. One pin is attached to ground the other to digital pin 2. Figure 1-14 shows the components needed and Figure 1-15 shows the setup of the Arduino.

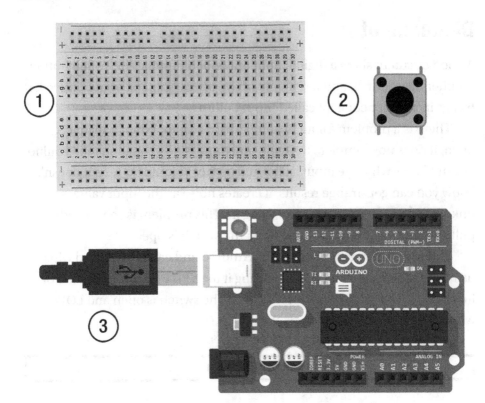

Figure 1-14. *Components for the digital input exercise:*
1. Breadboard, 2. Switch, 3. Arduino Uno

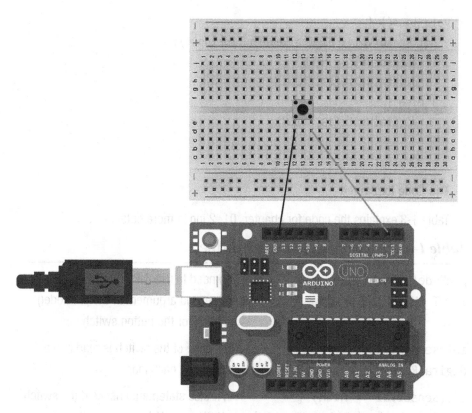

Figure 1-15. *Setup for the components for the digital input exercise*

Create a new sketch in the Arduino IDE, I called mine chapter_01_2, and copy in the code from Listing 1-3. Verify and upload the code to the Arduino. When you press the button the LED on the Arduino should light.

Listing 1-3. chapter_01_2.ino

```
int buttonInput = 2;
int LEDOutput = 13;

void setup() {
pinMode(buttonInput, INPUT_PULLUP);
  pinMode(LEDOutput, OUTPUT);
}
```

```
void loop() {
  int sensorVal = digitalRead(buttonInput);
  if (sensorVal == HIGH) {
     digitalWrite(13, LOW);
  } else {
     digitalWrite(13, HIGH);
  }
}
```

The Code Explained

Table 1-3 explains the code for chapter_01_2.ino in more detail.

Table 1-3. chapter_01_2.ino explained

pinMode(buttonInput, INPUT_PULLUP);	You need to use INPUT_PULLUP as the second argument in the pinMode() function for the button switch.
int sensorVal = digitalRead(buttonInput);	The value of the switch is read into a variable on each loop.

if (sensorVal == HIGH) {
   digitalWrite(LEDOutput, LOW);
} else {
   digitalWrite(LEDOutput, HIGH);
}
	An if/else statement checks if the switch is HIGH or LOW. Using the pullup means that the button's logic is reversed. If it's HIGH it means it's up and so the LED is off. When it is LOW it is being pressed, which switched the LED on.

Analog Input

Analog input is used with components such as photoresitors and potentiometers, components that give varying values. An Arduino Uno can register values between 0 and 5 volts; with this you can get an analog input value between 0 and 1023. An analog input sends a signal voltage. When the signal voltage is received it is checked against an internal reference. An example is illustrated in Figure 1-16.

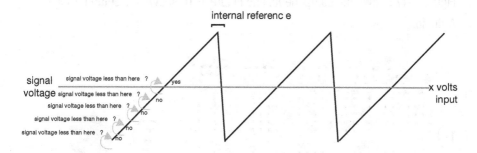

Figure 1-16. *An illustration of the analog input process*

When a signal voltage is received it is tested against the internal reference at multiple points on the line. For example, it checks if the input is greater than 0; if not, it checks if it's greater than the next number on the reference and keeps checking until it is. That point becomes the input number.

ANALOG INPUT

This exercise uses a potentiometer as an analog input. The potentiometer turns LED on the Arduino on and off when it is turned about halfway.
The components needed for this exercise are the following:

- 1 x Arduino Uno
- 1 x potentiometer

Figure 1-17 shows the components and Figure 1-18 shows the setup for the Arduino.

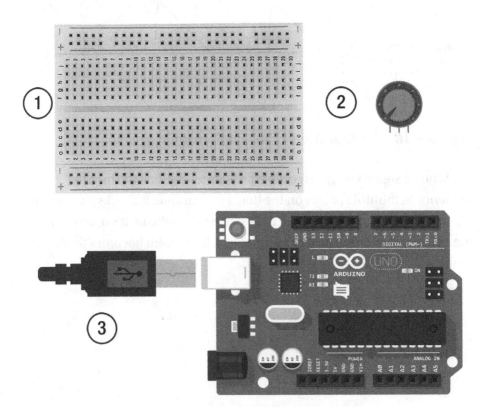

Figure 1-17. *Components for the analog input exercise:*
1. Breadboard, 2. Potentiometer, 3. Arduino Uno

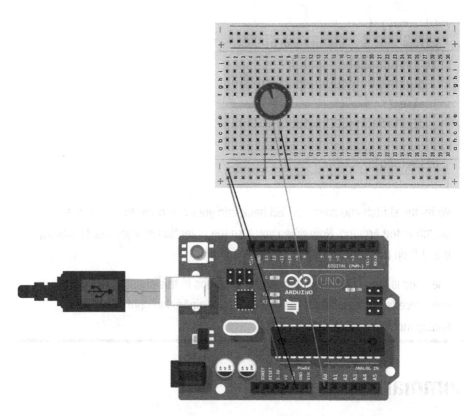

Figure 1-18. *Setup for the components for the analog input exercise*

Open a new sketch. I called it chapter_01_3; and then copy the code from
Listing 1-4.

Listing 1-4. chapter_01_3.ino

```
int pinAnalogInput  =  AO;
int LEDOutput = 13;
int valueLight =  0;

void setup() {
  pinMode(LEDOutput, OUTPUT);
}
```

```
void loop() {
  valueLight =  analogRead(pinAnalogInput);
  if (valueLight < 500) {
    digitalWrite(LEDOutput, LOW);
  } else {
    digitalWrite(LEDOutput, HIGH);
  }
  delay(500);
}
```

Verify the sketch and plug the USB back into your computer to upload the sketch to the Arduino. Now when you turn the potentiometer just past halfway, the LED on the Arduino should come off and on.

The code is very similar to the previous sketches in this chapter. The main difference is the variable for the analog pin int pinAnalogInput = A0; The analog input goes through pin A0;

Summary

This chapter was a basic introduction to the Arduino. It looked at how a circuit works and the analog and digital input and output. These are the basic blocks for Arduino that will be built on through the book. The next chapter will get you started with JavaScript and building a web server that will be able to receive data sent from an Arduino.

CHAPTER 2

Creating a Web Server

To get started on the web side of connecting Arduino to the Web, it is useful to have a basic understanding of web technologies. This chapter will go through some of the principles, including what a web server is, how a URL is constructed, what routes are, and what Node.js is. It will then get practical, and you will learn how to create a web server with Node.js and send data back and forth from the server to a web page. It will cover Node.js, ejs, and socket.io.

What Is a Web Server?

A web server serves pages to web browsers; it also processes information and stores data and assets for the pages. It allows requests to be processed using Hypertext Transfer Protocol (HTTP). This protocol allows networks to communicate with each other using addresses called Uniform Resource Locators (URLs), the address to your web page. URLs have a defined structure starting with the protocol, followed by the domain name, the domain extension, and an optional file and folder names; see Figure 2-1.

Figure 2-1. *URL structure*

© Indira Knight 2018

I. Knight, *Connecting Arduino to the Web*, https://doi.org/10.1007/978-1-4842-3480-8_2

A domain name is a translation into natural English of an Internet protocol (IP) address. An IP address is a series of numbers and anything that connects to the Internet has one. This includes smartphones and smart TV's; any piece of equipment connected to the Internet will have an IP address.

When computers on the Internet talk to each other they use their IP address. When you type a web address into your browser it is converted into an IP address. This tells the web server the address of the page you want. It is the route to that page. If the server finds the page it will return it back to your browser. If it can't, it will return an error page.

Web servers have a number of conventions to connect and transfer data from one computer on the network to another. One of these is representational state transfer, which is known as RESTful. It makes computer systems interoperable; this means however a server is set up, if it implements the RESTful web services it can talk to any other server that also implements them. When HTTP uses RESTful the requests GET, POST, PUT, and DELETE can be used. For example, POST allows you to fill in a form on a web page and post it to the browser.

You can create a web server on your own computer, and using Node. js is one way to do this. This means you can develop applications on your local machine and test them before deploying them. The local web server uses the domain name localhost, and this resolves to an IP address 127.0.0.1.

Routing

Without routes you would not be able to see web pages. Routing determines how a web server responds to a URL request from the web browser. Going back to example.com, the server has to know what page to serve when someone types in that URL. If you add on other pages such as example.com/about there will have to be a route in the server for this page as well. A route also tells the server how it should respond to a request.

It does this using RESTful commands; if a route starts with GET the server knows it needs to get content for a page. If it starts with POST, the server knows it will be receiving data from a web page and the route will define what should be done next.

What Is Node.js?

Node.js is a runtime environment for executing JavaScript server code. It means you can use the same language, JavaScript, on the browser and on the server. Using Node.js you can create routes to web pages, connect to localhost, connect to a database, and send data to web pages with JavaScript. It allows you to build web applications using the same language throughout.

Node.js works really well with Arduinos. Using the serial port you can use the server to pass data from an Arduino to a web page and pass Data from the web to an Arduino.

Apart from downloading Node.js you will need to download other packages that make it simpler to create the application you want. You do this with a package manager; there are a few different ones, but node package manager (npm) is used in this book.

Using a Command-Line Interface

A command-line interface is a way of sending instructions to your computer using text. You can use it for many things including moving around your computer's directories and to create new files and running code.

To work with Node.js you need to use a command-line interface. You use it to install new modules, start the server, and see messages and errors from the application.

Windows and Mac come with inbuilt command-line interface applications. In Windows it is called a command prompt or cmd.exe, and on a Mac it is called a terminal. Both will open a console window for the typing in of commands.

It is a very powerful tool and needs to be used with caution as you can wipe your system or make changes that are hard to undo.

The command-line interface is implemented in what is called a command-line shell. The shell is a program that accepts text commands and translates them into a language the operating system will understand.

When you open a console window, it should be displaying the home directory for the logged-in user. This is the top directory for that user and from it you can navigate to the files and folders of that user.

USING THE MAC TERMINAL

The Mac terminal application is located inside the utilities folder that is inside the application's folder. The path to it is the following:

Hard drive/Applications/Utilities/Terminal

When the application is open you should see a console window showing your home directory followed by $: for example:~ <username>$

Try out the following commands and review Table 2-1 for some additional ones you may find useful:

1. Open the terminal, and a new console window will open.

2. Type ls + return and you will see a list of all the files and folders at the current directory.

3. Type cd <folder name> + return and you will move into that directory.

4. Use ls to list files and directories then type cd and the directory name to move into another directory.

5. Type cd .. + return, and you will move up one folder in the directory.

6. Type cd + return, and you will move to your home directory.

7. Type Ctrl + l or Cmd+k, and both of these will clear the console screen. Crtl+l just clears the screen, and Cmd+k also clears the terminal buffer.

Table 2-1. *Some useful terminal Commands*

Command	Result
pwd	Writes the full path of the current directory
ls	Lists the content of a directory
cd <directory name>	Path to directory 1 level below
cd <directory name>/<directory name>	Path to directory 2 levels below
cd ..	Move up a directory
cd	Moves back to the home directory
mkdir <directory name>	Will make a new directory in the current directory
touch <file name.extension>	Will create a new file with that name and extension

USING THE WINDOWS COMMAND PROMPT

The windows console is called the command prompt or cmd.exe. There are a number of ways to open a command prompt console window, and these will change depending on which version of windows you are running (see Table 2-2). You can use Windows search to find the command prompt; the search is Cortana on Windows 10. Start to type in "command prompt" in the search field; the best match should be the desktop app "Command Prompt." Click on "Command Prompt" to open a console window.

When the application is open you should see a console window showing your home directory followed by a > It should look like this: C:\Users\Username>, and you start typing after the >.

Try out a few commands:

1. Open the command prompt, and a new console window will open.

2. Type dir + enter, and you should see all the files and folders in the current directory.

3. Type cd <folder name> + enter, and you will move into that folder.

4. Use ls to list files and directories and cd to move into another directory.

5. Type cd .. + enter, and you will move up one folder in the directory.

6. Type cd %userprofile% + enter to return to the home directory.

7. Type cls + enter, and the console screen will be cleared.

You can have optional arguments in a command. If you use the dir command you will see a lot of information about each file or folder in the directory. If you just wanted to see the names you would type dir /b.

Table 2-2. *Some useful command prompt commands*

Command	Result
echo %cd%	Writes the full path of the current directory dir
cd <directory name>	path to directory 1 level below the current directory
cd <directory name>/<directory name>	Path to directory 2 levels below the current directory
cd ..	Move up a directory
cd	Moves back to the home directory
mkdir <directory name>	Will make a new directory in the current directory
NUL> <filename.extension>	Will create a new file with that name and extension

Note   If you start writing a directory name in the console window and then press the tab key, the rest of the directory name will be filled in for you, as long as it is the only directory with those letters.

To move back and forward to previous commands, use the up and down arrows on the keyboard.

The Mac console is case sensitive. The Mac console is white space sensitive.

Setting Up a Node.js server

Now that the background has been covered, it's time to start coding. If you don't have Node.js installed on your computer, you will need to install it along with the node package manager. Depending on what you already have installed on your computer, it might take some time, but once it's done, further downloads are a lot quicker.

Installing Node.js

First, if you are not sure if you have Node.js installed on your computer, you can check in a console window.

CHECK IF NODE.JS IS INSTALLED

1. Open a console window.

2. At the console prompt type node -v if Node.js is installed you should see your version number (e.g., v6.10.3).

3. At the console prompt type npm -v and if npm is installed you should see the version number (e.g., 3.10.10),

If you see version numbers skip the next step on installing Node.js and go straight to the "Creating an Application" section.

INSTALL NODE.JS ON WINDOWS

In Windows you can install Node.js straight from the Node.js website.

1. Go to `https://nodejs.org/en/`.

2. Download the version for Windows(x64). For this book I downloaded v6.10.3.LTS (.msi).

3. Run the installer; to do this:

    a. Double-click on the downloaded file; it should be in your downloads folder with a name similar to node-v6.10.3.x64.

    b. The installer window should appear' press the run button, and this opens the Node.js Setup Wizard, then press the next button.

    c. The license agreement will appear, and you need to agree to the license to install Node.js. If you agree, check the check box and press the next button.

    d.   You can accept the default settings by pressing the next button until you see the finish button, and the default setting will install Node.js to a default directory.

    e.   Press the finish button to complete the installation.

4.   At the prompt, let the app make changes to your device.

5.   Restart your computer.

6.   Check that Node.js and npm have been installed by following the instructions in the "Check if node.js Is Installed" section above.

INSTALL NODE.JS ON A MAC

On a Mac there are a number of ways to install Node.js. The easiest way is to download the application from the Node.js website. While this is the simplest way it does have a disadvantage. It installs Node.js in a way that means you may need admin privileges to install supplemental modules and libraries. You can install these modules and libraries using the sudo command before the install command. The sudo command gives you admin privileges for that installation. sudo stands for Super-User DO and is used with UNIX-style operating systems. This allows you to install the package as an admin user.

Using sudo is not considered best practice as having admin rights means you can make unwanted changes to your computer. Using sudo can also affect how some of the modules work.

Another way to install Node.js is to use a Node version manager(NVM); it installs it so you don't need admin privileges to install other modules and libraries. It is slightly harder to install as you need Xcode installed and you will need a .bashprofile file. There is another advantage: you can easily change between different versions of Node.js.

Installing Node.js from the Node.js Website

If you install Node.js this way you may get errors when you install new modules for your application and they won't download. If this happens you will need to install the module again with admin privileges. To do this you type sudo before the install command. You will then be prompted to write your password.

1. Go to `https://nodejs.org/en/`.

2. Download the version for macOS(x64); for this book I downloaded v6.10.3.LTS (.pkg).

3. Run the installer and follow through its requests, and let it install at the default directory.

4. Let the app make changes to your device.

5. Restart your computer.

6. Check that Node.js and npm have been installed.

Installing Node.js Using a Node Version Manager(NVM)

To install with an NVM you need to have Xcode installed on your Mac and a .bashprofile.

If you don't have Xcode installed, install it from the app store; this can take a couple of hours.

1. Open a terminal window, and make sure you are at the root ~ <name>$ if not at the prompt type cd.

2. Check you have a .bashprofile file. At the $ prompt, type open -a TextEdit.app .bash_profile and if you have a .bashprofile it will open, or you can close the file.

3. If you don't have a .bash_profile at the prompt type touch .bash_profile.

4. To install the NVM at the console prompt type:
   curl `https://raw.githubusercontent.com/`
   `creationix/nvm/v0.25.0/install.sh` | bash.

5. To install the latest stable version of Node.js at the
   prompt type nvm install stable.

6. At the prompt type nvm use node.

7. Install the version on Node.js used in this book at
   the prompt type nvm install 6.11.0.

8. Make version 6.11.0 the default version when you
   open a console window. At the prompt type nvm
   alias default 6.11.0.

9. Start using this version of Node.js and at the prompt
   type nvm use 6.11.0.

10. You can see the versions of Node.js you have
    installed: type nvm ls.

11. Check that Node.js and npm have been installed.

You can find more information about nvm and how to use it on the
github page `https://github.com/creationix/nvm`.

Create a Node.js Application

By the end of this chapter you will have built a small application that uses
socket.io to send out updates from the server to connected browsers. You
will build up to this by going through a number of steps including creating
a web server, creating a route to a web page, some basic styling of a web
page, and sending data from the server to the browser. You will send data
from the server in two different ways: first through the route function to the
web page and then by using a web socket.

To write and edit the code you will need a specialized text editor. This can be a source code editor or an integrated development environment (IDE). They are easy to download and install. There are a number available such as Sublime Text, Atom, and Visual Studio code.

The first thing you need to do is create the directory for the application. I called mine chapter_02, so this will be the name of the application.

CREATE THE APPLICATION DIRECTORY

1. Open a console window.

2. Move to the directory you want to store the project, in terminal type cd <path>/<to>/<directory>.

3. Create a new folder for the project, in terminal type mkdir <directory name>.

4. Move into the new directory, in terminal type cd <new directory name>.

The Directory Structure

When you create a web application you will need a directory structure. The main folder for your application will be the root of the application. All other files and folders relating to the application should be in this folder. The files that make up your application will refer to files and folders in this structure. You will create some of these files and folders, and others are created automatically during the initial setup or when you download modules.

Figure 2-2 shows the directory structure for this chapter. The package. json file will be created on setup and the node modules folder will be created automatically when you download new modules. The "/" character represents the root of the application.

```
./
        node_modules/
        public/
                css/
                        main.css
        views/
                index.ejs
        index.js
        package.json
```

Figure 2-2. *The directory structure for the application*

USING NPM INIT TO CREATE AN APPLICATION

npm stands for node package manager. It hosts hundreds of thousands of packages of reusable code that you can download and use in projects.

npm also has a command called npm init, a useful way to create a Node.js application. It will ask a series of questions and then create a package.json file. You can press Ctrl+C to quit the process at any time.

It is easy to create the skeleton of the Node.js server using npm:

1. Open a console window.

2. Navigate to the folder you will use for your application.

3. At the console prompt type npm init+enter.

4. Change the default answers or press enter to accept them. Keep the default entry point as index.js.

5. Open up the project folder in a code editor. Open the root folder for the application, as you want to be able to see all the files and folders connected to the project. At the moment there you should see one file package.json.

Figure 2-3 shows an example of a package.json file.

```
{
  "name": "set-up-server",
  "version": "1.0.0",
  "description": "a basic node server using express",
  "main": "index.js",
  "scripts": {
    "test": "echo \"Error: no test specified\" && exit 1"
  },
  "author": "",
  "license": "ISC"
}
```

Figure 2-3. *An example of a package.json file*

package.json is an important file, it holds the metadata for the application and is used to handle the application's dependencies. As you start to install libraries there will be a reference to them in the package.json file. If you share your application files you wouldn't include all the libraries files. As the package.json has a reference to them, you can use npm install to install them at the copied location.

Note   The name has to be in lowercase letters without spaces though you can use underscores and dashes.

CREATE A NODE.JS SERVER

In Node.js you create a JavaScript file that will start the server. It is stored in the root of the project and will be the entry point for the application. This file is often called app.js or index.js. When I used npm init to create the package. json, I kept the default for the entry script of index.js so now the index.js file needs to be created.

Create a new file at the root of your application called index.js. This can be created in your text editor or using the console. Make sure you are in the applications directory at the same level as package.json.

In the newly created index.js file write in the following code from Listing 2-1.

Listing 2-1. index.js code

```
var http = require('http');
var express = require('express');
var app = express();
var server = http.createServer(app);
server.listen(3000, function() {
  console.log('Listening on port 3000...');
});
```

Listing 2-1 shows the basic code for setting up a web server using Express.js. Express.js is not part of the Node.js library so it will have to be installed in a minute, but first I will explain the code in Table 2-3.

The Code Explained

Modules, such as Express.js, needed for the server are loaded at the top of the page and assigned to variables. JavaScript uses the var keyword to create a variable.

45

Table 2-3. *index.js code explained*

`var http = require('http');`	This line brings in the HTTP interfaces to the application; this allows the server to communicate with the browser via the HTTP protocol.
`var express = require('express');`	This includes the express framework that we will be using to create the server and the routes. Express comes with a number of functions that make it easier to set up a node server. It is not part of the Node.js library and so it needs to be installed.
`var app = express();`	The express application is called and the return value is placed in a variable. This holds a new express application.
`var server = http.createServer(app);`	This creates a server object that is called when a server request is made.
`server.listen(3000, function() {` `});`	This tells the server to listen for requests to the server on the port 3000.
`console.log ('Listening on port 3000...');`	console.log is a JavaScript function that will output messages to the console. It is used here to tell you that the server is running.

USING NPM TO INSTALL LIBRARIES

At the moment if you ran this code, there would be an error. It is using an external library called Express.js, which is not part of Node.js. Express.js makes it a lot easier to create a web server. It needs to be downloaded and a reference to it saved in the package.json. This can be done using npm:

1. Open a console window and make sure you are in the same directory as the package.json file.

2. At the command line type npm install express@4.15.3 --save + enter.

3. Once it's downloaded start the server. In the console make sure you are at the root of the application, the same level as index.js. At the prompt type node index.js.

If you get an error installing Express.js and are on a Mac it may be that you need admin rights to install it. Try installing again, this time type sudo npm install express@4.15.3 --save then type in the computer's password at the password prompt.

In the console you should now see the console log Listening on port 3000.

If you are using Windows you may see a security alert that Windows firewall has blocked some features of this app. Tick the box that says: Private networks, such as my home or work network.

If you open a web browser and type in localhost:3000 you should see: **Cannot GET /**

That is because there isn't a route yet so the server does not know what page to serve to the browser. You will be creating routes in a minute.

If you look at your applications directory you will see there is a new folder called node modules. This is created the first time you install a new library into your application. If you look inside you will see that the files and folders for Express.js are in it.

Note   You use--save to save a reference to the downloaded module in the package.json file.

In this book I will use @ to install new modules. This means you will install the same version I have been using. Without the @ it will install the latest module.

CREATING A ROUTE TO A WEB PAGE

To create a simple route that sends some text to a web page, using the code in Listing 2-1, add into your file the following commands in bold, which are described further in Table 2-4:

```
var http = require('http');
var express = require('express');
var app = express();
var server = http.createServer(app);

app.get('/', function (req, res) {
  res.send("Hi There!");
});

server.listen(3000, function() {
  console.log('Listening on port 3000...');
});
```

The Code Explained

Now if you restart the server you should see the text **Hi There** on the web page.

1. Type Ctlr+c to stop the server.

2. In the terminal type node index.js again to restart the server.

3. Refresh the web browser.

Table 2-4. *index.js code explained*

`app.get('/', function` `(req, res) {` `res.send('Hi There!');` `});`	The function app.get creates a route to the root of the application. '/' represents the root which would be the main URL or in this case localhost:3000. If you wanted to send the message to a different web page, for example, to an about page you would use app.get('/about', function (req, res).

Add a second app.get below the first app.get to the code in Listing 2-1.

```
app.get('/about', function (req, res) {
  res.send("this is an about page");
});
```

Now you need to restart the server so it picks up the new route:

1. Press Ctlr+c to stop the server.

2. In terminal type node index.js again to restart the server.

3. Refresh the web browser and go to localhost:3000/about.

You should now see the words this is an about page on the web page. You can delete the about route.

NodeMon

Every time you make a change to the server you have to stop and restart the server for the change to be picked up. There is a useful library called nodemon that will notice when you make a change to a file that it is watching and restarts the server for you. It is easy to install using it in a console window. It should be installed globally so it is accessible to all your Node.js applications.

INSTALLING NODEMON

1. Open a console window and make sure you are at the home directory; you can go to the home directory on a Mac by typing cd and on a Windows pc by typing cd %userprofile%

2. At the prompt type npm install nodemon -g (-g installs it globally).

3. In the console navigate to the root of the chapter_02 application, do this with the cd command, for example cd Documents/code/chapter_02

4. When you are at the root of your Node.js application in the console, start the server by typing nodemon and press the enter key.

Now if you make a change in the index.js file you can refresh the browser and see the update. Nodemon automatically starts the main JavaScript file listed in package.json.

You don't need to save this to the package.json as it is not part of your application; it is a helper when developing the application.

Creating a Web Page

So far you have sent data to a web browser but it is just printing out a message from the router. Now you need to create a web page. Normally web pages are created in files with an .html extension. These are static web pages. As you will be updating the page with data from the server, you need to create a dynamic page that can take this data.

One way to do this is for the .html page to make AJAX requests to the server, which in turn returns some data. This relies on the browser page making a request for data from the server.

Another approach, which is more efficient, is to let the server update a web page with the data it has. In Node.js this is done with template engines.

Template Engine

A template engine allows you to create variables throughout a web page that the server can update without the web page making a request. Later in the book we will be passing data from an Arduino to the server. As the web page will be created with a template engine, the page will be updated automatically with the new data.

There are a number of different template engines you can use, some of which I have listed in Appendix B. This book uses ejs, embedded JavaScript.

SET UP THE SERVER

Some code needs to be added to the index.js file to use ejs but first ejs has to be added to the project:

1. Either open a console window and navigate to the root of the application directory, or navigate to the root of the application directory; or if the server is running at the root of the application press Ctlr + c to stop it.

2. At the console prompt at the root of the application type npm install ejs@2.5.6 --save + enter.

You should now be able to see ejs in your package.json file. It is just one line of code to include ejs in the project. Update your index.js file from code (Listing 2-1) with the line of code in bold:

```
var http = require('http');
var express = require('express');
var app = express();
var server = http.createServer(app);

app.set('view engine', 'ejs');

app.get('/', function (req, res) {
  res.send('Hi There!')
});

server.listen(3000, function() {
  console.log('Listening on port 3000...');
});
```

This new line of code will allow you to use ejs in the project.

Up to now in the route you have used res.send. Using res.send in a route allows you to send simple data to a web page, but for most applications you would want to be able to send pages that can hold a lot more information. To do this you use the function res.render; this allows you to specify a file that will render in the browser and also send it new data.

Change your index.js file from code (Listing 2-1) with the code in bold; this adds a couple of variables and changes the route so it uses res.render instead of res.send:

```
....

app.set('view engine', 'ejs');

var title = "Some Arduino components starting with p"
var componentArray = ['potentiometer', 'piezo', 'phototransistor',
'pushbutton'];

app.get('/', function (req, res) {
    res.render('index', {
                title: title,
                components: componentArray
    });
});

server.listen(3000, function() {
  console.log('Listening on port 3000...');
});
```

The Code Explained

The new code starts with two variables that hold the data to be passed to the browser (see Table 2-5).

Table 2-5. index.js code explained

`var title = "Some Arduino components starting with p"`	The title variable holds some text. In JavaScript strings are surrounded by either " " or ' '.
`var componentArray = ['potentiometer', 'piezo', 'phototransistor', 'pushbutton'];`	In JavaScript, [ ] is used to create an array. An array is a collection of data that can be accessed by its index (position) within the array. componentArray is an array of four elements that are all strings. The index in a JavaScript array starts at 0. To access the first element of the array you would use componentArray[0], which would return the string potentiometer. componentArray[3] would return the string pushbutton.

`res.render('index', {`
   `title: title,`
   `components:`
   `componentArray`
`});`
	Now instead of rendering a string you are telling Node.js which page you would like to render. In this case it is the index.js file. You then list the data you want passed to the page, in this case the title and the componentArray.

1. Start the server at the application route. Make sure you are in the same folder as the index.js file. At the console prompt type nodemon.

2. Refresh your web page, and you should see an error.

You should see an error on the page and in the console window that looks something like this:

Error: Failed to lookup view "index" in views directory "/Users/indie/ Documents/web/book/chapter 2/03_set-up-ejs/views"

This is because now you are asking it to find an index page that doesn't exist.

SET UP THE WEB PAGE

An ejs page looks similar to an html page except it uses .ejs suffix rather then .html. You can pass ejs page data from the server as a variable. On the page you still use the same html tags but you can also use ejs syntax. Pages created with ejs need to be put in a folder called views.

1. At the root of the application create a new folder called views.

2. Create a new file called index.ejs inside the views folder. To do this in a console window:

    a. at the root of the application type cd views

    b. on a Mac type $ touch index.ejs

    c. on a Windows pc type NUL> index.ejs

In Windows you might get a console response of Access is denied but the file should have been created.

In the newly created index.ejs file write in the code from Listing 2-2.

Listing 2-2. index.ejs code

```
<!DOCTYPE html>
<html>
<head>
    <title>an ejs page</title>
</head>
<body>
    <h1>EJS</h1>
    <p>This page is an ejs page and will show data from the
    server</p>
</body>
</html>
```

In a console window, make sure you are at the root of the project and restart the server. On the browser go to http://localhost:3000/ and there should no longer be an error. You should now see the text on the web page. You created this page with some simple HTML. HTML, which stands for HyperText Markup Language, is the common markup language used to create web pages. I will go into more detail about HTML in Chapter 4. It sets out the structure of the page and the elements within it.

ADDING DATA TO THE WEB PAGE

The server has passed to the browser the data from res.render. It has passed a string called title that contains the text "Some Arduino components starting with P" and an array called components that contains ['potentiometer', 'piezo', 'phototransistor', 'pushbutton']. Using ejs the browser now has access to this data.

Update the index.ejs from Listing 2-2 with the text in bold:

```
<!DOCTYPE html>
<head>
    <title>an ejs page</title>
</head>
<body>
    <h1>EJS</h1>
    <p>This page is an ejs page and will show data from the
    server</p>

    <h2><%= title %></h2>
    <% components.forEach(function(component) { %>
        <p>component: <%= component %> </p>
    <% }); %>

</body>
</html>
```

The Code Explained

<% %>, or <%= %> are part of the ejs library.

The <% %> tags are used when you are writing JavaScript, it will run the JavaScript inside the tags, and the text won't appear on the page. Usually when you want to add JavaScript to a web page you have to wrap it in script tags <script></script> that you will be using later. EJS has its own version of the script tag, <% %>, which you use when writing code that accesses the data passed from the server.

When the <%= %> tags are used, then content inside them is seen on the page. Inside the tags you can reference the variable from the server that was passed to the browser and see it on the web page. See Table 2-6.

Table 2-6. index.ejs code explained

`<h2><%= title %></h2>`	The title is part of the data passed from the server. As you want to see the title you use <%= %>. You can wrap the EJS in any HTML tags you like. In this case the ejs is wrapped in a H2 tag.

`<% components.forEach`
`(function(component) { %>`
`<p>component:`
`<%= component %> </p>`
`<% }); %>`
	This uses a JavaScript forEach function to iterate over the array data passed from the server and writes out each element of the array.

ADDING CSS

CSS stands for Cascading Style Sheet, and it is used to style elements on a web page. A web page without CSS looks very basic. While CSS can be added in the .ejs page it is best practice to create a separate .CSS file to hold the styles. You then need a link to the .css file in the .ejs page.

In a web application there are files called static files that are not created by the server and are used on the web page. These include CSS files, images, and JavaScript files. To use them in a .ejs file you need to know the path from the static file to the .ejs file. Express.js has a middleware function called express. static to help with this. You create a folder at the root of your application that will hold all your static files; this folder is normally called public. In the index. js file the express.static function is used to register the public folder. This means that the .ejs recognizes this folder as the root folder for your static files and you don't have to write the absolute path the to the .css file when you are calling it. You will write something like this: **`<link href="/css/main.css" rel="stylesheet" type="text/css">`**

To add CSS to the page first create a static folder.

1. At the root of the application create a new folder called public.

2. Inside this folder create another folder called css.

3. Inside the css folder create a file called main.css.

4. Update the index.js file to include the static function, with the updated code below.

Now update the index.js file from Listing 2-1 with the code in bold:

```
...

app.set('view engine', 'ejs');

app.use(express.static(__dirname + '/public'));

var title = "Some Arduino components starting with P"
var componentArray = ['potentiometer', 'piezo',
'phototransistor', 'pushbutton'];

...
server.listen(3000, function() {
  console.log('Listening on port 3000...');
});
```

The Code Explained

There is one line of code needed to register the static files folder (Table 2-7).

Table 2-7. *index.js code explained*

`app.use(express.static(__dirname + '/public'));`	This tells the app that all the static files will be served from a folder called public.

Now open the main.css file you just created and add in the CSS (Listing 2-3):

Listing 2-3. main.css

```css
*{
    margin: 0;
    padding:0;
}
body{
    background-color: #F2F3F4;
    font-family: Verdana, Arial, Helvetica, sans-serif;
}

h1, h2, p{
    padding: 10px;
}

h1{
    background-color: #4ABCAC;
    color: white;
}

#components{
    margin: 10px;
    border: #F78733 solid 2px;
    display: inline-block;
}
```

You will also need to update the index.ejs file to tell it where to find the CSS file. Update the index.ejs file (Listing 2-2) with the HTML in bold:

```
<!DOCTYPE html>
<head>
    <title>an ejs page</title>
    <link href="/css/main.css" rel="stylesheet" type="text/css">
</head>
<body>
    <h1>EJS</h1>
    <p>This page is an ejs page and will show data from the
    server</p>
    <h2><%= title %></h2>
    <div id="components">
        <% components.forEach(function(component) { %>
            <p>component: <%= component %> </p>
        <% }); %>
    </div>
</body>
</html>
```

So with the server running, refresh your web page, and you should now see the new style; it is using the HTML tags and an id to style the content.

package.json and Version Control

Now that you have installed a few packages for your application it's a good time to have another look at the package.json file. It holds information about the application including the names of the dependencies (modules) you installed followed by their version number.

These dependencies are written by different people and are updated at different times. These updates can break your code. Semantic versioning is used to track the changes. This means that each number of a version number has a particular meaning. The version number, as seen in Figure 2-4, is made up of three numbers separated with a full stop. The numbers increase with each new version and each number represents a different kind of update.

Figure 2-4. *Version control numbers*

In the package.json file you can see the dependencies.

```
{
  "name": "set-up-routes",
  "version": "1.0.0",
  "description": "setting up simple routes",
  "main": "index.js",
  "scripts": {
    "test": "echo \"Error: no test specified\" && exit 1"
  },
  "author": "Indira",
  "license": "ISC",
  "dependencies": {
```

```
   "ejs": "^2.5.6",
   "express": "^4.15.3"
  }
}
```

Next to each installed module is its version number. You might also see a symbol such as * or ~. When you run npm install from the package.json these symbols give some flexibility to the version that can be downloaded.

= or v This makes sure that exactly the same version of the package is installed. For example v2.5.6 would make sure that version 2.5.6 of the package is downloaded.

~ This fixes the major and minor version but allows for a higher patched version. For example, ~2.5.6 would make sure that the version installed would be greater or equal to 2.5.6 but less than 2.6.0.

^ This fixes the major version number but allows for a different minor or patched version. For example, ^2.5.6 would make sure the installed version could be greater or equal to 2.5.6 and less than 3.0.0.

* This is a wildcard so it means that any version can be installed. For example, 2.* means that any version starting with 2 can be installed.

SETTING UP A WEBSOCKET WITH SOCKET.IO

Now back to creating an application. At the moment the server passes the web page data when it loads. If the data updated, the web page would not reflect the change. You could write a script that pinged the server at regular intervals to see if there is a change but that wouldn't be efficient; you would be making wasted calls if there was no new data and when new data does arrive the page would have to wait until the next call to be updated.

The WebSocket protocol solves this: new data will be sent straight to the web page and the page can send data back to the server to update other browsers connected to the server. This book will be using the socket.io library to make web socket calls.

First, socket.io needs to be installed as socket.io is not installed with Node.js.

1. Open a console window and navigate to the root of your application.

2. At the prompt type npm install socket.io@1.7.3 –save.

You can now include socket.io into the index.js file. Index.js will no longer be using the variables title and componentArray to send data to the browser, so they can be deleted. The app.get function is also updated so the variables are no longer being sent to index.ejs. Update the index.js file so it matches the code in Listing 2-4, and the new code is in bold:

Listing 2-4. index.js updated

```
var http = require('http');
var express = require('express');
var app = express();
var server = http.createServer(app);
var io = require('socket.io')(server);

app.set('view engine', 'ejs');
app.use(express.static(__dirname + '/public'));

app.get('/', function (req, res) {
  res.render('index')
});

io.on('connection', function(socket){
    console.log('Connection to client established');
    socket.on('disconnect',function(){
        console.log('Server has disconnected');
    });
});

server.listen(3000, function() {
  console.log('Listening on port 3000...');
});
```

The Code Explained

Socket.io changes the way that the data is passed to the browser; it is no longer sent in the route but via a socket (Table 2-8).

Table 2-8. index.js updated code explained

```var io = require('socket.io')``` ```(server);```	This code includes socket.io and attaches the server to it.

```app.get('/', function (req, res) {```
```   res.render('index')```
```});```
	This creates a route from the server to the index.ejs page at the URL root. This time you are not sending the data through the route.

```io.on('connection',```
```function(socket){```
```   console.log('Connection to client```
```   established');```
	The io.on function will tell the socket what to do when there is connection by the web page to a server. You will see a console log each time a browser connects to the server.

```socket.on('disconnect',function(){```
```   console.log('Server has```
```   disconnected');```
```});```
	This function will run when a browser disconnects to the server.

REWRITE THE INDEX.EJS FILE TO INCLUDE SOCKET.IO

The index.ejs needs to display data coming from the socket. You no longer need the CSS or a number of the HTML components that were displaying the data from the server. There are new HTML components that will display the data from the socket. The socket uses JavaScript. There has to be a corresponding socket in the index.ejs file that references the socket in index.js, so there has to be a reference to socket.io in index.ejs. The <script> </script> tags are used to add JavaScript code into index.ejs (see Table 2-9). Update index.ejs with the code in Listing 2-5, and notice that a lot of the code from the previous version of index.ejs has been deleted.

Listing 2-5. index.ejs

```
<!DOCTYPE html>
<head>
    <title>WebSockets</title>
</head>
<body>

    <div class="wrapper">
        <h1>Using socket.io</h1>
        <p>This page will update with socket.io</p>
    </div>
<script src="https://cdn.socket.io/socket.io-1.2.0.js"></script>
<script>
    var socket = io();
</script>
</body>
</html>
```

The Code Explained

In the console make sure you are at the root of the application and start the application.

Try opening and closing the page on different web browsers and browser tabs and have a look at the console. Every time there is a new connection to the server ,you should see Connection to client established. Every time you close the connection to the serve by closing the page, you should see Server has disconnected.

Table 2-9. *index.ejs code explained*

`<script src="https://cdn.socket.io/socket.io-1.2.0.js"></script>`	Calls in the socket.io library to the web page; without this the page wouldn't have access to the library.
`var socket = io();`	Creates a variable for the socket.io functions.

How Sockets Work

Socket.io has a number of functions that broadcast and listen for data. socket.emit broadcasts data and socket.on listens for data.

The functions use a matching pair of id's on the server and the browser. These matching pairs of id's will listen for updates from each other and can send data to each other.

The structure is:

```
socket.emit('an_example_id', message);

socket.on('an_ example_id', function(message){
    Do something with the message from socket.emit
});
```

socket.emit will send the data to the function socket.on with a matching id. Socket.on will listen for data from socket.emit with a matching id.

This means you can have multiple sockets with different ids and the data doesn't get confused between the different sockets.

SENDING DATA TO A WEB PAGE WITH SOCKET.IO

You will now create a simple socket on the server and on the browser page that will pass information between them. There will be a button on the web page that will update a number when it is clicked. The message that the button has been clicked will be sent to the server via socket.io. The number will be changed and then socket.io on the server side will send the information back to the connected web pages.

In index.js add in the code in bold:

```
var http = require('http');
var express = require('express');
var app = express();
var server = http.createServer(app);
var io = require('socket.io')(server);

app.set('view engine', 'ejs');
app.use(express.static(__dirname + '/public'));

app.get('/', function (req, res) {
  res.render('index')
});

var buttonValue = 0;

io.on('connection', function(socket){
    console.log('Connection to client established');
    io.emit('clicked message', buttonValue);
```

```
socket.on('clicked message', function(msg){
    buttonValue = 1 - buttonValue;
        io.emit('clicked message', buttonValue);
        console.log('Received message from client!',msg);
});

socket.on('disconnect',function(){
        console.log('Server has disconnected');
    });
});

server.listen(3000, function() {
    console.log('Listening on port 3000...');
});
```

The Code Explained

Table 2-10 breaks down the code you just added.

Table 2-10. *index.js code explained*

`var buttonValue = 0;`	This variable holds a value that will be changed by someone clicking a button on a browser.

`socket.on('clicked`
`message', function(msg){`
`buttonValue = 1 -`
`  buttonValue;`
`  io.emit('clicked`
`message', buttonValue);`
`    console.log('Received`
`message from client!',`
`buttonValue);`
`});`
	In this code the socket id is 'clicked message'. This socket will be listening for messages from the browser sent by a function io.emit('clicked message', msg). When it receives one it will carry out the instruction buttonValue = 1 - buttonValue; this will change the value of buttonValue to either zero or one. It will then send out the new value using io.emit('clicked message', buttonValue) to the web browsers listening for the change.

The index.ejs from Listing 2-5 also needs to be updated with the code in bold:

```
<!DOCTYPE html>
<head>
    <title>WebSockets</title>
</head>
<body>
    <div class="wrapper">
        <h1>Using socket.io</h1>
        <p>This page will update with socket.io</p>
        <button id="clicked">click me</button>
        <div id="updates"></div>
    </div>
<script src="https://cdn.socket.io/socket.io-1.2.0.js"></script>
<script>
    var socket = io();
    var button = document.getElementById('clicked');

    button.onclick = function(e){
        socket.emit('clicked message', 'clicked');
    }
    socket.on('clicked message', function(msg){
        document.getElementById('updates').innerHTML = msg;
    });
</script>
</body>
</html>
```

The Code Explained

You should now have a working server that interacts with and updates a web page (Table 2-11). If you click on the button on the page, it will update and also update other pages with the same URL; you should also see a message in your console.

69

Table 2-11. *index.ejs code explained*

`var button = document.` `getElementById('clicked');`	This line of code is some basic JavaScript. In the HTML there is a button element with an id of 'clicked'. The variable button will hold a reference to this element so it can be referenced in the JavaScript.

`button.onclick = function(e){`
  `socket.emit('clicked`
    `message','clicked');`
`}`
	onclick is a function that is executed when the button on the web page is clicked. The function socket. emit('clicked message', 'clicked'); is called. This will pass the message 'clicked' to the server to its matching socket.io function socket.on('clicked message') .

`socket.on('clicked message',`
`function(msg){`
`document.getElementById`
`('updates').innerHTML = msg;`
    `});`
	This code is listening to messages from the server with an id of 'clicked message' and when it gets one it uses the JavaScript function document.getElementById to find an element on the page with an id of 'updates' and change its inner html to the data passed in from the server.

Summary

This chapter introduced you to web technologies and how to create a web server to send data to and from a web browser.

You will use these skills in the next chapter to create a server that will import data from an Arduino and display it on a web page.

CHAPTER 3

Arduino to Front End Part I

In Chapter 2 you learned how to create a web server with Node.js and use it to send data to a web page. In this chapter you will start sending data from an Arduino to a Node.js server and use the data on a web page.

The data will be coming from a switch button connected to an Arduino and into your computer via a serial port. You can import this data into a Node.js server and use it on a web page. By the end of this chapter, you will have a web page with a colored square on it, and the square will change color each time you press the Arduino button. Figure 3-1 is an example of what you will have made by the end of the chapter.

© Indira Knight 2018
I. Knight, *Connecting Arduino to the Web*, https://doi.org/10.1007/978-1-4842-3480-8_3

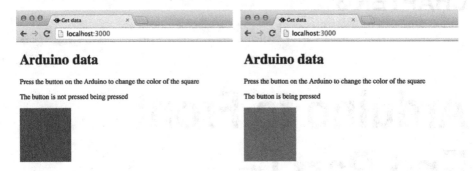

Figure 3-1. *Two possible outcomes of the exercise in Chapter 3*

Introduction to Serial Port

A serial port transfers data in and out of a computer in single bits one after another. A bit can have a value of 0 (low/off/false) or 1 (high/on/true). These bits can be joined together to transfer more complex data, and different numbers of bits have different names. Eight bits is a byte, a KiloByte (KB) is 1024 bytes (1024 x 8 bits), and a Megabyte (MB) is 1024 kilobytes. As the bits can only be 0 or 1 they are called binary data.

With Arduino's you can send serial data back and forth from your computer through the USB port. Every Arduino has a serial port, some more than one. The Arduino Uno uses RX(pin 0) and TX(pin 1) to communicate. If you are using serial you cannot attach anything to pins 0 and 1. The Arduino IDE has a built-in serial monitor to view serial data.

When you connect your Arduino to your computer it will be attached to one of the computer's serial ports. You need to know which port it is attached to, as you will need to reference it in your Node.js application.

Finding the Serial Port

On a Mac and a Windows PC the serial port number looks slight different. On a Mac it will look something like this: /dev/tty.<type of input and port number> or /dev/cu.<type of input and port number>. In Windows it will looks something like this: COM<port number>.

There are a number of ways you can find out the serial port the Arduino is attached to:

1. With the Arduino attached, open the Arduino IDE. In the menu click on the Tools menu and then hover over the Port menu; you will see all the devices attached to serial ports, and the serial port for the Arduino will look something like this: /dev/tty.usbmodem<port number> (Arduino/Uno) on a Mac and on a PC it will look like COM<port number>.

2. On a Mac open a terminal window and type ls /dev/tty.usbmodem*. You should get an output similar to /dev/tty.usbmodem<port number>.

3. On a PC, open the device manager and open the Ports (COM & LPT) menu, and you should see something like Arduino Uno COM<port number>.

Serial Data and Arduino

There are a number of functions that help you transfer serial data to and from an Arduino. They use a library called Serial. Table 3-1 shows some of the functions available in the library.

Table 3-1. *Arduino serial functions*

Command	Result
Serial.begin(9600)	The begin function sets the transmission rate for the serial data; it is measured in bits per second and is called the baud rate.
Serial.end()	Signals the end of serial communication and releases pins RX and TX so they can be used for other inputs and outputs.
Serial.write()	Writes binary data to the serial port.
Serial.println()	Prints out serial data.

The Baud Rate

The Baud rate sets the rate for transmitting data through the serial port. It is measured in bits per second. The rates that can be used with an Arduino are 300, 600, 1200, 2400, 4800, 9600, 14400, 19200, 28800, 38400, 57600, or 115200. The maximum speed you can set a baud rate will depend on your device. If the device can't process the higher speed then some of the data won't be registered, and you will lose data. The rate 9600 is a common baud rate for an Arduino.

SETTING UP THE ARDUINO CIRCUIT

In this chapter you will be connecting a switch button to an Arduino and using the Serial functions to find out if the button is pressed down or not.

The set up for the Arduino in this chapter will use an Arduino Uno, a breadboard, a switch button, a 220 ohm resistor, and jump leads. Figure 3-2 shows the kit you'll need.

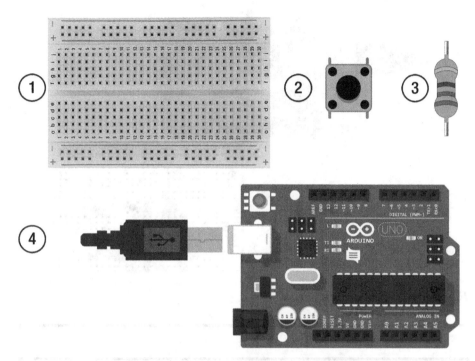

Figure 3-2. *1. Breadboard, 2. Switch button, 3. 220 ohm resistor, 4. Arduino*

Once you have the kit together you need to set it up as shown in Figure 3-3, and connect it to a USB port on your computer. Make sure the Arduino is not connected to the computer or any other power supply when you are connecting the components.

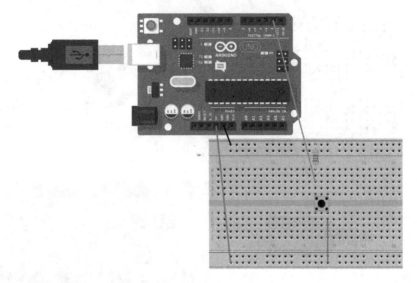

Figure 3-3. *The circuit setup*

WRITE THE ARDUINO CODE

When the Arduino is connected to your computer, open the Arduino IDE. There are two things to set up in the IDE: the type of board connected and the port it's connected to. The following sets up the IDE:

1. In the Arduino IDE menu choose Tools/Board and choose Arduino/Genuino Uno.

2. In the Tools/port menu choose the port that the Arduino is connected to, and it will say something like COM3 (Arduino/Genuino Uno) on a PC or /dev/cu.usbmodem621 (Arduino/Genuino Uno) on a Mac.

Then choose file/new to open a new file. Save the file as chapter_3. Copy the code from Listing 3-1.

Listing 3-1. chapter_3 code

```
int switchButton = 2;
void setup() {
    Serial.begin(9600);
    pinMode(switchButton, INPUT);
}
void loop() {
    int buttonState = digitalRead(switchButton);
    if(buttonState == HIGH){
    Serial.println("1");
    }else{
    Serial.println("0");
    }
    delay(500);
}
```

The Code Explained

Table 3-2 describes the code in Listing 3-1.

Table 3-2. *chapter_3.ino code explained*

`int switchButton = 2;`	This code creates a variable to hold the number for the switch input into the Arduino. On the Arduino it is connected to digital pin 2.
`Serial.begin(9600);`	This function sets the baud rate that the data will be transferred at.
`pinMode(switchButton, INPUT);`	pinMode is a function that sets the mode for the pins, and INPUT is the default and sets it up to receive data. It is being passed to the switchButton variable that holds the digital pin number.
`int buttonState = digitalRead (switchButton);`	The variable buttonState holds the data coming from digital pin 2, which the button is connected to. It will either be high if the button is being pressed or low when it's not.

`if(buttonState == HIGH){`
`  Serial.println("1");`
`}else{`
`  Serial.println("0");`
`}`
	The if statement checks if the buttonState is HIGH. If it is, the button is being pressed and Serial.println will send "1" to the serial port. If it's not it, the else statement will send "0" instead.

`delay(500);and`	As the code is in a loop you can delay the loop starting again. If you don't do this, code might not have finished executing before the loop starts again and you can lose data. The delay function uses milliseconds, and 500 is half a second. You need to get the balance right with the delay; you don't want to lose data but if you make the delay too long, you might miss the button being pressed.

RUN THE ARDUINO CODE

Check that the code is correct by clicking on the tick icon, and then send the code to the Arduino by clicking on the arrow icon.

Once the code has uploaded, open the serial monitor in the IDE by clicking on it; it is shown in red in Figure 3-4.

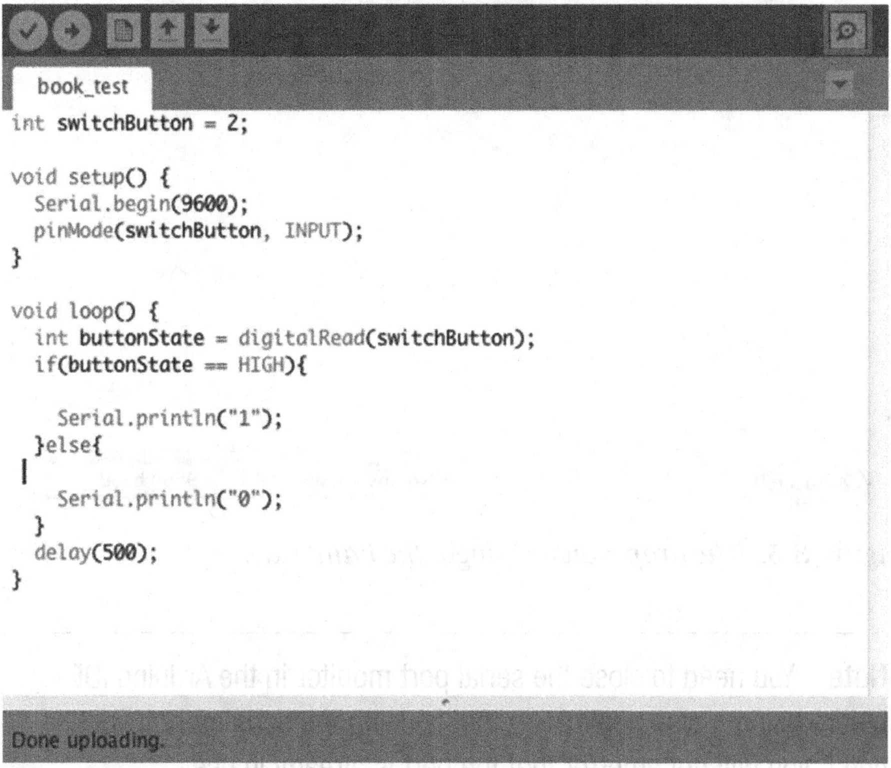

```
book_test
int switchButton = 2;

void setup() {
  Serial.begin(9600);
  pinMode(switchButton, INPUT);
}

void loop() {
  int buttonState = digitalRead(switchButton);
  if(buttonState == HIGH){

    Serial.println("1");
  }else{

    Serial.println("0");
  }
  delay(500);
}
```

Done uploading.

Figure 3-4. How to open the serial port monitor

You should start to see data in the serial port window. It might not be the 0
or 1 you expected to see, buy this happens if the baud rate in the serial port
monitor does not match the baud rate in the code. Figure 3-5 shows where
this can be changed in the serial port window. Go to this drop-down and
change the rate to 9600. When the button is pressed, you should see a series
of 1's printed; otherwise the output should be 0.

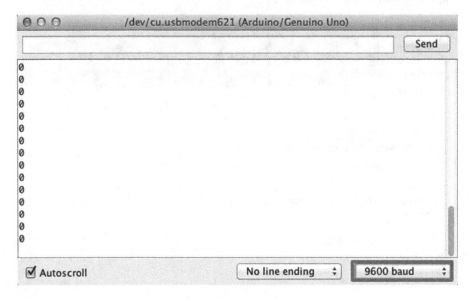

Figure 3-5. *The drop-down changes the baud rate.*

Note   You need to close the serial port monitor in the Arduino IDE
before using a web application that is using the serial port. If you
don't, you will get an error that the port is already in use.

Using the Data on the Front End

Now that you can see the serial data in the Arduino the next step is to send it to a Node.js server so that it can be displayed on a web browser. The Node.js application in this chapter will take in data from the Arduino and use Socket.io to pass the data to the front end.

SerialPort Library

One of the libraries you will import is the SerialPort library. This library allows you import data from the Arduino, via the serial port, into Node.js.

To open a port with the library in Node.js you need to include a path to the Library and create a new port object.

The data coming through the SerialPort library is a buffer object. A buffer object is the stream of bits (binary data) that is coming through the serial port. JavaScript does not handle binary data very well. SerialPort has a readLine parser that converts the binary data into strings. The code looks like this:

```
serialport.parsers.readline("\n")
```

The "\n" is the way to create a new line in JavaScript. The readLine converts the binary data into lines of text. It knows that it is the end of the current data stream when it sees the newline character and so it separates the different streams of data.

There a number of functions in the SerialPort library, but we will be using a few in this book. You can find more information about the SerialPort library in Appendix B.

Downloading the SerialPort Library

You will be using npm to install the SerialPort library. On a PC you will need to download a couple of other packages before using npm to install SerialPort. On a Mac you will be able to download it without any extra libraries so you don't need to do the following steps.

If you are using a PC, follow the following steps to download the necessary support libraries for the SerialPort library.

1. First, install node-gyp, as it is used for compiling native add-on modules in Node.js. Open a console window and type in npm install -g node-gyp. You can find more information at https://github.com/nodejs/node-gyp#installation.

2. Extra build tools for windows also need to be installed. These have to be installed with a console window running in administration mode. Open the CMD.exe by right-clicking on the Windows menu and choose CMD.exe(run as Administrator) or type it in the search bar. In the console type npm install -g --production windows-build-tools. You can find out more about the tools at https://github.com/felixrieseberg/windows-build-tools; this might take a few minutes to install.

CREATE A NODE.JS APPLICATION

The directory structure for this chapter will be the following:

```
/chapter_03
    /node_modules
    /views
        index.ejs
    index.js
    package.json
```

The first thing to do is to create a new Node.js application for this chapter and install the necessary libraries.

1. Create a new folder to hold the application. I called mine chapter_03.

2. Open the command prompt (Windows operating system) or a terminal window (Mac) and navigate to the newly created folder.

3. When you are in the right directory type npm init to create a new application; you can press return through each of the questions, or make changes to them.

4. You can now start adding the necessary libraries; to download Express.js at the command line type npm install express@4.15.3 –save.

5. Then install ejs, type npm install ejs@2.5.6 –save.

6. When that's downloaded, install serial port. On a Mac type npm install serialport@4.0.7 --save on a Windows PC type npm install serialport@4.0.7 --build-from-source.

7. Then finally install socket.io, type npm install socket.io@1.7.3 –save.

If you look at your package.json file you should see the following dependencies:

```
"dependencies": {
    "ejs": "^2.5.6",
    "express": "^4.15.3",
    "serialport": "^4.0.7",
    "socket.io": "^1.7.3"
}
```

Now you can write the code for the application. In the root of the chapter_03 folder create a file called index.js copy in the code from Listing 3-2.

Note   Throughout this book you will be using the serial port library in index.js. You will need to add into index.js a reference to the serial port that your Arduino is connected to. In the code where it says <add in the serial port for your Arduino> on a Mac, change it to '/dev/tty.usbmodem<port number> ' and on a PC you change it to 'COM<port number> '. You need to keep the ' ' and remove the < > symbols

---

Listing 3-2. index.js code

```
var http = require('http');
var express = require('express');
var app = express();
var server = http.createServer(app);
var io = require('socket.io')(server);
var SerialPort = require('serialport');
var serialport = new SerialPort('<add in the serial port
for your Arduino>', {
```

```
        parser: SerialPort.parsers.readline('\n')
});
app.engine('ejs', require('ejs').__express);
app.set('view engine', 'ejs');
app.get('/', function (req, res){
    res.render('index');
});
serialport.on('open', function(){
    console.log('serial port opened');
});
io.on('connection', function(socket){
    console.log('socket.io connection');
    serialport.on('data', function(data){
        data = data.trim();
        socket.emit('data', data);
    });
    socket.on('disconnect', function(){
        console.log('disconnected');
    });
});
server.listen(3000, function(){
    console.log('listening on port 3000...');
});
```

Remember to add in the serial port you are using. If you run this code now there will be an error. It references an index.ejs file that hasn't been created yet.

The Code Explained

Table 3-3 describes the code in Listing 3-2.

Table 3-3. *index.js explained*

`var SerialPort = require('serialport');`	This brings the SerialPort library into the Node.js application and stores it as a variable.
`var serialport = new SerialPort('<serial port>'`	The code creates a new serial port object. You need to add in the serial port that your Arduino is connected to in between the < >. On a Mac it should look like /dev/tty. usbmodem<port number> and on a PC it should look like COM<port number>.
`{ parser: SerialPort. parsers.readline('\n') });`	The data gets parsed using readline, the '\n' creates a new line which separates each line of data.
`serialport.on('open', function(){`	The open event is emitted when the port is opened. You can specify events when the serial port is open, and in the code there is a console log so you know if it has opened.
`serialport.on('data', function(data){`	The data event starts to monitor for new data, and the function is passed to the new data.
`data = data.trim();`	The function gives you access to the new data, but first it needs to be trimmed of any white space before or after the character.
`socket.emit('data', data);`	The data is passed to the front end using the socket.io function emit; it has a reference id of 'data'.

INTERACTING WITH A WEB PAGE

The data from the Arduino is going to be used to update a web page. The color of a square will change each time the button is pressed. A variable will keep track of the current data sent from the Arduino. When new data comes into the page, there is a JavaScript function that checks if the new data is different from the current data.

If it is and the data is the string "1," then the function will pick at random an element from an array that is a list of colors. It then updates the color of the square. It also updates a piece of text and the current variable so the new data becomes the current data.

If the new data is "0" the color of the square doesn't change, but a piece of text gets updated. Again the current variable will be updated with the new data. You now need to create an index.ejs file in the views folder; first create a views folder in the root of your application and then create a file called index. ejs inside it. Copy the code from Listing 3-3 into the index.ejs file.

Listing 3-3. index.ejs code

```
<!DOCTYPE html>
<html>
    <head>
        <meta charset="UTF-8">
        <title>Get data</title>
    </head>
    <body>
        <h1>Arduino data</h1>
        <p>Press the button on the Arduino to change the
        color of the square</p>
        <p>The button is <span id="button-state"></span> </p>

        <svg width="120" height="120" viewBox="0 0 120
        120">
```

```
            <rect id="change-color"
             fill="LightSkyBlue"
             width="120"
             height="120"
             />
        </svg>
        <script src="/socket.io/socket.io.js"></script>
        <script>
            var socket = io();
            var current = "0";
            var shape = document.getElementById('change-color');
            var buttonState =
            document.getElementById('button-state');
            var colorArray = ["LightSkyBlue",
            "LightSlateGray","DarkOliveGreen", "orange",
            "DarkRed", "gold", "purple"];

            socket.on("data", function(data){
                if(data === "1"){
                    buttonState.innerHTML = "pressed";
                    if(data !== current){
                        var newColor = colorArray[Math.
                        floor(Math.random()*colorArray.length)];
                        shape.style.fill = newColor;
                    }
                } else{
                    buttonState.innerHTML = "not pressed";
                }
                current = data;
            });
        </script>
    </body>
</html>
```

Now in a console window navigate to the route of the application and type nodemon index.js or node index.js to start the application. Open a browser and go to http://localhost:3000/ to see the application running.

Each time you press the button the color of the rectangle will change. As the color in the array is picked at random it may pick the same color as the current color. If you wanted to make sure the rectangle changed color, you could create a variable for the current color and check that the new color is different.

The Code Explained

Table 3-4 describes the code in Listing 3-3.

Table 3-4. index.ejs explained

`<svg width="120" height="120" viewBox="0 0 120 120">`	This creates a scalable vector graphic (SVG) square with a width, height, and color. There will be details on SVG's in Chapter 4.
`var current = "0";`	This creates a variable that holds the current value of the serial data. This variable will be used to check if the data from the serial port has changed.
`var shape = document. getElementById('change-color');`	Shape is a variable that holds a reference to the SVG rectangle. The variable is used to update the color of the rectangle. It finds it using the SVG's id.
`var buttonState = document. getElementById('button-state');`	buttonState is a variable that holds a reference to a span element. It finds the element by its id and will update text within it.

(continued)

Table 3-4. (*continued*)

`var colorArray = ["LightSkyBlue", "LightSlateGray", "DarkOliveGreen", "orange", "DarkRed", "gold", "purple"];`	The variable colorArray holds an array of different color names.
`socket.on("data", function(data) {`	The socket.on function is listening for data coming from a socket.emit with the id of 'data' and passes the incoming data to a function.
`if(data === "1"){`	The if statement checks if the new data is the string "1." If it is, the text on the web page changes and another if statement is called.
`if(data !== "current"){`	This if statement checks if the new data is the not the same (!==, not equal to) the current data. If it is not the same it carries out the code within the statement.
`var newColor = colorArray[Math. floor(Math.random() *colorArray.length)];`	This piece of code chooses a color from the colorArray. The JavaScript Math.random() function is used to pick a random number between 0 and the number of the elements in the array. It's multiplied by (the * symbol) the length of the array so it only chooses a number within the array length.

(*continued*)

Table 3-4. (*continued*)

`shape.style.fill = newColor;`	Using the variable shape, the fill style of the SVG is changed to the new color.

`else{`
`buttonState.innerHTML = "not`
`pressed";`
`}`
	If the value of the new data is not "1," then the HTML of the span with the id button-state is changed to the string "not pressed."

`current = data;`	The variable holding the value of the current data needs to be updated with the value of the new data.

Summary

You should now have a working application with a web page that updates when you press the button attached to the Arduino. There were a lot of new concepts in this chapter, and Chapter 4 will look at these in more detail.

CHAPTER 4

Introduction to Creating Web Content

Before moving forward, it is good to understand Hypertext markup language (HTML), cascading style sheets (CSS), scalable vector graphics (SVG), and JavaScript. These four concepts will be used throughout the book to create interactive web applications, process data, and send data to and from an Arduino. If you are confident in some of these areas, just skip to the parts you would like to know more about. if you feel happy with all these subjects please skip ahead to Chapter 5.

HTML

Hypertext markup language (HTML) is used to create content on a web page. You don't need HTML to create content if you create a file with a .txt extension that will open up in a web browser as will a number of other file types. The reason that HTML is used is that it gives your page structure. It allows you to define headings and paragraphs, create different blocks of content on the page, and place images. The structure is made up of HTML elements; these elements can be styled with CSS and made interactive with JavaScript and CSS. Figure 4-1 shows the format of an HTML paragraph element.

© Indira Knight 2018
I. Knight, *Connecting Arduino to the Web*, https://doi.org/10.1007/978-1-4842-3480-8_4

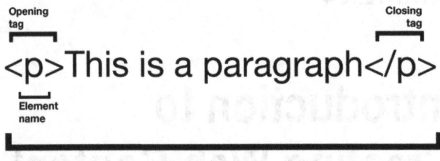

HTML Paragraph element

Figure 4-1. *The structure of a paragraph element*

HTML Elements

HTML elements are normally made up of an opening and closing tag. The opening tag contains a reference to the type of element it will be and attributes for the element.

Elements in HTML are usually either block or inline elements. Block elements follow on from each other on the page: for example, headings and paragraphs. Inline elements work within blocks and format the elements.

Block Elements

There are a wide range of block elements available. Table 4-1 lists some of them.

Table 4-1. *Some HTML block elements*

Command	Result
`<h1></h1>, <h2></h2>, <h3></h3>, <h4></h4>, <h5></h5>, <h6></h6>`	These are used to create headings; the lower the number, the more important the heading.
`<p></p>`	The paragraph element is for creating paragraphs of text,

`<ul>`
`<li>Orange</li>`
`<li>Melon</li>`
`</ul>`
	A <ul> tag creates an unordered list of elements; the <li> elements are the list items inside the list.

`<ol>`
`<li>Orange</li>`
`<li>Melon</li>`
`</ol>`
	An <ol> tag creates an ordered list element; the <li> tag creates the list items inside the list. An ordered list will have numbers or numerals to show the order of the items.

`<div></div>`	The div tag creates an element that is a container for other elements. It is used to define blocks of content.

Inline Elements

Table 4-2 lists some of the inline elements available in HTML.

Table 4-2. *Some HTML inline elements*

Command	Result
`<span></span>`	Span itself does not change the text it wraps around, but it can be used by CSS or JavaScript to select a span of text.
`<i></i>`	Italicizes text it is wrapped around.
`<b></b>`	Used to make text bold.
`<u></u>`	Underlines text,
` `	This element creates a line break; it does not have a closing tag.
`<a></a>`	This is an anchor element used to create a URL link to another page; it also contains the URL to the other page.
`<img>`	This is the tag used to add images to a web page; it doesn't have a closing tag but does need a source path to the image.

BASIC HTML PAGE STRUCTURE

There is a basic structure to all web pages.

In a text editor, create a new HTML file called structure.html and copy the HTML from Listing 4-1.

Listing 4-1. structure.html

```
<!DOCTYPE html>
<html>
    <head>
        <title>A basic web page</title>
        <meta charset="utf-8">

    </head>
    <body>
        <h1>Basics</h1>
```

```
    <p>This is a basic web page</p>
  </body>
</html>
```

The HTML Explained

Listing 4-1 shows the basic structure of a web page. The type of document is declared at the top, then the content is wrapped in an HTML element. Table 4-3 explains some of the elements in Listing 4-1.

Table 4-3. structure.html

`<!DOCTYPE html>`	This should be the start of any or your HTML files; it lets the browser know that it is reading HTML.
`<html></html>`	This is the html element, and it contains all the content of your web page.
`<head></head>`	The head element holds information about your page, but its contents don't appear on the page itself. It can hold metadata about the page such as the character encoding, or it can hold links to JavaScript libraries and CSS files.
`<title>A basic web page</title>`	This element holds the text that will appear in the tab of the web browser.
`<meta charset="uft-8">`	This tells the browser what character encoding it should use for the page.
`<body></body>`	This element holds the content of the web page, what appears on the screen.

You can open up the page in a web browser by choosing **File ➤ Open File** from the menu of a web browser and navigate to structure.html, where you will see a basic web page.

HTML Attributes

HTML attributes are a way to add additional information to elements. They are added into the opening tag of an element. They are usually a key value pair, in the format of "attribute name" = "value." One example is the link attribute; if you want to create a link to another web site from your web page, you use the anchor tag, and within this tag you add an attribute with the value of the other website's URL. Figure 4-2 shows the attributes for an anchor element.

Figure 4-2. A link attribute

Open up the structure.html file you created and add the following line into the body of the HTML:

```
<a href = "http://example.com/">go to example.com</a>
```

When you refresh the page, you will have a link to example.com.

Note   The value of an attribute cannot have white space in it, but it can have an underscore or a dash.

Two attributes that you will use a lot are ID and class. Both of these attributes allow you to create identifiers for an element. That identifier can be used to select the element in CSS and JavaScript.

ID Attribute

You can give an ID to any HTML element. An ID is a unique identifier for that element. As it is a unique identifier, it can only be used once on a page. This is an example of a paragraph element with an ID:

```
<p id="first_paragraph">This is the text of the first paragraph
on a page</p>
```

Class Attribute

A class attribute is also an identifier for elements but is different from an ID as it can be added to multiple elements on a page. This means that you can select all the elements with the same class and make changes to them all. This is an example of a paragraph element with a class:

```
<p class="first_paragraph">This is the text of the first
paragraph on a page</p>
```

Nested Elements

When you create a web page, you will put elements inside elements, which can be put inside other elements; these are nested elements.

Parent, Child, and Sibling Elements

HTML has a tree-like structure of parent, child, and sibling elements. A child element inherits some style properties from its parent but can also override those. The following HTML shows nested elements:

```
<!DOCTYPE html>
<html>
    <head>
        <title>A basic web page</title>
```

```
            <meta charset="utf-8">
        </head>
        <body>
            <h1>Basics</h1>
            <p>This is a basic web page</p>
            <div id="link-viewer">
                <div class="a-link">
                    <h2>a new link</h2>
                <a href = "http://example.com/">go to example.
                com</a>
                <p>This is an example web page</p>
            </div>
            <div class="a-link">
                <h2>a new link</h2>
                <a href = "http://example.com/">go to example.
                com</a>
                <p>This is an example web page</p>
            </div>
        </div>
    </body>
</html>
```

Figure 4-3 describes the family links between the different elements.

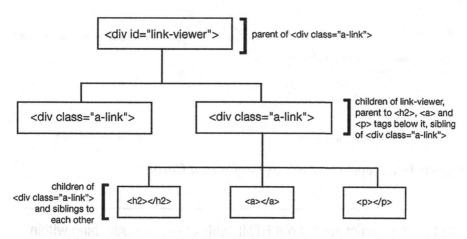

Figure 4-3. *The family of the div "link-viewer"*

Document Object Model

When the browser displays a web page, it has turned the HTML and the CSS into a document object model (DOM). The browser first reads in and parses the HTML, and it creates a tree-like structure of nodes to represent the elements. It then parses the CSS and combines the relevant CSS to the elements in the DOM. The browser then uses the DOM to create the web page.

Browser Developer Tools

Most browsers have tools that help developers to view pages and debug their code. In both Firefox and Chrome, you open them on a Mac by pressing option + command + i and Ctrl + shift + i on Windows.

Try opening structure.html in Firefox or Chrome. Open up the developer tools; in Firefox click on the Inspector tab, and in Chrome click on the Elements tab – you can see the structure of the web page. You can edit the CSS and HTML inside the tools and see how changes work straight away. When you refresh the page, it will go back to the save version of the HTML. Figure 4-4 shows the tabs on the developer tools in Firefox and Chrome.

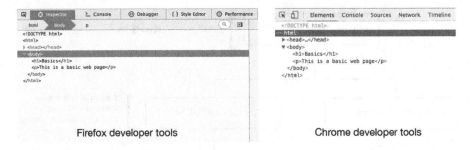

Firefox developer tools

Chrome developer tools

Figure 4-4. Developer tools in Firefox and Chrome

Note You can comment out HTML with < ! -- -->. Anything within those brackets will not appear on the page.

In most text editors, if you are on a line of code and you press **Ctrl + /** it will comment or uncomment your code.

CSS

Cascading style sheets (CSS) are used to define how a web page will look, and they set the layout of a page and how it is styled. It means that there is a separation of content (HTML) and style (CSS). With CSS the same HTML can look very different and without it very basic.

CSS also allows you to create dynamic layouts that change depending on the device the page is being viewed on. These responsive layouts change the size and position of the HTML elements so they fit whatever device the viewer is seeing them on.

CSS changes the style of elements on a web page by using the tag names or an element's attributes; it can hook onto these and attach a style to them. Hooks to the HTML elements are called selectors. CSS is made up of rules. Figure 4-5 Shows the construction of a CSS rule for the HTML body element.

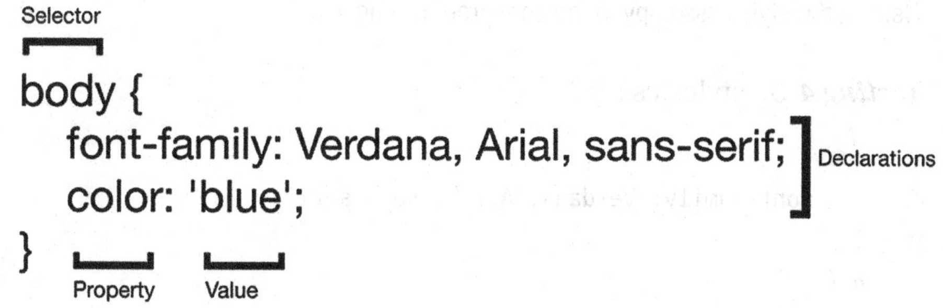

Selector

body {
    font-family: Verdana, Arial, sans-serif;] Declarations
    color: 'blue';
}   Property   Value

Figure 4-5. *A CSS rule*

Most browsers will implement some styles to HTML elements that will be overridden by your CSS.

ADD CSS TO HTML

Create two new files in the same folder: one called styles.html and one called styles.css. In styles.html copy in the HTML from Listing 4-2.

Listing 4-2. styles.html

```
<!DOCTYPE html>
    <html>
        <head>
            <title>starting CSS</title>
            <meta charset="utf-8">
            <link rel="stylesheet" type="text/css" href="styles.css">
        </head>
        <body>
            <h1>Using CSS</h1>
            <p>This paragraph text will is styled with CSS so
            that it is blue.</p>
        </body>
    </html>
```

103

Next, in the styles.css copy in the code from Listing 4-3.

Listing 4-3. styles.css

```css
body{
    font-family: Verdana, Arial, sans-serif;
}
h1{
    color: green;
    border: black solid 1px;
}

p{
    color: blue;
}
```

Open styles.html in a web browser, and you will see the effects of the CSS on HTML content.

You can write the CSS in the head of the HTML, but it is good practice to create a separate file and link it to the HTML page.

The Code Explained

Table 4-4 explains styles.html and styles.css.

Table 4-4. styles.html and styles CSS explained

```<link rel="stylesheet"```
```type="text/css"```
```href="styles.css">```
	The <link> tag is used to import the CSS into the HTML file. The attribute href has a value of the path to the CSS file.

```body{```
```font-family: Verdana,```
```Arial, sans-serif;```
```}```
	A CSS is rule is created for the body of the HTML page. The font-family declaration lists the fonts you want the page to use. If the browser does not have a font, it will try the next one on the list.

```{```
``` parser: SerialPort.```
``` parsers.readline('\n')```
```});```
	The data gets parsed using readline, and the '\n' creates a new line that separates each line of data.

```h1{```
``` color: green;```
``` border: black solid```
``` 1px;```
```}```
	A CSS rule is created for H1 elements. There are two declarations; color changes the font color and border creates a border around the element.

```p{```
``` color: blue;```
```}```
	A CSS rule is created for the p elements, changing the font color to blue.

CSS Selectors

In CSS selectors, select an element or elements on an HTML page. There are different types of selectors.

Type Selector

These are selectors that will select any HTML element on a page with the same tag name. For example, the selector for an h1 tag is:

```
h1{
    background-color: orange;
}
```

Class Selector

You can use an HTML elements class name as a selector. The class selector uses the class name of the element with a period (.) before it; for example, the following rule would select all elements on an HTML page with the class chosenElement:

```
.chosenElement{
    background-color: orange;
}
```

ID Selector

You can use an HTML elements ID as a selector. The ID selector uses the ID of the element with a hash (#) before it; for example, the following rule would select the element on an HTML page with the ID of chosenElement:

```
#chosenElement{
    background-color: orange;
}
```

Attribute Selectors

You can select an HTML attribute by its key or its key and value. The example below shows the href attribute for an anchor tag being styled:

```
a[href]{
  background-color: orange;
}
```

Universal Selectors

The universal selector is a star symbol (*) and can go before any selector and will match any element of that type; it can be used as a simple reset of CSS rules at the beginning of your CSS.

```
*{
  margin: 0;
  padding: 0;
}
```

Selectors give you an enormous amount of control: you can have multiple selectors in a CSS rule, and you can choose child and sibling elements and elements in a particular nested position.

This can get confusing with elements having multiple styles attached to them. The Cascading in CSS implements a number of rules to let you control what element has what style.

Cascading Rules

When you have nested elements, a style is attached to elements above and will cascade down to the elements below. The decision on which style will be applied to an element is dependent on a set of three rules: importance, specificity, and source order. Importance will win over specificity and source order and specificity will win over source order.

Specificity

Specificity looks at how specific a selector is. An ID is more specific than a class because an ID is unique. A class is more specific then a tag name.

Importance

In CSS, !important can be added at the end of a declaration; for example:

```
color: orange !important;
```

It will override any other color rule that is applied to an element. If you are having conflicts with CSS it is better to work them out without using !important; only use it when it is really necessary if the style can't be overridden in any other way.

Source Order

In the style sheet you might have selectors with the same importance and specificity; if this is the case rules that are later in the style sheet will win.

The Box Model

The CSS box model forms the layout of the page. All elements on the page are seen as having a box around them. The box model consists of the content, padding, border, and a margin. Figure 4-6 shows the box model.

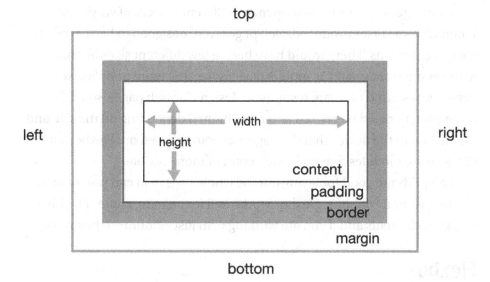

Figure 4-6. *The CSS box model*

Note   Browsers adopt CSS rules and JavaScript at different rates. On caniuse.com you can check which browsers support the CSS or JavaScript you want to use.

Display Layout

There are a few types of display layouts; these determine how HTML elements are positioned on a web page in relation to other elements. Block and inline layouts were explained earlier in the chapter. Others include position, float, inline block, Flexbox, and CSS grid.

Flexbox and CSS grid are new and overcome a number of problems with CSS layouts. As they are new, older browsers do not support them and while their rules might change, the underlying concepts will not.

109

Web pages are now viewed on many different devices of varying sizes. When CSS was first introduced, web pages were designed to be viewed on computer screens. There would have been a few different sizes but not as many as there are today. As mobile devices became more popular, web developers started to create responsive designs for web pages, so that the same content could be resized and repositioned depending on the size and orientation of the device that the page was being viewed on. Flexbox and CSS grid are modules that make web content more flexible.

CSS grids are good for laying out the whole page; you can use them to create rows and columns. Flexbox works well for aligning content within blocks of elements and if you are working with just columns or just rows.

Flexbox

Flexbox was introduced in CSS3 and is in the candidate recommendation stage. It allows for flexibility in the layout when aligning elements, ordering elements, sizing elements, and directing elements.

Flexbox is a module and not a single CSS property. Some of the module's properties are designed for parent containers while others are for child elements. With Flexbox you have a flex container and flex items.

USING FLEXBOX

Create an HTML file called flex.html and copy the code from Listing 4-4.

Listing 4-4. flex.html

```
<!DOCTYPE html>
<html>
<head>
    <style>
        .container {
            display: flex;
```

```
        justify-content: space-between;
        flex-direction: row;

    }
    .item {
        background: YellowGreen;
        width: 200px;
        height: 220px;
        margin-top: 10px;
        line-height: 220px;
        color: white;
        font-weight: bold;
        font-size: 32px;
        text-align: center;
        list-style: none;
    }
    </style>
</head>
<body>
    <ul class="container">
      <li class="item">box 1</li>
      <li class="item">box 2</li>
      <li class="item">box 3</li>
    </ul>

</body>
</html>
```

Open flex.html in a web browser, and try changing the justify-content property to center, flex-start, flex-end, and space-around, refreshing the page each time and seeing the differences. Table 4-5 explains some Flexbox CSS.

The CSS Explained

Table 4-5. *Flexbox CSS*

display: flex	This sets the display mode to Flexbox.
body{ justify-content: space-between;	The justify-content property defines the alignment of the main axis.
flex-direction: row;	This sets the direction of the content, and there are four values in a row: default, row-reverse, column, and column-reverse.

CSS Grid

As CSS grid is new, it will not work on older browsers. CSS grid breaks the page into columns and rows. You define the width and height of the columns and rows and define how many columns and rows an HTML element will take up.

Grid lines divide each row and column; it is these lines that are used to define the space an HTML element will take up on the page. Figure 4-7 shows the grid lines on a CSS Grid.

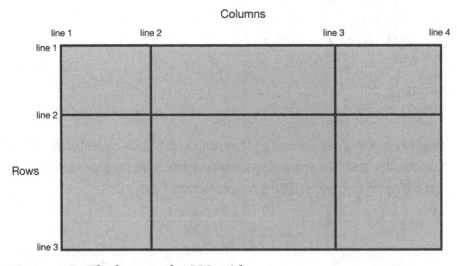

Figure 4-7. *The layout of a CSS grid*

Three columns of 1Fr each column will take up 1 fraction of the available space. All the columns will have an equal width on the page. You can place elements across the cells of the grid. Figure 4-8 Shows div elements placed on a CSS Grid.

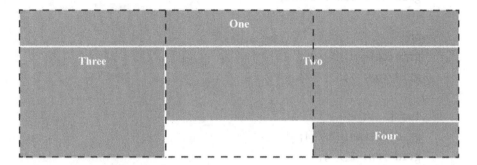

Figure 4-8. *HTML elements on a CSS Grid*

USING CSS GRID

Create a new HTML file called grid.html, and copy the code from Listing 4-5, which should replicate Figure 4-8.

Listing 4-5. grid.html

```
<!DOCTYPE html>
<html>
<head>
  <style>
    .wrapper > div {
      background-color: YellowGreen;
      text-align: center;
      color: white;
      line-height: auto;
      font-weight: bold;
      font-size: 32px;
      padding-top: 20px;
    }
```

113

```
    .wrapper {
     display: grid;
     grid-template-columns: repeat(3, 1fr);
     grid-gap: 5px;
     grid-auto-rows: 100px;
    }
    .one {
     grid-column: 1 / 4;
     grid-row: 1;
    }
    .two {
     grid-column: 2 / 4;
     grid-row: 2 / 4;
    }
    .three {
     grid-column: 1;
     grid-row: 2 / 5;
    }
    .four {
     grid-column: 3;
     grid-row: 4;
    }
  </style>
</head>
<body>

<div class="wrapper">
  <div class="one">One</div>
  <div class="two">Two</div>
  <div class="three">Three</div>
  <div class="four">Four</div>
</div>

</body>
</html>
```

The CSS Explained

Table 4-6 explains the grid css.

Table 4-6. Grid CSS explained

`.wrapper > div {`	This adds style to any div's that are children of the div with the class "wrapper."
`display: grid;`	This sets the display mode to CSS Grid.
`grid-template-columns: repeat(3, 1fr);`	This property sets the number of columns and the fraction of the width they will use on the page. Repeat is a way to add the same formatting to a number of columns, and there will be 3 columns each with 1fr.
`grid-gap: 5px;`	This is the gap between each grid item.
`grid-auto-rows: 100px;`	Sets the height of the rows; there are a number of options including max-content, min-content, and auto.
`grid-column: 1 / 4;`	This specifies how many column grid lines the div will go across. In this example there are 3 columns and 4 grid lines so a div set to 1 / 4 will start at the first grid line and go across to the fourth grid line, across the whole page.
`grid-row: 2 / 5;`	This specifies how many row grid lines the div will go across; in this case it will start at the second grid line and go to the fifth.

Appendix B lists some good resources for Flexbox and CSS Grid.

Color

Color can be represented in a number of ways when building a web application. So far, elements have been given colors with names. There are a certain amount of set color names for the most common colors. You are not restricted to these colors and can use precise color values to define the colors on the page. You can define colors by their red, green blue (RGB) value; their hexadecimal value; and the hue, saturation, and lightness (HSL) value.

RGB

An RGB color is made up of three numbers. The first number represents red, the second green, and the third blue. That number can be between 0 and 255. In CSS it is written as rgb(120, 0 , 0), which would be a dark red color.

Hexadecimal

A hexadecimal color is made up of three hexadecimal numbers. Hexadecimal numbers use the base 16 number system; it uses 16 symbols to represent all numbers. These symbols are 0, 1, 2, 3, 4, 5, 6, 7, 8, 9, A, B, C, D, E, F. In CSS it is written as #780000, which would be a dark red color. The first two digits (78) represent red, the second two (00) green, and the third pair (00) blue. The hexadecimal number 78 is 120 in the decimal system.

HSL

HSL defines a color by hue saturation and lightness. In CSS it is written as hsl(0, 100%, 47%). The first number is hue and then saturation and lightness are represented by percent.

Scalable Vector Graphics (SVG)

SVG is a markup language based on XML. It is a way to describe 2D vector-based graphics. There are advantages to SVG's. They are searchable and can be referenced by JavaScript. They don't lose quality when they are scaled, and they can be manipulated and animated on a web page. You can create basic shapes easily with SVG, and you can create more complex illustrations in software such as InkScape and Illustrator and export illustrations as SVG's. Some primitive shapes defined in SVG are rectangles, circles, and lines.

CREATE AN SVG

Create a new file and call it rectangle.svg and copy in the code in Listing 4-6.

Listing 4-6. rectangle.svg

```
    <svg width="120" height="120" viewBox="0 0 120 120"
  xmlns="http://www.w3.org/2000/svg">
 <rect x="10" y="10"
      width="100" height="100"
      fill="orange" fill-opacity="0.8"
/>
</svg>
```

Open the file in a browser and you should see something similar to Figure 4-9.

Figure 4-9. rectangle.svg in a web browser

117

SVG Explained

Table 4-7 explains rectangle.svg.

Table 4-7. rectangle.svg

`<svg></svg>`	Creates an SVG element.
`width="120" height="120"` `viewBox="0 0 120 120"`	Defines the width and height of the element and its viewBox.
`<rect x="10" y="10"` `width="40"` `height="40"` `fill="orange"` `fill-opacity="0.8"` `/>`	This defines a rectangle that is positioned 10 pixels from the top and left of the SVG area with a width and height of 100 pixels. It also has a fill color that has an opacity.

SVG elements have their own coordinate system that is outside the box model system of HTML elements.

The SVG canvas is where the SVG is drawn; it has a viewport that defines the visible area of the SVG. Any part of the graphic outside of the viewport will be clipped or invisible. <svg width="120" height="120"> defines the width and height of the viewport. If you don't specify units in SVG's, they are considered pixels.

The viewport has a coordinate system with an x- and y-axis that starts at 0,0 at the top left of the SVG. The positive x-axis moves from left to right and the positive y-axis is from the top down.

SVG Scaling

As the coordinate system of an SVG starts at 0,0 on the top left, if you change the height of an SVG it scales upward toward 0 on the y-axis. Make the height value smaller in the code in Listing 4-6 and refresh the browser; the bottom of the rectangle has moved up.

Sometimes you want the height to scale from the bottom of an SVG, for example, if you are animating a bar on a bar chart. Using a scale transform can do this. Open the code from Listing 4-6 and make the changes in bold.

```
<svg width="120" height="120" viewBox="0 0 120 120"
    xmlns="http://www.w3.org/2000/svg">
  <rect x="10" y="-110"
            width="100" height="100"
            fill="orange" fill-opacity="0.8"
            transform="scale(1, -1)"
/>
</svg>
```

A scale transform has been added to the SVG. The scale has two arguments for the x- and y-axes. By scaling it by -1 in the y-axis, the second argument, the rectangle is the same height as before, but it is scaling in a negative direction. The y position has to be moved down by 120 so that you can see the rectangle as the negative scale has scaled it upward, and it is now outside the viewBox. If you save the code and refresh the browser the SVG should look the same. Now try decreasing the height, and in the browser you will notice that the rectangle is scaling from the bottom.

Viewbox

The viewbox allows for a new mapping onto the viewport coordinate system. The viewBox parameters are viewBox = "min-x min-y width height." The min-x and min-y define the upper-left corner of the viewbox. If you change the viewBox in the code to viewBox="10 10 120 120" the result will be that the rectangle will move up and left 10 pixels. The coordinates 0,0 have been remapped so the left corner is now 10,10. If you change the code to svg width="120" height="120" viewBox="0 0 60 60," the Viewbox width and height of 60 will map to the viewport's width and height of 120; this will scale the rectangle up.

Computer Programming

A computer needs to understand the instructions that it is sent so it can carry out the commands. A programming language is a way of writing instructions a human can understand and that can be processed (compiled) into a language a computer understands.

There are some concepts and rules that are true across the majority of programming languages; each language will have a different syntax and implementation, but the concepts are often the same. If you already know one computer language you will see similarities in JavaScript. This section will describe a number of general programming concepts and then how they are implemented in JavaScript.

Variables

A variable is a named storage location for data in the program. It is made up of a key and a value. The key can be any string that isn't a reserved word in that programming language. A variable can be used throughout the code instead of that value. In some languages you can create variables that can't be changed once defined or define what type of data a variable can hold.

In JavaScript you don't have to define the type of a variable. You use the var or let keyword; for example, var x = 10; creates a variable called x that holds the numerical value of 10. The content of x can be changed once it has been created.

Operators

Operators perform actions on variables or values. Some of the common operators in JavaScript are the following:

+ add

- minus

* multiply

/ divide

= assign a value to

== equal to

=== strong equal, the type and value are the same

!== not equal to

&& logical and

|| logical or

++ increments by 1

-- decrements by 1

Types

Types are the ways you can represent data in a programming language. For example, 2 could be a number type or a string type. Different languages have different types. Strings, numbers, and Boolean are all types. What you can do with a variable can depend on what type it is and how it will respond to operators.

JavaScript has seven data types: Boolean, Null, Undefined, Number, String, Symbol, and Object.

Boolean

A Boolean can have a value of true or false. If you had a variable with a Boolean value, you could use that in a conditional statement, for example:

```
var isDay = true;
if(isDay){
    console.log("it is daytime");
} else {
    console.log("it is nighttime");
}
```

Null

Null can only have the value of null. You define a variable and give it a value of null. Null has to be assigned.

Undefined

A variable has the value of undefined if it has been declared but not assigned a value. It is different from Null, as Null has to be assigned and undefined is the value when no value has been assigned.

Number

In JavaScript there is just one type for numbers called Number. Its value is between $-(2^{53}-1)$ and $2^{53}-1$. Floating point numbers can be represented as can +Infinity, -Infinity, and NaN (not-a-number).

String

The String type represents all text in JavaScript whether it's a single character or a paragraph. Strings are bounded by either double quotes " " or single quotes ' '

Symbol

Symbols are new to JavaScript; they are unique and immutable and can be used as a key to an object.

Objects

These are collections of data that you would want to group together. They are sets of key/value pairs.

Statements

Statements are simple instructions that perform an action: for example, var x = 1 + 1 is a statement. When this statement is executed, the variable x will hold the value of 1 + 1.

Expressions

Expressions yield or evaluate a value; 1+1 is an expression.

Data Structures

Data structures are ways of organizing data. They will be grouped together, and there will be a process of extracting the data from the structure.

Array and object are the data structures in JavaScript. An array holds multiple values, called array elements, which don't have a key. An object can hold multiple key/value pairs. The values can be different types within the same array or object.

As the values in an array don't have keys, they are referenced by their place in the array, for example:

```
var fruits = ["oranges", "peaches", "mangoes", "bananas"];
```

The variable fruits hold a number of fruit names. You access an element of array by its position in the array. Array positions start at 0.

```
Fruits[0]; //returns "oranges"
Fruits[3]; //returns "bananas"
```

An object is made up of key/value pairs, for example:

```
var navelOrange = {
    fruit: "orange",
    color: "orange",
    genus: "citrus"
};
```

You access the values using the keys, for example:

```
var navelOrangeType = navelOrange.genus; //returns "citrus"
```

You can also add data to an object:

```
navelOrange.pips = "yes";
```

Conditional Statements

These are statements that will execute code under set conditions. For example, if a variable is equal to something. They are often called if/then statements or if/then/else statements.

In JavaScript you can create an if statement, an if/else statement, or an if/ else if, for example:

```
var fruit = "orange";

if(fruit === "orange") {
    console.log("it is an orange");
}

if(fruit === "orange") {
    console.log("it is an orange");
} else if (fruit === "apple"){
    console.log("it is an apple");
} else {
    console.log("it is not an apple or an orange");
}
```

Loops

Loops let you keep running the same piece of code over and over again until a condition becomes true or false. In JavaScript there are for loops and while loops. For example, loops are a good way of iterating over an array:

```
var fruits = ["oranges", "peaches", "mangoes", "bananas"];

for(var i = 0; i < fruits.length; i++){
    console.log(fruits[i]);
}
```

The for loop defines a variable i that is a counter; there is a check that i is less than the number of elements in the array i < fruits.length;, then i is incremented, i++;. The function console.log then prints out the element of the array fruits with the current counter number. When it becomes greater than the length of the array, the loop stops running.

125

Note   You can test JavaScript code in the developer tools in a browser.

1. Open a browser and press Cmd + Opt + I on a Mac or Ctrl + Shift + I on a Windows PC.

2. Choose the Console tab.

3. At the > type in 2+2 you should see the number 4 on the next line.

There are also while loops:

```
var x = 0;

while(x < 10){
    console.log(x);
    x++;
}
```

The while loop will run as long as x is less than 10. The output will be 0 – 9.

With loops you need to make sure that there is a condition that ends them. If there isn't the loop will go on forever. In the while loop the x is incremented each time the loop executes so it will become greater than 10.

Functions

You can create a short piece of code that does a particular thing and give it a name. These are called functions. For example. if you have code that adds up two numbers you can put it inside a named function. then call it throughout your code. It means you aren't duplicating code and allows you to create code in blocks that are easier to debug.

In JavaScript there are a number of ways to create functions, and one is by creating a named function. For example:

```
function add(number1, number2){
    return number1 + number2;
}
var addUp = add(2, 6);   //addUp holds the value of 8
```

The name of the function is add, and it is passed by two arguments, number1 and number2; it will add these together and return them.

You call a function by its name and in the parentheses pass in the parameters you want to be added up.

Scope

Scope is the range of the code that a variable is accessible in. If you create a variable inside a function it only has scope inside that function, if you try to access it outside the function you will get an error.

Summary

This chapter was a deeper dive into the different components that make up a web application. It explained the concepts behind, building, and styling a web page and some of the concepts of computer programming; these will be used throughout the book. In the next chapter you will create an application that creates a web page that controls components on an Arduino.

CHAPTER 5

Front End to Arduino

So far you have used the serial port to send data to a web server, but the serial port can be a two-way stream of data; it can send and receive data. In this chapter you will start sending data to the Arduino through a web server via the serial port. With an interactive web page, you will be controlling components connected to an Arduino.

The Applications

You will be creating two web applications in this chapter. One will turn on and off LED's connected to an Arduino. Figure 5-1 shows the web page.

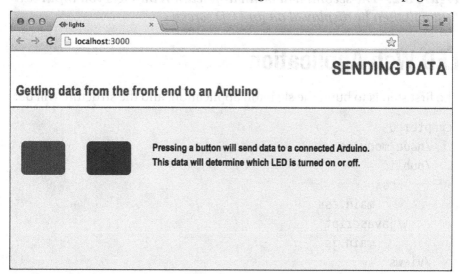

Figure 5-1. *The web page for the first application*

© Indira Knight 2018
I. Knight, *Connecting Arduino to the Web*, https://doi.org/10.1007/978-1-4842-3480-8_5

The second will be an application that lets you input text that will then be displayed on an LCD screen. Figure 5-2 shows the final web page.

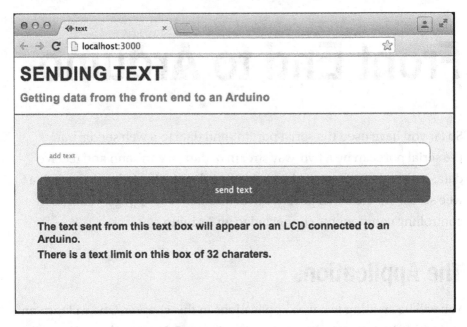

Figure 5-2. *The second will be an application that lets you input text that will then be displayed on an LCD screen*

LED Web Application

The first step is to build the skeleton application, and the structure will be:

```
/chapter_05
    /node_modules
    /public
        /css
            main.css
        /javascript
            main.js
    /views
        index.ejs
    index.js
```

The node modules folder will be created automatically on installation of the modules. The setup for creating the server is the same as in Chapter 3:

1. Create a new folder to hold the application. I called mine chapter_05.

2. Open the command prompt (Windows operating system) or a terminal window (Mac) and navigate to the newly created folder.

3. When you are in the right directory, type npm init to create a new application, and you can press return through each of the questions, or make changes to them.

4. You can now start adding the necessary libraries; to download Express.js at the command line, type npm install express@4.15.3 --save.

5. Then install ejs, and type npm install ejs@2.5.6 --save.

6. When that's downloaded install serial port. On a Mac type npm install serialport@4.0.7 --save; on a Windows PC type npm install serialport@4.0.7 --build-from-source.

7. Then finally install socket.io, type npm install socket. io@1.7.3 --save.

CREATE A NODE.JS SERVER

In the route of the application create a file called index.js and copy in the code
from Listing 5-1.

Listing 5-1. index.js code

```
var http = require('http');
var express = require('express');
var app = express();
var server = http.createServer(app);
var io = require('socket.io')(server);

app.engine('ejs', require('ejs').__express);
app.set('view engine', 'ejs');

app.use(express.static(__dirname + '/public'));

app.get('/', function (req, res){
    res.render('index');
});

io.on('connection', function(socket){
    console.log('socket.io connection');

socket.on('disconnect', function(){
        console.log('disconnected');
    });
});

server.listen(3000, function(){
    console.log('listening on port 3000...');
});
```

The Code Explained

The server has a route to a web page and also creates a web socket. The
function app.get creates a route so that an index file will be rendered when the
application is opened.

CREATE A WEB PAGE

The initial page will contain two blocks of color, one red and one green. When the user clicks on a block, it will change to its on or off color. Each block of color will be created by a div with a background color.

If you haven't created the index.ejs, main.css and main.js files do that now; make sure they are in the right directory. As main.css and main.js are referenced in the index.ejs file, they need to be created, even though there is no code in them at this point. In the index.ejs file copy the code in Listing 5-2.

Listing 5-2. index.ejs code

```
<!DOCTYPE html>
<html>
<head>
    <meta charset="UTF-8">
    <title>lights</title>
    <link href="/css/main.css" rel="stylesheet" type="text/css">
</head>
<body>
    <header>
        <h1>SENDING DATA</h1>
        <h2>Getting data from the front end to an Arduino</h2>
    </header>
    <div id="content">
        <div class="container">
            <div id="red-block" class="color-block"></div>
            <div id="green-block" class="color-block"></div>
            <div class="text-block">
                <p>Pressing a button will send data to a
                connected Arduino.</p>
                <p>This data will determine which LED is turned
                on or off.</p>
```

133

```
            </div>
        </div>
    </div>
    <script src="/socket.io/socket.io.js"></script>
    <script src="javascript/main.js"></script>
</body>
</html>
```

The Code Explained

Each block of color has its own div. The id is used in the CSS to color the block and the class is used to style both color blocks. There is no child content in the div.

You can check out how the page looks so far by navigating to the application in a console window and type nodemon index.js or node index.js to start the application. Open a browser and go to http://localhost:3000/ to see the application running.

ADD STYLE

The style will be added in the main.css file in the public/css folder. Open or create the main.css file and copy in the code from Listing 5-3.

Listing 5-3. main.css CSS

```
*{
    margin: 0;
    padding: 0;
}
body{
    font-family: "Arial Narrow", Arial, "Helvetica Condensed",
    Helvetica, sans-serif;
    color: #5a5b5a;
```

```css
    background-color: #f4f4f4;
}
h1{
    letter-spacing: 1px;
    padding: 10px;
    direction:rtl;
    text-align:justify;
}
h2{
    letter-spacing: 0.5px;
    padding: 0 0 15px 10px;
}
p{
    font-weight: bold;
    margin-bottom: 5px;
    color: black;
}
header{
    border-bottom: 2px solid #5a5b5a;
    background-color: white;
}
.container {
    display: flex;
    flex-wrap:wrap;
    margin-top: 40px;
}
#red-block{
    background-color: #C80002;
}
.red-block-on{
    background-color: #ff0036 !important;
```

```css
    box-shadow: rgba(0, 0, 0, 0.2) 0 -1px 7px 1px, inset #441313
    0 -1px 9px, rgba(255, 0, 0, 0.5) 0 2px 12px;
}
#green-block{
    background-color: #1f5900;
}
.green-block-on{
    background-color: #1eff00 !important;
    border: 10px;
    box-shadow: rgba(0, 0, 0, 0.2) 0 -1px 7px 1px, inset #304701
    0 -1px 9px, #89FF00 0 2px 12px;
}
.color-block, .text-block{
    margin: 20px;
}
.color-block{
    flex-basis:40px;
    height: 60px;
    border-radius: 8px;
    flex-grow: 1;
    cursor: pointer;
}
.text-block{
    flex-basis:200px;
    height: 200px;
    flex-grow: 8;
    font-size: 18px;
}
```

The Code Explained

Table 5-1 explains the CSS in main.css.

Table 5-1. main.css CSS explained

`h1{`
`  letter-spacing: 1px;`
`  padding: 10px;`
`  direction:rtl;`
`  text-align:justify;`
`}`
	letter-spacing increases the space between letters, and this can make words written in uppercase easier to read.
	direction: rtl is a style that changes the direction of the text from right to left instead of left to right.

`flex-wrap:wrap;`	This will make the items in the Flexbox fall below each other when the browser is smaller.

`.red-block-on{`
`background-color: #F00`
`!important;`
`box-shadow: rgba(0, 0,`
`0, 0.2) 0 -1px 7px 1px,`
`inset #441313 0 -1px 9px,`
`rgba(255, 0, 0, 0.5) 0 2px`
`12px;`
`}`
	Both the red and green box have an on state when they are clicked. This is achieved by adding a class with a box shadow to create the impression of a light being on. !important is used with background-color to override the div's original color. The box shadow is being used to create the lighter edge around the div.

`.color-block{`
`  border-radius: 22px;`
`  flex-grow: 1;`
`  cursor: pointer;`
`}`
	The flex-grow:1 command determines how much space in the Flexbox the item will take up.
	cursor: pointer is used to change the cursor when it hovers over a box.

If your server is still running with nodemon you should be able to refresh the page and see the changes the CSS has made. If you're not using nodemon, restart your server and refresh the page.

A Bit More About Flexbox

It a good time to gain a bit more understanding of Flexbox and look at some of the values. Table 5-2 lists some Flexbox values.

Table 5-2. *Flexbox values*

flex-direction	The default is row; this means that items will be placed horizontally by default.
justify-content: flex-start	The items will stack at the start of the line.
align-items:stretch	The items will stretch to fill the container.
flex-wrap: nowrap	The items will stay in a single line.
Flex-shrink: 1	The items are allowed to shrink.
flex-grow	flex-grow determines the amount of space the item will take up in the flex container in relation to other items. In the CSS in Listing 5-3 the two color blocks have a flex-grow value of 1, and the text box has a flex-grow value of 8. The text box will be given more space than the color blocks.

ADD INTERACTION

JavaScript is used to add in the action when each colored block is clicked. The JavaScript will be added in the main.js file in the public/javascript folder. Open the empty main.js file you created earlier or create a main.js file and copy in the code in Listing 5-4.

Listing 5-4. main.js code

```
var redBlock = document.getElementById("red-block");
var greenBlock = document.getElementById("green-block");

redBlock.addEventListener("click", function(){
    redBlock.classList.toggle("red-block-on");
});

greenBlock.addEventListener("click", function(){
    greenBlock.classList.toggle("green-block-on");
});
```

The Code Explained

There are two variables that hold a reference to the color block elements on the page, "redBlock" and "greenBlock." Event listeners are added to these variables. A JavaScript event listener is always listening for a certain event to happen. When it does happen it can call a function. In this case the function changes the color of the block. It does this by adding or removing a class called "red-block-on" or "green-block-on." It is common practice to add or remove classes to make a change to an element. It means that all the CSS for the change is in one place. Table 5-3 explains main.js.

Table 5-3. *main.js explained*

`redBlock.addEventListener` `("click", function()`	A click event listener is added to the redBlock div. This listener listens for the div to be clicked. When it is clicked a function is called.
`redBlock.addEventListener` `("click", function()`	A click event listener is added to the redBlock div. This listener listens for the div to be clicked. When it is clicked a function is called.
`redBlock.classList.` `toggle("red-block-on");`	This line of code uses two JavaScript functions classList and toggle. classList is normally used with add or remove to add or remove a class. By using it with toggle it will determine if the div has the class; if it does it removes it, if it doesn't, it adds it.

Now in a console window navigate to the route of the application and type nodemon index.js or node index.js to start the application. Open a browser and go to http://localhost:3000/ to see the application running.

When you click on the red or green button you should see it change so it looks like a light being switched on or off.

SENDING DATA FROM THE FRONT END

Now the basic application is set up, it's time to send data from the front end to an Arduino. Each time a button is pressed in the web browser, data will be sent to the SerialPort functions, so it can be sent to an Arduino via the serial port.

To do this code will be added to Listing 5-1 and Listing 5-4.

First update the main.js file from Listing 5-4; the updates are in bold.

```
(function(){
    var socket = io();

    var redBlock = document.getElementById("red-block");
    var greenBlock = document.getElementById("green-block");

    redBlock.addEventListener("click", function(){
        var redClick = redBlock.classList.toggle("red-block-on");
        socket.emit('red', redClick + "_red");
    });

    greenBlock.addEventListener("click", function(){
        var greenClick = greenBlock.classList.toggle("green-
        block-on");
        socket.emit('green', greenClick + "_green");
    });
})();
```

The Code Explained

Table 5-4 expains the code in main.js

Table 5-4. *main.js update explained*

```(function(){ })();```	The JavaScript has been wrapped in an anonymous function that calls itself. It is know as an Immediately-invoked function expression (IIFE). It keeps the JavaScript in a block and avoids conflict if you name something in your code the same as a library you are importing. For example, you don't have to worry if the library you are importing has a variable called greenClick as it is in the function you created; it is within its own namespace and scope.
```var greenClick = greenBlock.classList. toggle("green-block-on");```	The Node.js application will send data to an Arduino telling it to turn a LED on or off depending on if the button on the front end is in on or off mode. The function toggle() returns a Boolean, a true or false value, depending on the state of the toggle. This value can be used to determine if the class that puts the button into the on state has been applied to the HTML element. The variable greenClick and redClick will hold this value.
```socket.emit('red', redClick + "_red");```	When the button has been clicked a socket.emit() function is triggered, sending the information about which button has been clicked and its state to the server.

Finally update the index.js file from Listing 5-1. The updates are in bold.

```
var http = require('http');
var express = require('express');
var app = express();
var server = http.createServer(app);
var io = require('socket.io')(server);
var SerialPort = require('serialport');
var serialport = new SerialPort('<add in the serial port for
your Arduino>', {
    parser: SerialPort.parsers.readline('\n')
});

app.engine('ejs', require('ejs').__express);
app.set('view engine', 'ejs');

app.use(express.static(__dirname + '/public'));

app.get('/', function (req, res){
    res.render('index');
});

serialport.on('open', function(){
    console.log('serial port opened');
});

io.on('connection', function(socket){
    console.log('socket.io connection');

    socket.on('red', function(data){
        serialport.write(data + 'T');
    });

    socket.on('green', function(data){
        serialport.write(data + 'T');
    });
```

```
    socket.on('disconnect', function(){
        console.log('disconnected');
    });
});

server.listen(3000, function(){
    console.log('listening on port 3000...');
});
```

Delete <add in the serial port for your Arduino> and add in your own serial port into the new SerialPort() function.

Most of the additions are code you have used in previous chapters. The SerialPort library is included in the application along with the port id for the Arduino. The serialport.on() function is called to open the serial port.

There are two socket.on() functions that link to the socket.emit() functions in the front-end JavaScript code. What is new is the serialport.write() function.

The Code Explained

Table 5-5 explains index.js.

Table 5-5. *index.js update explained*

serialport. write(data + 'T');	This function sends data from the application to the serial port. In this case data from the front end will be sent to the serial port. The character "T" is also added to the data. This is a terminating character. It could be any character you choose. You need a terminating character, as when an Arduino receives the data it doesn't know what the end of the data is. It receives a stream of data and needs to know what one piece of data is and what is the next. The "T" is used in the Arduino program to let it know that it is the end of one piece of data

Setting Up the LED

The setup for the Arduino in this chapter will use an Arduino Uno, a breadboard, a green and a red LED, two 220 ohm resistors, and jump leads. Figure 5-3 shows the kit you'll need.

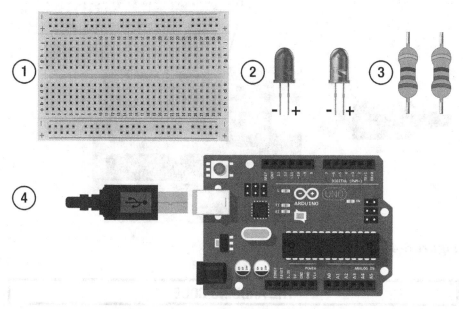

Figure 5-3. *1. Breadboard, 2. A red and a green LED, 3. Two 220 ohm resistors, 4. An Arduino*

Once you have the kit together you need to set it up as shown in Figure 5-4 and connect it to a USB port on your computer. Make sure the Arduino is not connected to the computer or any other power supply when you are connecting the components.

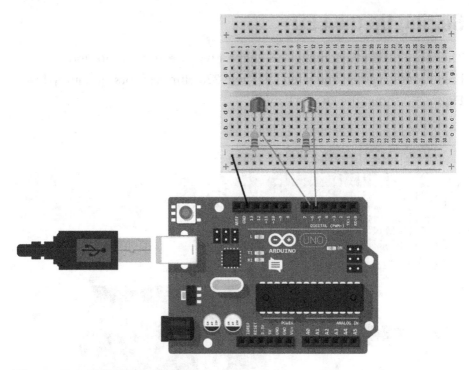

Figure 5-4. *The LED circuit*

THE ARDUINO CODE

Open the Arduino IDE. In the tools menu make sure the correct Arduino type is chosen in board and that the port the Arduino is connected to is registering.

Create a new sketch and call it chapter_05, and copy the code from Listing 5-5.

Listing 5-5. chapter_05.ino

```
const int redLed = 6;
const int greenLed = 5;

char charRead;
String inputString ="";
```

```
void setup() {
  Serial.begin(9600);
  pinMode(redLed, OUTPUT);
  pinMode(greenLed, OUTPUT);
}

void loop() {
  if (Serial.available()) {
    charRead = Serial.read();
    if(charRead != 'T'){
      inputString += charRead;
    } else {

      if(inputString == "true_red"){
        digitalWrite(redLed, 1);
      } else if(inputString == "false_red") {
        digitalWrite(redLed, 0);
      } else if(inputString == "true_green") {
        digitalWrite(greenLed, 1);
      } else if(inputString == "false_green") {
        digitalWrite(greenLed, 0);
      }
      inputString = "";
    }
  }
}
```

Verify the script, and then upload it to the Arduino. Make sure that the Node.js application is turned off. If it is still running, the code will not be uploaded to the Arduino as the serial port is already being used by the application.

The Code Explained

Table 5-6 explains the code in chapter_05.ino.

Table 5-6. *chapter_05.ino explained*

`const int redLed = 6;` `const int greenLed = 5;`	There are two constant variables that hold the digital pin numbers of the two LEDs.
`char charRead;`	A variable with the type of char (a single character) is created to hold each character of data from the serial port.
`String inputString ="";`	inputString is a variable of type string, and it will be used to join together all the characters coming in through the serial port for a specific piece of data.
`if (Serial.` `available()) {`	The if statement checks if there is serial data coming into the Arduino.
`charRead = Serial.` `read();`	The Serial.read() function is called to get the data from the serial port. The data will be a single character, which is stored in the variable charRead.

`if(charRead != 'T'){`
`  inputString +=`
`  charRead;`
`}`
	The if statement checks that charRead is not equal to the character "T." If it isn't it means that the current character isn't the terminating character so it is added to the inputString.

`else{`	If the character is "T" it means that all the current data has been received and the else statement is triggered.

`if(inputString ==`
`"true_red"){`
`   ...`
`digitalWrite`
`(greenLed, 0);`
`}`
	Inside the else statement are a series of if statements that check what the data is and determine which light should be turned on or off.

`inputString = "";`	Once the data has been used to turn on or off an LED, the inputString is reset to empty, so it is ready for the next piece of data.

Once the program has been uploaded to the Arduino, restart the Node.js server and go to http://localhost:3000/. When you click on the red or green button, the equivalent button should be turned on or off on the circuit.

LCD Web Application

The second application in this chapter will send text data to the Arduino that will be displayed on a liquid crystal display (LCD). The application will need a new directory, with the following structure:

```
/chapter_05_lcd
    /node_modules
    /public
        /css
            main.css
        /javascript
            main.js
    /views
        index.ejs
    index.js
```

Create the skeleton application for the application:

1. Create a new folder to hold the application. I called mine chapter_05_lcd.

2. Open the command prompt (Windows operating system) or a terminal window (Mac) and navigate to the newly created folder.

3. When you are in the right directory, type npm init to create a new application, and you can press return through each of the questions, or make changes to them.

149

4. You can now start adding the necessary libraries; to download Express.js at the command line, type npm install express@4.15.3 --save.

5. Then install ejs, type npm install ejs@2.5.6 --save.

6. When that's downloaded, install serial port. On a Mac type npm install serialport@4.0.7 –save, and on a Windows PC type npm install serialport@4.0.7 --build-from-source.

7. Then finally install socket.io, type npm install socket.io@1.7.3 --save.

Create the folders for the directories and you can also create the files.

Note   When using npm init, names cannot contain capital letters.

Create the Server

The Node.js server is almost identical to the final version of Listing 5-1. Open or create a index.js file for the chapter_05_lcd application and copy in the code from Listing 5-6.

Listing 5-6. index.js

```
var http = require('http');
var express = require('express');
var app = express();
var server = http.createServer(app);
var io = require('socket.io')(server);
var SerialPort = require('serialport');
```

```
var serialport = new SerialPort('<add in the serial port for
your Arduino>', {
    parser: SerialPort.parsers.readline('\n')
});

app.engine('ejs', require('ejs').__express);
app.set('view engine', 'ejs');

app.use(express.static(__dirname + '/public'));

app.get('/', function (req, res){
    res.render('index');
});

serialport.on('open', function(){
    console.log('serial port opened');
});

io.on('connection', function(socket){
    console.log('socket.io connection');

    socket.on('input-text', function(data){
        serialport.write(data + 'T');
    });

    socket.on('disconnect', function(){
        console.log('disconnected');
    });
});

server.listen(3000, function(){
    console.log('listening on port 3000...');
});
```

There is a new socket.on() function id called 'input-text'. This will listen for the socket.emit with the same id, which will be on the front end. It will send the text to the Arduino.

CREATE THE WEB PAGE

The web page will be very simple, a text box and an enter button. Open or create the index.js file in the views folder and copy the code from Listing 5-7.

Listing 5-7. index.ejs

```
<!DOCTYPE html>
<html>
<head>
    <meta charset="UTF-8">
    <title>text</title>
    <link href="/css/main.css" rel="stylesheet" type="text/css">
</head>
<body>
    <header>
        <h1>SENDING TEXT</h1>
        <h2>Getting data from the front end to an Arduino</h2>
    </header>
    <div id="content">
        <input type="text" id="input-text" placeholder="add
        text" maxlength="32">
        <input id="send-text" type="submit" value="send text">
        <div class="text-block">
            <p>The text sent from this text box will appear on
            an LCD connected to an Arduino.</p>
```

```
            <p>There is a text limit on this box of 32
            charaters.</p>
        </div>
    </div>
    <script src="/socket.io/socket.io.js"></script>
    <script src="javascript/main.js"></script>
</body>
</html>
```

The HTML uses input boxes. In HTML there are a number of elements for creating forms. These forms can be sent to the server to be processed.

The Code Explained

Table 5-7 explains the code in index.ejs.

Table 5-7. index.ejs explained

`<input type="text" id="input-text" placeholder="add text" maxlength="32">`	This creates a text input by making type = "text." It has placeholder text that holds default text. There is also a character limit that is sent with maxLength.
`<input id="send-text" type="submit" value="send text">`	This input is a submit button, and its type has been set to submit. It has a value that will appear on the button.

MAKE THE WEB PAGE INTERACTIVE

Open or create a main.js file in the public/javascript folder and copy into it the code in Listing 5-8.

Listing 5-8. main.js

```
(function(){
    var socket = io();

    var sendTextButton = document.getElementById("send-text");

    sendTextButton.addEventListener("click", function(){
        var sendText = document.getElementById("input-text").value;
        socket.emit('input-text', sendText);
    });
})();
```

The Code Explained

Table 5-8 explains the code in main.js.

Table 5-8. *main.js explained*

var sendTextButton = document.getElementById("send-text");	The variable sendTextButton holds a reference to the input button.
sendTextButton.addEventListener ("click", function(){	A click function is added to the input button.
var sendText = document.getElementById("input-text").value;	When the input button is clicked, a variable gets the value that is in the text input box.
socket.emit('input-text', sendText);	The text from the input box is sent to the server with a socket.emit function.

STYLE THE PAGE

There are some differences to the CSS for this application from Listing 5-3. It doesn't use Flexbox and there is styling for the inputs. Open or create a main. css file in the public/css folder and copy in the CSS in Listing 5-9.

Listing 5-9. main.css

```css
*{
 margin: 0;
 padding: 0
}

body{
 font-family: Arial, "Helvetica Condensed", Helvetica,
 sans-serif;
 color: #3a3b3a;
 background-color: #F4F4F4;
}

h1{
  letter-spacing: 1px;
  padding: 10px;
}

h2{
 letter-spacing: 0.5px;
 font-size: 19px;
 padding: 0 0 15px 10px;
 color: #E37222;
}
```

```css
p{
 font-weight: bold;
 margin-bottom: 5px;
}
header{
 border-bottom: 2px solid #07889B;
 background-color: white;
}

#content {
  margin: 40px;
}

input[type=text], select {
  width: 100%;
  padding: 12px 20px;
  margin: 8px 0;
  display: inline-block;
  border: 1px solid #E37222;
  border-radius: 12px;
  box-sizing: border-box;
}

input[type=submit] {
  font-size: 14px;
  width: 100%;
  background-color: #07889B;
  color: white;
  padding: 14px 20px;
  margin: 8px 0;
  border: none;
  border-radius: 12px;
  cursor: pointer;
}
```

```
.text-block{
  width: 100%;
  font-size: 18px;
  margin-top: 20px;
}
```

The CSS Explained

Table 5-9 explains the CSS in main.css.

Table 5-9. *main.css explained*

input[type=text], select {	This selects the input text box.
display: inline-block;	Elements with inline-block can have a width and height.
box-sizing: border-box;	This makes the corners of the box rounded.
input[type=submit] {	This selects the submit button.

Set Up the LCD

There are quite a few pins on the LCD that control the component. There is a register select (rs) pin; this controls where the data will go to in the LCDs memory. The Enable (en) pin allows writing to registers. There are eight data pins (d0 – d7).

A potentiometer is also part of the circuit. This changes the contrast of the screen. The equipment needed for this application is shown in Figure 5-5.

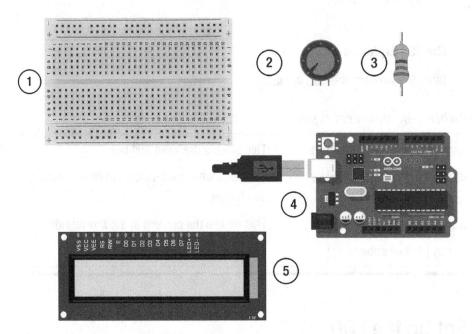

Figure 5-5. *1.breadboard, 2. 10k ohm potentiometer, 3. A 220 ohm resistor, 4. An Arduino, 5. An LCD screen*

The setup for the Arduino is shown in Figure 5-6 Make sure that the Arduino is not connected to power when putting it together.

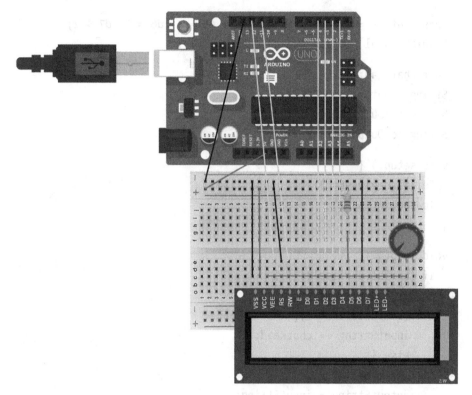

Figure 5-6. *Setup for the LCD*

THE ARDUINO CODE

Open the Arduino IDE and create a new sketch. Connect the Arduino to your computer and make sure that it shows up in the port and is the correct board. Copy the code in Listing 5-10 into the new sketch. Save it as chapter_05_lcd. ino, verify it, and then upload it to the Arduino.

Listing 5-10. chapter_05_lcd.ino

```
#include <LiquidCrystal.h>

const int rs = 12, en = 11, d4 = 5, d5 = 4, d6 = 3, d7 = 2;
LiquidCrystal lcd(rs, en, d4, d5, d6, d7);

char charRead;
String inputString = "";
String outputString = "";
String newOutputString = "";

void setup() {
  Serial.begin(9600);
  lcd.begin(16, 2);
}

void loop() {
  if (Serial.available()) {
    charRead = Serial.read();
    if(charRead != 'T'){
      inputString += charRead;
    } else {
      lcd.clear();
      outputString = inputString;
      inputString = "";
    }
  }

  if(newOutputString != outputString){
    lcd.print(outputString);
    newOutputString = outputString;
  }

  lcd.scrollDisplayLeft();
  delay(500);
}
```

The Code Explained

Table 5-10 explains the code in chapter_05_lcd.ino.

Table 5-10. chapter_05_lcd.ino explained

`#include <LiquidCrystal.h>`	Brings the LiquidCrystal library into the sketch. This library is needed to control the LCD.

`const int rs = 12, en = 11,`
`d4 = 5, d5 = 4, d6 = 3,`
`d7 = 2;`
	A number of integer variables are created to hold information on the pins used on the LCD. Pin 12 is the register select; pin 11 is the Enable pin; d4, d5, d6, and d7 are the data pins.

`LiquidCrystal lcd(rs, en,` `d4, d5, d6, d7);`	A LiquidCrystal object, called lcd, is created.

`char charRead;`
`String inputString = "";`
`String outputString = "";`
`String newOutputString = "";`
	A number of variables are created to hold the text data.

`lcd.begin(16, 2);`	This initializes the LCD and species the width and height of the display.
`lcd.clear();`	The clear() function clears the screen so it is ready to display the new data.
`outputString = inputString;`	Put the new string into the variable that holds the data to be displayed.
`inputString = "";`	Resets the inputString ready for new data.
`if(newOutputString !=` `outputString){`	Check that the outputString isn't the same as the current string. As the code is in the loop function, without the check the same string would be added to the output string every time the loop went around.

(continued)

161

Table 5-10. (*continued*)

`lcd.print(outputString);`	If it is a new string the LiquidCrystal library's print() function is called, and the string is passed and displayed on the LCD.
`newOutputString = outputString;`	The variable newOutputString is updated ready for the next loop.
`lcd.scrollDisplayLeft();`	The scrollDisplayLeft() function makes the text scroll left.

Once the Arduino has been updated, go to the root of the application in a console window and start the application by either typing nodemon index.js or node index.js. Open a web browser and go to http://localhost:3000/. Type some text into the box and send it; it will take a few seconds but it will then appear on the LCD screen.

Use the potentiometer to change the contrast of the screen. If you don't see anything on the screen, it might be that the contrast is turned down.

Caution   As there a quite a few wires in this setup, if you are not getting data shown on the screen or if there are strange characters on the screen, check all the wires. Also turn the potentiometer as this changes the contrast of the screen.

Summary

In this chapter you started sending data from a server to an Arduino to change components. Now you know the main principles of sending data to and from an Arduino using a web server. The next chapter will combine this knowledge to create a project that sends data from an Arduino to a web page and use that information to update a component connected to an Arduino.

CHAPTER 6

Arduino to Front End Part II

This chapter looks in depth how Arduino components interact with web page elements. You will use analog and digital data, JavaScript data structures, and simple calculations on the data. By the end of this chapter, you will have created an interactive application using potentiometers to answer web-based questions, make calculations with the data, and visualize it on an Arduino.

Analog and Digital Signals

Arduinos have both digital and analog pins that can send and receive either analog or digital signals. An analog signal is continuously variable; a digital signal counts in fixed units. Figure 6-1 shows an analog and digital signal.

© Indira Knight 2018
I. Knight, *Connecting Arduino to the Web*, https://doi.org/10.1007/978-1-4842-3480-8_6

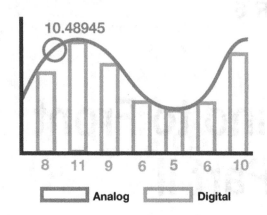

Figure 6-1. *An analog and digital signal*

A digital signal has a limited number of values, a limited number of steps in a range. An analog signal is continuously variable. So a digital signal could register 11 or 12 where an analog signal could register any number between 11 and 12.

An Arduino has both analog and digital pins. There is an analogRead function that lets you read in data from an analog pin and an analogWrite function that lets you use that data to control other components, for example, the brightness of an LED.

The analogRead function has a range of 0 to 1023, and the analogWrite function has a range of 0 to 255. The read function maps the input voltage into values between 0 and 1023. The data from the read has to be mapped so that it fits into the range of the analogWrite.

The Application

In this chapter you will be creating an event feedback application. It will allow you to get feedback from attendees of an event and work out how successful the event is. There will be questions on the screen that will be answered using physical potentiometers. That data will then be used to work out how successful the event is, displayed on the web page, and sent back to an Arduino.

SET UP THE ARDUINO

The circuit for the events metric application will consist of two potentiometers and a button. The potentiometers are used to answer questions and the button to submit the data. You will need two potentiometers, an Arduino, a button, and leads. The components are shown in Figure 6-2.

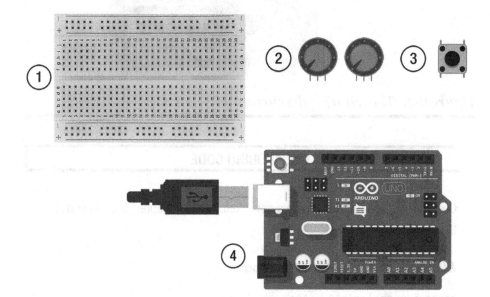

Figure 6-2. Components for the application: 1. Breadboard, 2. 2 x potentiometers, 3. Button, 4. Arduino Uno

Connect the components to the Arduino as shown in Figure 6-3.

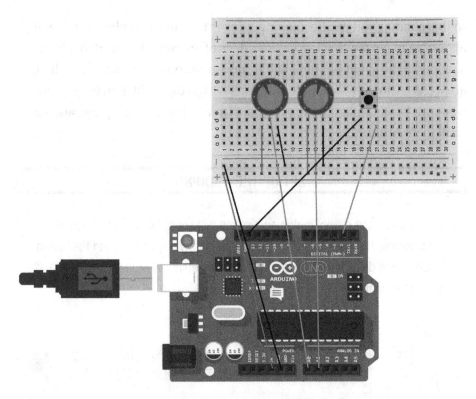

Figure 6-3. *The setup for the circuits*

THE ARDUINO CODE

Open the Arduino IDE and create a new sketch called chapter_06, and copy in the code from Listing 6-1.

Listing 6-1. Chapter_06.ino code

```
const int analogInA0 = A0;
const int analogInA1 = A1;
const int pushButton = 2;
```

```
bool lastButtonState = 0;

int a0Value = 0;
int a0LastValue = 0;

int a1Value = 0;
int a1LastValue = 0;
String a0String = "A0";
String a1String = "A1";
String pushButtonString = "BP";

void setup(){
  Serial.begin(9600);
  pinMode(pushButton, INPUT_PULLUP);
}
void loop(){
  int buttonStateUp = digitalRead(pushButton);

  a0Value = analogRead(analogInA0);
  a1Value = analogRead(analogInA1);

  a0Value = map(a0Value, 0, 1023, 0, 10);
  a1Value = map(a1Value, 0, 1023, 0, 10);

  a0LastValue = CheckValue(a0Value, a0LastValue, a0String);
  a1LastValue = CheckValue(a1Value, a1LastValue, a1String);
  if(lastButtonState != buttonStateUp){
      lastButtonState = buttonStateUp;
    if(buttonStateUp == false){
        Serial.println(pushButtonString + a0Value
        + "," + a1Value);
    }
  }
}
```

```
int CheckValue(int aValue, int aLastValue, String aString)
{
  if(aValue != aLastValue){
    Serial.println(aString + aValue);
    aLastValue = aValue;
  }
  return aLastValue;
}
```

Connect your Arduino to your computer, compile, and upload the code.

The Code Explained

In this sketch there are two potentiometers that are connected to Analog outputs A0 and A1. There is also a button connected to a digital output 2.

This code sends two types of data to the server, one type if a potentiometer is turned and another type if the button is pressed. On every loop the value from each potentiometer is sent to a function called CheckValue.

This function checks if the value has changed. If it has, it sends the new value to the serial port. The function is called twice in a loop to check each potentiometer. Each potentiometer has an identifier string that is sent to the serial port along with its value. To check if the value has changed, the function needs the value of the potentiometer from the previous loop as well as the value in the current loop.

The state of the button is also checked on each loop. If it changes and the change is it being pressed, the current value of each potentiometer is sent to the serial port along with an identifier that the data is connected to the button press. Table 6-1 explains the code in detail.

Table 6-1. *Chapter_06.ino explained*

```const int analogInA0 = A0;```
```const int analogInA1 = A1;```
```const int pushButton = 2;```
    ```text-align:justify;```
	There are three variables that hold a reference to the pin number for the potentiometers and the button.

```bool lastButtonState = 0;```	This variable holds the state the button was in, 0 for up 1 for down.

```int a0Value = 0;```
```int a0LastValue = 0;```
```int a1Value = 0;```
```int a1LastValue = 0;```
	These variables will hold the current and last values of the potentiometers.

```String a0String = "A0";```
```String a1String = "A1";```
```String pushButtonString = "BP";```
	There is a reference string for each of the interactive components.

```int buttonStateUp =``` ```digitalRead(pushButton);```	The current state of the button is registered at the start of each loop.
```a0Value = analogRead(analogInA0);``` ```a1Value = analogRead(analogInA1);```	The value of each potentiometer is read into a variable.

```a0Value = map(a0Value, 0, 1023,```
```0, 10);```
```a1Value = map(a1Value, 0, 1023,```
```0, 10);```
	The values are mapped. This is because the potentiometers values go between 0 and 1023, and for the application they need to be between 0 and 10.

```a0LastValue = CheckValue(a0Value,```
```a0LastValue, a0String);```
```a1LastValue = CheckValue(a1Value,```
```a1LastValue, a1String);```
	The value of the potentiometer is sent to a function called CheckValue. Check value is passed three arguments: the current value, the last value, and the identifier string

(continued)

169

Table 6-1. (*continued*)

```int CheckValue(int aValue, int aLastValue, String aString){ if(aValue != aLastValue){ Serial.println(aString + aValue); aLastValue = aValue; } return aLastValue; }```	The CheckValue() function has an if statement that checks if the new value is different from the old value (using not equal to). If it is different the Serial.println() function is called, passing the string identifier ("A0" or A1"). The last value is changed to the current value and is returned from the function.
```if(lastButtonState != buttonStateUp){```	This if statement checks if the state of the button has changed.
```lastButtonState = buttonStateUp;```	If the button state has changed the variable lastButtonState is updated to reflect the change.
```if(buttonStateUp == false){ Serial.println(pushButton String + a0Value + "," + a1Value); }```	If the buttonStateUp is false it means the button is pressed down; if it is down then the identifier "BP" is concatenated with the value of both the potentiometers, and this piece of data is sent through the serial port.

Note   Unlike JavaScript functions, the return value of the function needs to be declared when defining functions in .ino files. So far there have been two functions, setup and loop. Both of these don't return anything so they start with the keyword void. In this chapter the function CheckValue is called. It returns an integer, so when it's defined the int keyword comes before the name of the function: int CheckValue(int aValue, int aLastValue, String aString).

The Node.js Application

The web application will be sent data when a potentiometer is turned. The web application will need to work out which potentiometer has been turned and then update the web page. Figure 6-4 shows what the application will look like.

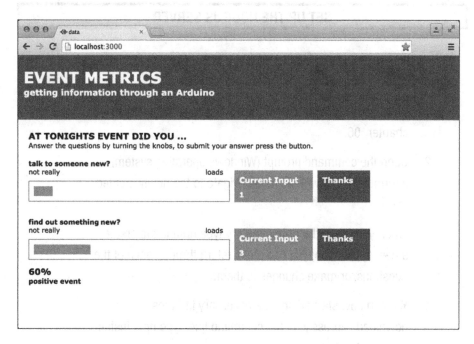

Figure 6-4. *The event feedback front end*

The directory structure for the application will look like this:

```
/chapter_06
    /node_modules
    /public
        /css
            main.css
```

```
/javascript
      main.js
/views
    index.ejs
index.js
```

SET UP THE NODE.JS SERVER

The Node.js server in this chapter is set up in the same way as previous chapters:

1. Create a new folder to hold the application. I called mine chapter_06.

2. Open the command prompt (Windows operating system) or a terminal window (Mac) and navigate to the newly created folder.

3. When you are in the right directory type npm init to create a new application; you can press return through each of the questions, or make changes to them.

4. You can now start adding the necessary libraries; to download Express.js at the command line, type npm install express@4.15.3 --save.

5. Then install ejs, type npm install ejs@2.5.6 --save.

6. When that's downloaded install serial port. On a Mac type npm install serialport@4.0.7 –save, and on a Windows PC type npm install serialport@4.0.7 --build-from-source.

7. Then finally install socket.io, type npm install socket.io@1.7.3 --save.

CREATE A NODE.JS SERVER

The Node.js server is similar to previous chapters. The main difference is that the data coming from the Arduino could be sent from either of the potentiometers or from the button. This means that the data has to be cleaned depending on the input and sent to the right function. In the root of the application, create a file called index.js and copy in the code in Listing 6-2.

Listing 6-2. index.js code

```
var http = require('http');
var express = require('express');
var app = express();
var server = http.createServer(app);
var io = require('socket.io')(server);
var SerialPort = require('serialport');
var serialport = new SerialPort('<add in the serial port for
your Arduino>', {
    parser: SerialPort.parsers.readline('\n')
});
app.engine('ejs', require('ejs').__express);
app.set('view engine', 'ejs');

app.use(express.static(__dirname + '/public'));

app.get('/', function (req, res){
    res.render('index');
});

serialport.on('open', function(){
    console.log('serial port opened');
});
```

```
io.on('connection', function(socket){
    console.log('socket.io connection');
    serialport.on('data', function(data){
        console.log(data);
        var dataKey = data.slice(0,2);
        var dataString = data.slice(2);
        dataString = dataString.replace(/(\r\n|\n|\r)/gm,"");

        if(dataKey === "BP"){
            var dataArray = dataString.split(",");
            console.log(dataArray);
            socket.emit("button-data", dataArray);
        } else {
            var dataObject = {
                dataKey: dataKey,
                dataString: dataString
            }
            console.log(dataObject);
            socket.emit("bar-data", dataObject);
        }
    });
    socket.on('disconnect', function(){
        console.log('disconnected');
    });
});
server.listen(3000, function(){
    console.log('listening on port 3000...');
});
```

Delete <add in the serial port for your Arduino> and add in your serial port to the new SerialPort() function.

The Code Explained

The server needs to process two different types of data, the potentiometer data and the button data. Two sockets are created, one for each type of data, with ID's of "bar-data" and "button-data."

There are a few new functions and concepts used in this code. They are related to a potentiometer being turned or a button being pressed and creating data structures with that data.

The console logs are useful to see what data is being sent to the front end. Table 6-2 explains index.js.

Table 6-2. index.js explained

`serialport.on('data', function(data){ console.log(data);`	The data passed via the serial port could come from either the potentiometer or the button. If it is the potentiometer connected to A0, the data will be something like "A03," with "A0" being the identifier and "3" being the data from the potentiometer. If it is the potentiometer connected to A1 it will be something like "A13." If the button is pressed then the data will be something like "BP2,4." "BP" is the identifier for the button and "2,4" is the data passed by the button.
`var dataKey = data. slice(0,2);`	slice() is a JavaScript function that removes elements of a JavaScript string. When the function is passed (0,2), it starts slicing from index 0 of the string and slices two characters. The two sliced characters are stored in the dataKey variable.

(continued)

Table 6-2. (*continued*)

`var dataString = data.` `slice(2);`	By passing one argument to the slice function, the characters from that index point to the end of the string will be returned.

`dataString = dataString.`
`replace(/(\r\n|\n|\r)`
`/gm,"");`
	The replace function in JavaScript can replace a certain character with another character. In this case there is a new line at the end of the string that needs to be replaced with an empty string "". The first argument is a regular expression (\r\n|\n|\r)/ that looks for any type of return or newline on the string, and the second argument it's replaced with is an empty string "".

`if(dataKey === "BP"){`
`...`
`} else {`
`...`
`}`
	The data key defines what has been interacted with on the Arduino. There is an if/else statement to check that component. The if statement checks what the dataKey variable holds. If it is "BP" it means the button has been pressed, if not it means a potentiometer has been turned.

`var dataArray =` `dataString.split(",");`	The split() function splits a string and puts it into an array. The argument "," tells split what to split the string on, in this case a comma. The result here will be an array with the two numbers from the potentiometer in it; for example, ['3', '4'].
`socket.emit("button-` `data", dataArray);`	This emits the array to a socket called "button-data."

(*continued*)

Table 6-2. (*continued*)

```var dataObject = { dataKey: dataKey, dataString: data String }```	If the else statement is used, the data is from a potentiometer. In this case you need to pass an identifier to show which potentiometer has been turned, as well as the data. An object called dataObject is created that can be passed to the front end with the identifier and the data.
```socket.emit("bar-data", dataObject);```	This data is then sent via a socket called "bar-data."

Note   Regular expressions are used to search for different characters in a string. They are made up of defined set symbols that describe a search pattern. For example, using \n matches a newline and \r matches a carriage return.

CREATE THE FRONT END

The front end in this chapter will do a number of things; it will give the user of the Arduino feedback and it will show information about what previous users have said. To start you will create a web page that gives feedback on the Arduino inputs. Create a views folder in the root of the application and create a file in it. Copy the HTML from Listing 6-3.

Listing 6-3. index.ejs code

```
<!DOCTYPE html>
<html>
<head>
    <meta charset="UTF-8">
```

```
<title>data</title>
<link href="/css/main.css" rel="stylesheet" type="text/css">
</head>
<body>
    <header>
        <h1>EVENT METRICS</h1>
        <h2>getting information through an Arduino</h2>
    </header>
    <div id="content">
        <h2>AT TONIGHTS EVENT DID YOU ...</H2>
        <p>Answer the questions by turning the knobs, to submit
        your answer press the button.</p>
        <div id="bar-A0" class="container">
            <div  class="bar">
                <p>talk to someone new?</p>
                <div class="response-container">
                    <p class="flex-item">not really</p>
                    <p class="flex-item">loads</p>
                </div>
                <svg width="400" height="20" viewBox="0 0 400
                20">
                    <rect id="A0"
                    x="0"
                    y="0"
                    fill="#6BCAE2"
                    width="320"
                    height="20"/>
                </svg>
            </div>
```

```
<div class="text-block">
    <h3>Current Input<h3>
    <p></p>
</div>
<div class="text-block-response hidden">
    <h3>Thanks<h3>
</div>
</div>
<div id="bar-A1" class="container">
    <div  class="bar">
        <p>find out something new new?</p>
        <div class="response-container">
            <p class="flex-item">not really</p>
            <p class="flex-item">loads</p>
        </div>
        <svg width="400" height="20" viewBox="0 0
        400 20">
            <rect id="A1"
            x="0"
            y="0"
            fill="#6BCAE2"
            width="320"
            height="20"/>
        </svg>
    </div>
    <div class="text-block">
        <h3>Current Input<h3>
        <p></p>
    </div>
```

```
            <div class="text-block-response hidden">
                <h3>Thanks<h3>
                <p></p>
            </div>
        </div>
    </div>
    <script src="/socket.io/socket.io.js"></script>
    <script src="javascript/main.js"></script>
</body>
</html>
```

The Code Explained

The server needs to process two different types of data, the potentiometer data and the button data. Two sockets are created, one for each type of data, with ID's of "bar-data" and "button-data."

The front end needs to give feedback to the user of their interaction with the Arduino; this includes information about the value of the potentiometer and feedback to let them know the button press has been registered.

The main thing to notice is that there are two very similar blocks of HTML, one for each of the potentiometers. They both have the same structure, with a class of "container," "bar, "text-block," and "text-block-response" as well as an SVG. Each block also has id references as a reference to the potentiometer it is visualizing. Table 6-3 goes into more detail about the code in index.ejs.

Table 6-3. *index.ejs explained*

`<div id="bar-A0" class="container"> <div id="bar-A1" class="container">`	There are similar blocks of HTML for each potentiometer, so they get the right data; each has an id relating to a potentiometer.
`<div class="text-block-response hidden">`	In each container block there is a div with the class hidden. Its content will only be shown when someone presses the button so it has a second class on it called hidden, which will hide the div.

ADD STYLE

Create a public folder in the root of the application and in it create a folder called CSS; in that create the main.css file. Copy the CSS in Listing 6-4 into the newly created file.

Listing 6-4. main.css

```
*{
  margin: 0;
  padding: 0;
}
body{
  font-family: Verdana, Arial, sans-serif;
}
h2{
  font-size: 18px;
}
h3{
  font-size: 16px;
}
```

```
p{
  font-size: 14px;
}
header{
  background: #FE8402;
  color: white;
}
header h1{
  padding-top: 25px;
}
header h2{
  padding-bottom: 45px;
}
header h1,header h2, header h3, header p{
    padding-left: 12px;
}
#content{
  margin: 22px;
}
.container{
    display: flex;
    flex-direction: row;
    margin-top: 20px;
}
.response-container{
  display: flex;
}
.flex-item:nth-child(2){
  margin-left: 305px;
}
```

```css
.bar > p{
  font-weight: bold;
}
.text-block{
    background: #6BCAE2;
    color: white;
    width: 145px;
    height: 45px;
    margin-top: 22px;
    margin-bottom: 10px;
    margin-right: 10px;
    padding: 10px;
    font-size: 16px;
}
.text-block-response{
    background: #FE8402;
    color: white;
    width: 90px;
    height: 45px;
    margin-top: 22px;
    margin-bottom: 10px;
    margin-right: 10px;
    padding: 10px;
    font-size: 16px;
}
.text-block p{
  padding-left: 0px;
  padding-top: 12px;
}
```

```
.container svg{
  border: #FE8402 solid 1px;
  padding: 10px;
  margin: 10px 10px 10px 0;
}
.hidden{
  visibility: hidden;
}
```

The Code Explained

The CSS is similar to previous chapters, using Flexbox for the main content. Table 6-4 explains some of the CSS in main.css.

Table 6-4. *main.css explained*

header h1,header h2, header h3, header p{}	This selects just the h1, h2, h3, and p tags that are in the header.
.flex-item:nth-child(2){ margin-left: 305px; } <div class="response-container"> <p class="flex-item">not really</p> <p class="flex-item">loads</p> </div>	nth-child is a CSS command that chooses a child with an element or class name in a certain position. In this case there are two p tags with the class "flex-item"; nth-child(2) picks the second one and gives it a margin on the left of 305 pixels; this is so it sits at the end of the bar.

(continued)

Table 6-4. (*continued*)

`.bar > p{`
`font-weight: bold;`
`}`
	The > character in CSS selects the children but not the grandchildren of the element before it. In this case it will pick the paragraph within the div of class "bar" but not any paragraphs in divs that are children of "bar."

`.hidden{`
`visibility: hidden;`
`}`
	The class hidden uses visibility to hide whatever element has the class. This can then be added and removed with JavaScript to hid and unhide an HTML block.

MAKE THE PAGE INTERACTIVE

Finally add the code to make the elements on the front end interactive. In the public folder create a new folder called JavaScript and create a file called main.js. Copy the code in Listing 6-5 into main.js.

Listing 6-5. main.js code

```
(function(){
    var socket = io();
    socket.on("bar-data", function(data){
        var current = data.dataKey;
        var svgBar = document.getElementById(current);
        var newWidth = data.dataString * 40;
        svgBar.setAttribute("width", newWidth);
        currentInputValue(data);
        addRemoveClass("add");
    });
```

```
    socket.on("button-data", function(data){
        addRemoveClass("remove");
    });
    function addRemoveClass(action){
        var buttonResponse = document.getElementById("bar-A0").
        getElementsByClassName("text-block-response")[0];

        buttonResponse.classList[action]("hidden");
        buttonResponse = document.getElementById("bar-A1").
        getElementsByClassName("text-block-response")[0];
        buttonResponse.classList[action]("hidden");
    }
    function currentInputValue(data){
        var targetP = document.getElementById("bar-" + data.
        dataKey).getElementsByClassName("text-block")[0].
        getElementsByTagName("p")[0];
        targetP.innerHTML = data.dataString;
    }
})();
```

The Code Explained

The CSS is similar to previous chapters, using Flexbox for the main content.

The JavaScript will receive data from two sockets, "bar-data" and "button-data" depending if a potentiometer is turned or a button is pressed. When the button is pressed a notification needs to be given to the user. When a potentiometer is turned the user will see a representation of the data in a bar and as a number.

When the potentiometer is turned, the front end is sent an object that contains the identifier for the potentiometer and the value. The Table 6-5 goes into more detail about the code in main.js.

Table 6-5. *main.js explained*

```socket.on("bar-data",```
```function(data){```
```   var current = data.dataKey;```
	The first thing the socket.on function does is get the key for the potentiometer and store it in a variable.

```var svgBar = document.``` ```getElementById(current);```	The correct SVG bar is then stored in a variable.
```svgBar.setAttribute("width",``` ```newWidth);```	The width attribute is updated on the svg.
```currentInputValue(data);```	A function is called that updates the text value of the potentiometer.
```addRemoveClass("add");```	A function is called that hides the button pressed notification.

```socket.on("button-data",```
```function(data){```
```   addRemoveClass("remove");```
```});```
	When the button is pressed a function is called to remove the hidden class from the notification block.

The ```AddRemoveClass(action)``` function	This function adds or removes the class hidden from the div that notifies the user that they have pressed the button.

```var buttonResponse = document.```
```getElementById("bar-A0").```
```getElementsByClassName("text-```
```block-response")[0];```
	This selects the first element with the class name text-block-response"bar-A0" in the element with the id "bar-A0."

(*continued*)

Table 6-5. (*continued*)

`buttonResponse.classList[action]` `("hidden");`	classList is a JavaScript function that either adds or removes a class name from an element. As the function is being used to add or remove a class, those keywords are passed into the AddRemoveClass function as the argument action and passed to the classList function in square brackets[].
The `currentInputValue(data)` `function`	This function first stores the element it wants to change and then changes its innerHTML to the current data string from a potentiometer,

Note   You may have noticed the [0] at the end of the call "document.getElementsByClassName." This is because it returns an array like object of all elements with that class name. To access the element in that array that you want, you ask for it by its position in the array using brackets. Even though there would only be one element returned in the call you made, it still needs to be referenced by its position in the array, which would be position 0.

Note   You would normally see the function called like this:

buttonResponse.classList.add("hidden"); or
buttonResponse.classList.remove("hidden");

The add and remove keywords are written after the ".". In this code the words "add" or "remove" are strings sent as an argument to the function. As they are strings, not keywords, they cannot be added after the dot and need to be put in square brackets instead. The square brackets are used for any function that is being passed a string when it expects a keyword.

You can check out how the page looks so far by navigating to the application in a console window and then type nodemon index.js or node index.js to start the application. Make sure the Arduino is connected to your computer and open a browser and go to http://localhost:3000/ to see the application running.

Extending the Application

Now that you have the data there is a lot you can do with it. The application will be extended to include an overall rating for the evening.

These calculations can be carried out on the server or the front end. In this case they will be carried out on the front end. If you refresh the page, the data will be lost as it is only being stored locally on the browser.

You can set up databases connected to a Node.js server and store data, this is not covered in this book; there is some information on where to find out information on setting up a data base in Appendix B.

The setup of the Arduino is the same and so is the code for the Node.js server.

The calculation works out what percent of people chose 5 or over for each question.

UPDATE THE CODE

To update the application open up the index.ejs file from Listing 6-3 and copy in the HTML in bold.

```
<!DOCTYPE html>
<html>
...
            <div class="text-block">
                <h3>Current Input<h3>
                <p></p>
            </div>
            <div class="text-block-response hidden">
                <h3>Thanks<h3>
                <p></p>
            </div>
        </div>
        <div>
            <h2><span id="percent">0</span>%</h2s>
            <p>positive event</p>
        <div>
        </div>
        <script src="/socket.io/socket.io.js"></script>
        <script src="javascript/main.js"></script>
</body>
</html>
```

The added div will show the percentage of positive feedback. The span has an id so that it can be accessed by JavaScript and updated with a percentage.

Next open the main.js from Listing 6-5 and add in the code in bold.

```
(function(){
    var socket = io();
    var totalClickCounter = 0;
    var accumulatorArrayA0 = [0,0,0,0,0,0,0,0,0,0,0,0];
    var accumulatorArrayA1 = [0,0,0,0,0,0,0,0,0,0,0,0];
    socket.on("bar-data", function(data){
        var current = data.dataKey;
        var svgBar = document.getElementById(current);
        var newWidth = data.dataString * 40;
        svgBar.setAttribute("width", newWidth)
        currentInputValue(data);
        addRemoveClass("add");
    });
    socket.on("button-data", function(data){
        var percetageSpan = document.getElementById('percent');
        totalClickCounter = totalClickCounter + 2;
        accumulatorArrayA0[data[0]] =
        accumulatorArrayA0[data[0]] + 1;
        accumulatorArrayA1[data[1]] =
        accumulatorArrayA1[data[1]] + 1;

        var positiveTotal1 = sumPositiveResponses
        (accumulatorArrayA0);
        var positiveTotal2 = sumPositiveResponses
        (accumulatorArrayA1);
        var positiveTotals = positiveTotal1 + positiveTotal2;
        var positivePercentage = (positiveTotals/
        totalClickCounter) * 100;
        percent.innerHTML = Math.floor(positivePercentage)
        addRemoveClass("remove");
    });
```

```
function sumPositiveResponses(dataArray){
  var positiveTotal = 0;
  for(var i = 5; i< dataArray.length; i++){
    positiveTotal = positiveTotal + dataArray[i];
  }
  return positiveTotal;
}
function addRemoveClass(action){
    var buttonResponse = document.getElementById("bar-A0").
    getElementsByClassName("text-block-response")[0];
    buttonResponse.classList[action]("hidden");
    buttonResponse = document.getElementById("bar-A1").
    getElementsByClassName("text-block-response")[0];
    buttonResponse.classList[action]("hidden");
}

function currentInputValue(data){
    var targetP = document.getElementById("bar-" + data.
    dataKey).getElementsByClassName("text-block")[0].
    getElementsByTagName("p")[0];
    targetP.innerHTML = data.dataString;
}
})();
```

The Code Explained

Table 6-6 explains the code in main.js.

Table 6-6. *The updated main.js explained*

`var totalClickCounter = 0;`	A counter is created that keeps track of how many times the button has been pressed.
`var accumulatorArrayA0 = [0,0,0,0,0,0,0,0,0,0,0];` `var accumulatorArrayA1 = [0,0,0,0,0,0,0,0,0,0,0];`	There are two arrays: one for each of the questions with 11 elements, one for each of the possible choices on the potentiometer.
`totalClickCounter = totalClickCounter + 2;`	The counter is incremented by 2 each time the button is clicked as the percentage needs to be worked out over two questions.
`accumulatorArrayA0[data[0]] = accumulatorArrayA0[data[0]] + 1;` `accumulatorArrayA1[data[1]] = accumulatorArrayA1[data[1]] + 1;`	The data from each question is added to the appropriate array. If some has entered 3 for the first question then the third position in the array is updated by 1.
`var positiveTotal1 = sumPositive Responses(accumulatorArrayA0);` `var positiveTotal2 = sumPositive Responses(accumulatorArrayA1);`	A function is called that adds up how many elements there are in the array that are five or over.
`var positiveTotals = positiveTotal1 + positiveTotal2;`	The totals from the two questions are added together.

(*continued*)

Table 6-6. (*continued*)

```var positivePercentage = (positiveTotals/totalClickCounter) * 100; console.log(Math. floor(positivePercentage));```	The percentage is worked out.
```percent.innerHTML = Math. floor(positivePercentage)```	The span on the index.ejs is updated with the percentage. Math.floor() is a JavaScript function that makes sure the value is an integer; without this you could end up with a long floating-point number.

Finally, update the CSS, open the main.css file from Listing 6-4, and add the addition CSS to the bottom.

```
#responses{
  color: black;
  font-weight: normal;
  margin: 12px;
}
#responses .text-block{
    background-color: white;
    border: #6BCAE2 solid 2px;
    color: black;
    width: 260px;
    height: 48px;
    margin-top: 22px;
    margin-bottom: 10px;
    margin-right: 10px;
    padding: 10px;
```

```
font-size: 14px;
font-weight: normal;
}
```

Now if you restart the server, you should see the percentage change depending on the inputs from the Arduino.

Visualizing the Data on an Arduino

Now that you have a number that represents how much people are enjoying the event, you can also represent that using components attached to an Arduino. This final section of the chapter updates the Arduino circuit and the code so that the brightness of an LED depends on the enjoyment rating.

The percentage is sent back to the Arduino from the Node.js server using the serialport.write() function. The Arduino then processes this data so it can be used to light an LED.

UPDATE THE FRONT-END JAVASCRIPT

The JavaScript used in the front end needs to be updated so that the calculated percent is sent to the server. This uses the socket.emit function.

Open the updated main.js file add in the code in bold in the socket.on() function with an id of "button-data."

```
socket.on("button-data", function(data){
    var percetageSpan = document.getElementById('percent');
    totalClickCounter = totalClickCounter + 2;

    accumulatorArrayA0[data[0]] = accumulatorArrayA0[data[0]] + 1;
    accumulatorArrayA1[data[1]] = accumulatorArrayA1[data[1]] + 1;
    var positiveTotal1 = sumPositiveResponses(accumulatorArrayA0);
```

```
        var positiveTotal2 = sumPositiveResponses(accumulatorArrayA1);
        var positiveTotals = positiveTotal1 + positiveTotal2;
        var positivePercentage = (positiveTotals/totalClickCounter) * 100;
        positivePercentage = Math.floor(positivePercentage);
        percent.innerHTML = positivePercentage;
        socket.emit('percentData', positivePercentage);
        addRemoveClass("remove");
});
```

The Code Explained

Table 6-7 explains the code in the updated main.js file.

Table 6-7. *The updated main.js explained*

positivePercentage = Math. floor(positivePercentage);	The positivePercentage variable is updated to hold the result of the Math. floor() function. This is so the Math. floor() function does not need to be called twice. The value being sent by socket.emit needs it as well as the innerHTML.
socket.emit('percentData', Math.floor(positivePercentage));	The socket emit functions id is 'percentData', and the positive percent number is sent to any socket.on function that matches that id.

UPDATE THE NODE.JS SERVER

Open up the index.js file, Listing 6-2, and update the io.on() function with the code in bold.

```
io.on('connection', function(socket){
    console.log('socket.io connection');
    serialport.on('data', function(data){
            // console.log(data);
            var dataKey = data.slice(0,2);

            var dataString = data.slice(2);
            // console.log(dataString);
            dataString = dataString.replace(/(\r\n|\n|\r)/gm, "");

            if(dataKey === "BP"){
                var dataArray = dataString.split(",");
                // console.log(dataArray);
                socket.emit("button-data", dataArray);
            } else {
                var dataObject = {
                    dataKey: dataKey,
                    dataString: dataString
                }
                // console.log(dataObject);
                socket.emit("bar-data", dataObject);
            }
    });
    socket.on('percentData', function(data){
        serialport.write(data + 'T');
    });
    socket.on('disconnect', function(){
        console.log('disconnected');
    });
});
```

The socket.on() function is connected to the socket.emit() function in main.js. When new data is received, it is sent through the serial port with the terminating character "T" added to it.

UPDATE THE ARDUINO

The Arduino circuit and code need to be updated. For the circuit you will need the following:

1 x LED
1 x 220 ohm resister

Figure 6-5 shows how the LED should be added to the circuit.

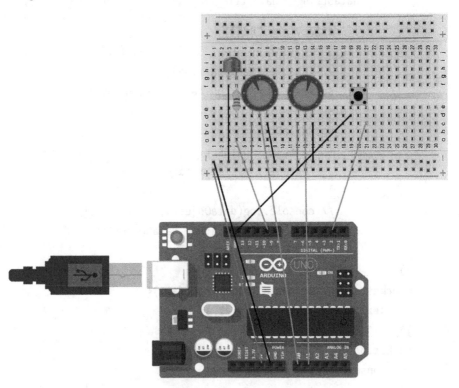

Figure 6-5. *The updated circuit*

Remember to unplug the Arduino when updating the circuit. The anode of the LED (the longer positive leg) is connected to the 220 ohm resistor, which is connected to digital pin 9. The cathode of the LED (the shorter negative leg) is connected to ground.

UPDATE THE ARDUINO

Open up the chapter_06.ino code from Listing 6-1 and update it with the code in bold.

```
const int analogInA0 = A0;
const int analogInA1 = A1;
const int pushButton = 2;

const int ledPin = 9;

bool lastButtonState = 0;

int a0Value = 0;
int a0LastValue = 0;

int a1Value = 0;
int a1LastValue = 0;

String a0String = "A0";
String a1String = "A1";
String pushButtonString = "BP";

int serverValueRemapped = 0;
char charRead;
String inputString ="";
```

```
void setup(){
  Serial.begin(9600);
  pinMode(pushButton, INPUT_PULLUP);
}
void loop(){
  int buttonStateUp = digitalRead(pushButton);
  a0Value = analogRead(analogInA0);
  a1Value = analogRead(analogInA1);
  a0Value = map(a0Value, 0, 1023, 0, 10);
  a1Value = map(a1Value, 0, 1023, 0, 10);
  a0LastValue = CheckValue(a0Value, a0LastValue, a0String);
  a1LastValue = CheckValue(a1Value, a1LastValue, a1String);
  if(lastButtonState != buttonStateUp){
   lastButtonState = buttonStateUp;
    if(buttonStateUp == false){
        Serial.println(pushButtonString  + a0Value + "," + a1Value);
    }
  }
  checkSerialRead();
}
void checkSerialRead(){
    if (Serial.available()) {
    charRead = Serial.read();
    if(charRead != 'T'){
      inputString += charRead;
    } else {
      int convertedString = inputString.toInt();
      serverValueRemapped = map(convertedString, 0, 100, 0, 255);
      analogWrite(ledPin, serverValueRemapped);
      inputString = "";
    }
  }
}
```

```
int CheckValue(int aValue, int aLastValue, String aString){
  if(aValue != aLastValue){
    Serial.println(aString + aValue);
    aLastValue = aValue;
  }
  return aLastValue;
}
```

You will have to stop the server to upload the code to the Arduino. Verify the code and then upload it onto the Arduino. Restart the server and refresh the browser. Now the brightness of the light should reflect the percentage.

The Code Explained

A new function has been added, called void checkSerialRead(), and this function is called in the loop and checks if there is new serial data coming from the server. It uses the Serial.available and Serial.read() function used in Chapter 5 and parses the new data and works out the value for the LED. Table 6-8 explains the code in the updated chapter_06.ino file in more detail.

Table 6-8. *updated chapter_06.ino explained*

`int serverValueRemapped = 0;`	A new variable is added that will hold the remapped value from the server.
`char charRead;` `String inputString ="";`	There are two variables that are used to parse the data from the server.
`checkSerialRead();`	The checkSerialRead() function is called in each loop.
`void checkSerialRead(){}`	The checkSerialRead() function is void as it doesn't return a value.
`int convertedString = inputString.toInt();`	The data string is converted into an integer.
`serverValueRemapped = map(convertedString, 0, 100, 0, 255);`	The value from the front end is converted to a value that can be used to light the LED using the map() function.
`analogWrite(ledPin, serverValueRemapped);`	The new value is used to send a value to the LED.

Summary

In this chapter you have used analog and digital data with an Arduino to create a system to find out how much people enjoyed an event. The data had to be mapped and parsed so it could work with the front end. You also started asking questions with the data and visualizing the answers. The next chapter goes further and starts using that data to answer more questions and visualize them using the JavaScript library D3.js.

CHAPTER 7

Visualizing Data

Being able to visualize data makes it easier to understand. It allows you to see patterns that might have otherwise been hidden as well as tell stories about your data. You can create data visualizations with pure JavaScript, but there are a number of JavaScript libraries that make it easier. The library you will be using in this book is D3.js. In this chapter you will create a bar chart with D3.js with data collected in the same way as in Chapter 6. At the end of the chapter you will have a bar graph with the data from one of the potentiometers.

Introduction to D3.js

D3 stands for data-driven documents; it is a data visualization JavaScript library. It allows you to bind data to the document object model (DOM) to display visualizations on a web page with DOM elements. These can be any DOM element: for example, text or a div. In the examples in this book SVG DOM elements will be used to display data.

D3.js has a number of functions to build different types of data visualizations. These include bar graphs, line graphs, choropleth maps, bubble charts, and a lot more. It works out the math to translate the data into data visualizations.

It allows you to use a number of different data file types including JSON, GeoJSON, and CSV.

© Indira Knight 2018
I. Knight, *Connecting Arduino to the Web*, https://doi.org/10.1007/978-1-4842-3480-8_7

There are other libraries you can use for creating data visualizations in JavaScript; I have listed some of them in Appendix B.

How D3.js Works

With D3.js you start by selecting an HTML element to hold the whole visualization, then decide what type of DOM element you want to use to hold each datum: for example, text, a div, or an SVG. Next you bind the data to these elements, and then append SVGs or DOM elements that will show the data. You can then position, scale, and color the shapes.

D3.js does the math for you. If you have a dataset of 2, 5, and 9, and you wanted to make three bar graphs you know that is your smallest number and 9 is the largest. You could create a graph with that scale that went from 0 to 9. But what would happen if the data was updated and went from -4 to 22, or a fourth number is introduced; the axis would be wrong. When working with live data you need to have axis that can scale with the data, and D3.js has functions that will do that.

The data values are the input domain, which are scaled to become the output range. The lowest and highest input numbers of the input domain are mapped to the lowest and highest numbers for the output range. Figure 7-1 shows the input domain, the input data of 0 to 55, and the output range from 0 to 500.

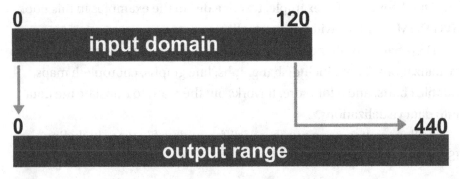

Figure 7-1. *The input domain and output range*

D3.js uses the general update patterns of enter, update, and exit for the data. Enter is used for the new data, it adds a DOM element, updates when data changes, no DOM elements are added or removed, and exits when the number of DOM elements decrease. Using this pattern allows for animated transitions of the DOM elements when the data updates, if the number of DOM elements needs to increase, or if the number of DOM elements needs to decrease. The functions for this pattern are shown in Figure 7-2.

.enter() – contains data elements not yet bound to a DOM object.

.exit() – selects DOM elements that no longer have data.

.remove - can be used to take the redundant elements off the page.

.selectAll() – if DOM elements already exist new data updates those elements.

Figure 7-2. *The functions for the general update pattern*

The function enter() is used if there is data that doesn't have a DOM element. When there is a DOM element that no longer has data exit() is used. The update() function is used when there is the same number of DOM elements as data but the data has changed. Figure 7-3 shows how these functions work.

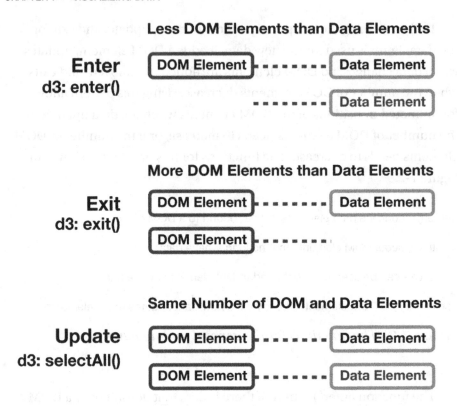

Figure 7-3. *How elements are added, updated, and removed from the DOM with D3.js*

TRY D3.JS

The best way to understand D3.js is to start using it. Before using D3.js with Arduino data, it's good to go through the basics by building a bar chart. The code in Listing 7-1 will make a bar chart using some random data. The data will define the height of the bars, the labeling of the axis, and the scale of the axis. A div with an id of "viz" will contain the visualization. Open a text editor and copy in the code from Listing 7-1.

Listing 7-1. bar_chart.html

```html
<!DOCTYPE html>
<html lang="en">
<head>
    <meta charset="utf-8">
    <title>D3.js</title>
    <script type="text/javascript" src="https://d3js.org/d3.v4.js">
    </script>

    <style type="text/css">
        body{
            font-family: arial;
        }
        h1{
            font-size: 22px;
          margin: 0px;
        }
        h2{
            font-size: 16px;
            margin: 0px;
            margin-top: 2px;
        }
        .axis text {
            font-family: arial;
            font-size: 12px;
            font-weight: normal;
            color: pink;
        }
        .axis path,
        .axis line {
            fill: none;
            stroke: #000;
            shape-rendering: crispEdges;
        }
```

```
        .bar {
            fill: #fd8f00;
        }
        h1, h2, p{
            margin-left: 40px;
        }
        p{
            font-size: 12px;
        }
    </style>
</head>
<body>
    <h1>A D3 bar chart</h1>
    <div id = "viz"></div>

    <script type="text/javascript">
        var margin = {top: 20, right: 20, bottom: 40, left: 40};
        var width = 480 - margin.left - margin.right;
        var height = 500 - margin.top - margin.bottom;

        var data = [
          {"amount": 5, "name": "column1"},
          {"amount": 11, "name": "column2"},
          {"amount": 55, "name": "column3"},
          {"amount": 23, "name": "column4"}
        ]

          var x = d3.scaleBand()
          .domain(data.map(function(d) { return d.name; }))
          .range([0, width], .1)
          .padding(0.1);

          var y = d3.scaleLinear()
          .domain([0, d3.max(data, function(d) { return +d.amount; })])
          .range([height, 0]);
```

```
    var dataviz = d3.select("#viz").append("svg")
      .attr("width", width + margin.left + margin.right)
      .attr("height", height + margin.top + margin.bottom)
      .append("g")
      .attr("transform", "translate(" + margin.left + "," +
      margin.top + ")");

    dataviz.selectAll(".bar")
      .data(data)
    .enter()
      .append("rect")
      .attr("class", "bar")
      .attr("x", function(d) { return x(d.name); })
      .attr("width", x.bandwidth())
      .attr("y", function(d) { return y(+d.amount); })
      .attr("height", function(d) { return height - y(+d.
      amount); });

      dataviz.append("g")
      .attr("transform", "translate(0," + height + ")")
      .call(d3.axisBottom(x));
      dataviz.append("g")
      .call(d3.axisLeft(y));
  </script>
</body>
</html>
```

Open a browser and open bar_chart.html file; you will see the data
visualization.

The Code Explained

Table 7-1 explains the code in bar_chart.html.

Table 7-1. bar_chart.html explained

```<script type="text/ javascript" src="https:// d3js.org/d3.v4.js"> </script>```	You can download D3.js or include it in your page from a URL.
```<style type="text/css"> </style>```	As D3.js attached data to DOM elements, those elements can be styled with CSS. Normally you would create a separate CSS file but in this example the CSS is on the HTML page.
```var margin = {top: 20, right: 20, bottom: 40, left: 40};```	If the visualization were the same size as SVG viewport there wouldn't be space to read the axis. The variable margin holds an object with the amount of space in pixels you want to leave around the visualization.
```var width = 480 - margin. left - margin.right; var height = 500 - margin. top - margin.bottom;```	The width and height variables hold the width and height of the SVG canvas – the margins.
```var data = [{"amount": 5, "name": "column1"}, ...]```	The variable data holds an array of objects; in this case there are two key/value pairs in each object.

(continued)

Table 7-1. (*continued*)

```var x = d3.scaleBand() .domain(data.map (function(d) { return d.name; })) .range([0, width]) .padding(0.1);```	The variable x holds the scale calculations for the x axis. The D3.js function scaleBand() is used for non-numerical data such as labels or ordinal data. The input domain is the name data; it takes one argument, the data. It runs through the data and works out how many values there are.
```var y = d3.scaleLinear() .domain([0, d3.max(data, function(d) { return +d.amount; })]) .range([height, 0]);```	The y variable holds the scale for the y-axis. This time the scaleLinear() function is used as the data is numerical. The input domain is an array from 0 to the largest number in the data set. The d3.max() function finds the largest number in the data set.
```var dataviz = d3.select ("#viz").append("svg") .attr("width", width + margin.left + margin. right) .attr("height", height + margin.top + margin. bottom) .append("g") .attr("transform", "translate(" + margin. left + "," + margin.top + ")");```	The d3.select() function lets you choose a DOM element to attach the visualization to. The append() function adds an SVG to the element. The next two attr() functions set the width and height of the element. You add the margin that was removed from the width and height. The append("g") adds a "g" element to the visualization. A "g" element isn't specific to D3.js; it is a container element that lets you group together graphical elements.
```dataviz.selectAll(".bar")```	The selectAll() function selects all the bar objects, even though there aren't any yet, and it makes a placeholder for the bars.

(*continued*)

Table 7-1. (*continued*)

`.data(data)`	The data() function attaches the data to the visualization.
`.enter()` `.append("rect")`	The enter() function is part of the update pattern, and append adds an SVG.
`.attr("class", "bar")`	A class is added to each bar so they can be styled and it also allows you to select them again.
`.attr("x", function(d) {` `return x(d.name); })`	This sets the position for the x-axis for each bar.
`.attr("width",` `x.bandwidth())`	The width attribute sets the width for each bar. It is worked out using the x scale set earlier. It knows how many items of data there are and the width of the visualization.
`.attr("y", function(d) {` `return y(+d.amount); })`	This sets the position for the top of the rectangle.
`+d.amount`	You use the + before the value to convert the amount data to a number. Sometimes you think the data is a number but it is actually a string.

`.attr("height", function(d)`
`{ return height - y(+d.`
`amount); });`
	This sets the height for the bar. The coordinates for SVGs start at 0 0 at the top left and any height is from top to bottom. In this graph you want the bars to grow from the bottom of the axis up, the height − y(+d.amount) works this out.

(*continued*)

Table 7-1. (*continued*)

```dataviz.append("g") .attr("transform", "translate (0," + height + ")") .call(d3. axisBottom(x));```	This appends a new group to the SVG that will contain the x-axis. D3.js has a function axisBottom() that creates a horizontal axis at the bottom of the SVG.
```dataviz.append("g") .call(d3.axisLeft(y));```	This appends a new group to the SVG that will contain the y-axis. D3.js has a function axisLeft() that creates a vertical axis at the left of the SVG.

Method Chaining

You may have noticed that in D3.js there are functions called one after the other with a "." between them. This is called method chaining and is used in JavaScript and JavaScript libraries. The code "dataviz.append("g"). attr("transform", "translate(0," + height + ")").call(d3.axisBottom(x));" is three functions called one after the other, append(), attr(), and call(). It makes code easier to read and to create blocks of function calls that naturally group together.

Visualizing Data from the Arduino with D3.js

This chapter will use the same Arduino setup and the same base JavaScript code as Chapter 6. The JavaScript will be updated to include the new visualization. Figure 7-4 shows the final outcome for this chapter, a bar chart that shows the number of times a certain score was picked for the first question: "At tonight's event did you talk to someone new?"

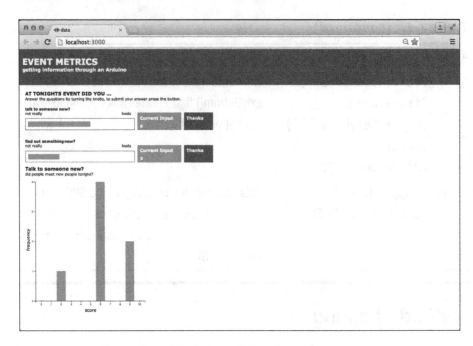

Figure 7-4. The web application with a bar chart

SET UP THE ARDUINO

The setup for the Arduino is exactly the same as in Chapter 6. The setup for the Arduino is in Figure 6-3. Once the components are connected, flash the Arduino with the code from Listing 6-1. You want to use the original code, not the updates that were added later in Chapter 6.

SET UP THE NODE.JS SERVER

The code for this will also be based on the original code in Chapter 6. The directory structure for the application will be:

```
/chapter_07
    /node_modules
    /public
        /css
            main.css
        /javascipt
            main.js
    /views
        index.ejs
    index.js
```

Creating the skeleton Node.js application will be the same as in previous chapters:

1. Create a new folder to hold the application. I called mine chapter_07.

2. Open the command prompt (Windows operating system) or a terminal window (Mac) and navigate to the newly created folder.

3. When you are in the right directory, type npm init to create a new application; you can press return through each of the questions, or make changes to them.

4. You can now start adding the necessary libraries; to download Express.js at the command line, type npm install express@4.15.3 --save.

5. Then install ejs, type npm install ejs@2.5.6 save.

215

6. When that's downloaded install serial port. On a Mac, type npm install serialport@4.0.7 –save, and on a Windows PC type npm install serialport@4.0.7 --build-from-source.

7. Then finally install socket.io, type npm install socket.io@1.7.3 --save.

In the index.js, file copy in the code from Listing 6-2. You want to use the original listing of the code, not the version updates from later in Chapter 6. Copy the code from Listing 6-3 into the index.ejs file, then the CSS from Listing 6-4 into the main.css file, and finally copy the code from Listing 6-5 into the main.js file.

Make sure that you update the <add in the serial port for your Arduino> to your own serial port in the new SerialPort() function.

You should now have the basic setup from the last chapter duplicated in the chapter_7 application. You can test that you have it by navigating to the chapter_07 application in a console window and starting the application with either nodemon index.js or node index.js. As long as the Arduino is connected, you should be able to interact with the potentiometers and button and see the result when you open a browser and go to http://localhost:3000.

UPDATE THE APPLICATION

Now you can up update the main.js. Open the file and add in the code in bold in Listing 7-2.

Listing 7-2. main.js

```
(function(){
    var socket = io();

    var accumulatorArrayA0 = [0,0,0,0,0,0,0,0,0,0,0,0];
        var accumulatorArrayA1 = [0,0,0,0,0,0,0,0,0,0,0,0];
```

```
var margin = {top: 20, right: 20, bottom: 40, left: 40};
var width = 480 - margin.left - margin.right;
var height = 500 - margin.top - margin.bottom;

var x = d3.scaleBand()
.range([0, width], .1)
.padding(0.1);

var y = d3.scaleLinear()
.range([height, 0]);

var bars = d3.select("#bar-chart").append("svg")
  .attr("width", width + margin.left + margin.right)
  .attr("height", height + margin.top + margin.bottom)
  .append("g")
  .attr("transform", "translate(" + margin.left + "," +
  margin.top + ")");

bars.selectAll(".bar")
  .data(accumulatorArrayA0)
.enter()
  .append("rect")
  .attr("class", "bar")
  .attr("x", function(d, i) { return x(i); })
  .attr("width", x.bandwidth())
  .attr("y", function(d) {return y(d); })
  .attr("height", function(d) {   return height - y(+d); });

  bars.append("g")
  .attr("class", "x axis")
  .attr("transform", "translate(0," + height + ")")
  .call(d3.axisBottom(x));

bars.append("g")
  .attr("class", "y axis")
  .call(d3.axisLeft(y)
    .ticks(0));
```

217

```
    bars.append("text")
    .attr("transform",
          "translate(" + (width/2) + " ," +
                         (height + margin.top + 20) + ")")
    .style("text-anchor", "middle")
    .text("score");

  bars.append("text")
    .attr("transform", "rotate(-90)")
    .attr("y", 0 - margin.left)
    .attr("x",0 - (height / 2))
    .attr("dy", "1em")
    .style("text-anchor", "middle")
    .text("frequency");

socket.on("bar-data", function(data){
    var current = data.dataKey;
    var svgBar = document.getElementById(current);

    var newWidth = data.dataString * 40;

    svgBar.setAttribute("width", newWidth);

    currentInputValue(data);
    addRemoveClass("add");
});

socket.on("button-data", function(data){
    accumulatorArrayA0[data[0]] = accumulatorArrayA0[data[0]] + 1;
    accumulatorArrayA1[data[1]] = accumulatorArrayA1[data[1]] + 1;

    updateBar(accumulatorArrayA0);
    addRemoveClass("remove");
});

function updateBar(data){

    x.domain(d3.range(data.length));
    y.domain([0, d3.max(data)]);
```

```
    var rect = bars.selectAll(".bar")
        .data(data);

    rect.enter().append("rect");

      rect.attr("class", "bar")
      .transition()
      .duration(1000)
      .attr("x", function(d, i) { return x(i); })
      .attr("width", x.bandwidth())
      .attr("y", function(d) {return y(d); })
      .attr("height", function(d) {  return height - y(+d); });
   bars.select(".x.axis")
            .transition()
            .duration(1000)
          .call(d3.axisBottom(x));

        bars.select(".y.axis")
            .transition()
            .duration(1000)
          .call(d3.axisLeft(y)
      .ticks(d3.max(data))
      .tickFormat(d3.format("d")));
 }

function addRemoveClass(action){
    var buttonResponse = document.getElementById("bar-A0").
    getElementsByClassName("text-block-response")[0];

    buttonResponse.classList[action]("hidden");

    buttonResponse = document.getElementById("bar-A1").
    getElementsByClassName("text-block-response")[0];

    buttonResponse.classList[action]("hidden");
 }
```

```
function currentInputValue(data){
    var targetP = document.getElementById("bar-" + data.
    dataKey).getElementsByClassName("text-block")[0].
    getElementsByTagName("p")[0];

    targetP.innerHTML = data.dataString;
  }
})();
```

The Code Explained

The D3.js used in the application is similar to the example in Listing 7-1, but there is some new functionality. Table 7-2 goes into more detail about the code in main.js.

Table 7-2. main.js explained

`.ticks(0));`	This function creates the ticks on the y-axis, as there isn't any data when the graph is created and it is set to 0; this will be updated when there is data.

`bars.append("text")`
`    .attr("transform",`
`        "translate`
`        (" + (width/2) + " ," +`
`                (height + margin.`
`                top + 20) + ")")`
`    .style("text-anchor", "middle")`
`    .text("score");`
	These functions add and align the label for the x-axis, and there is a similar set of functions for the y-axis.

`updateBar(data);`	When the button is pressed, the bar chart needs to be updated with the new data. The code for the update is in a function called updateBar(), which is passed the array of data.

(continued)

Table 7-2. (*continued*)

`x.domain(d3.range(data.length));` `y.domain([0, d3.max(data)]);`	Before, the domain and range of the x and y were declared at the same time. Now the domain will constantly change as new data is added to the array. This means that the domain of the x and y also needs to change. In this case the length of the data for the x will not change but the maximum value in the array will. This is used to change the height of the bar and so the y.domain goes from 0 to the maximum value in the array. This uses the d3.max() function, which can take an array as its data and work out the highest value in the array.
`.transition()` `.duration(1000)`	These functions make the new value of the bars animate from the old value, and the duration is in milliseconds.
`.ticks(d3.max(data))`	You need ticks on the y-axis but the maximum number will need to change as the maximum number in the array increases. Using the d3.max() function means the ticks will always be the same as the maximum number in the array.
`.tickFormat(d3.format("d")));`	There are a number of ways you can format your ticks; using "d" makes them integers.

You need to separate the creation of the visualization with the update. If you don't do this, you will be creating new SVG's each time new data is added. By separating the creation and update, you can update the same SVG with the new data.

UPDATE THE FRONT END

You don't need to do much to update the front end. Open up your index.ejs file and add in the code in bold from Listing 7-3. This is the code from Chapter 6 with small updates so I haven't written the old code in full.

Listing 7-3. Index.ejs

```
<!DOCTYPE html>
<html>
<head>
    ...
    <link href="/css/main.css" rel="stylesheet" type="text/css">
    <script type="text/javascript" src="https://d3js.org/d3.v4.js">
    </script>

</head>
<body>
    <header>
        <h1>EVENT METRICS</h1>
        <h2>getting information through an Arduino</h2>
    </header>
    <div id="content">
        <h2>AT TONIGHTS EVENT DID YOU ...</H2>
        <p>Answer the questions by turning the knobs, to submit
        your answer press the button.</p>
```

...

```
        <div class="text-block-response hidden">
            <h3>Thanks<h3>
            <p></p>
        </div>
    </div>

    <div id="bar-chart">
        <h2>Talk to someone new?</h2>
        <p>did people meet new people tonight?</p>

    </div>
    </div>
    <script src="/socket.io/socket.io.js"></script>
    <script src="javascript/main.js"></script>

</body>
</html>
```

The updates are to include the D3.js library and to add a div to hold the visualization.

UPDATE THE CSS

Open up the main.css file; you should already have copied the CSS from Chapter 6 so only the following code needs to be added:

```
.bar {
    fill: #6BCAE2;
}
```

This adds color to the bars in the graph.

On your browser, if you refresh the page you should be able to see the color on the bars.

Tidying Up the Code

You may have noticed that adding in the D3.js code has created a lot of global variables. It isn't a good idea to have global variables for a number of reasons, including the following:

1. They are in the global namespace. It is quite easy to forget what you have called a variable and create multiple variables with the same name. This can leave you with unexpected results. Also any function could use the variable.

2. If you bring in other libraries, they may have the same name as your global variable.

3. It can be difficult to see what variable belongs to what function.

The code for creating the visualizations is very different from the code used in the rest of the page, so it is a good candidate for having its own space in a separate JavaScript file. You do need to pass data from the main. js to the visualization and that can be done in a number of ways. In this chapter you will use the revealing module pattern to do this.

Revealing Module Pattern

There are a number of programming patterns in JavaScript. The revealing module pattern is one of them. It uses a variable that holds an immediately invoked function expression. The function is called when it loads. Within this function you can create variables and functions, which are encapsulated inside the main function. You can allow access to these functions and variables outside the module. Returning them at the end of the function does this. Any functions or variables that are not returned cannot be called outside the module.

Separating the Data Visualization

In the chapter_07 application create a new file in the public/javascript folder called BarChart.js. This will mean the directory structure for the chapter_07 application will look like this:

```
/chapter_07
    /node_modules
    /public
        /css
            main.css
        /javascipt
            main.js
            BarChart.js
    /views
        index.ejs
    index.js
```

USE THE REVEALING MODULE PATTERN

Open BarChart.js and copy in the code in Listing 7-4.

Listing 7-4. BarChart.js

```javascript
var BarChart = (function(){

    var margin = {top: 20, right: 20, bottom: 40, left: 40};
    var width = 480 - margin.left - margin.right;
    var height = 500 - margin.top - margin.bottom;
    var x;
    var y;
    var bars;
```

```
function setup(data){
    x = d3.scaleBand()
    .range([0, width], .1)
    .padding(0.1);

    y = d3.scaleLinear()
    .range([height, 0]);

    bars = d3.select("#bar-chart").append("svg")
      .attr("width", width + margin.left + margin.right)
      .attr("height", height + margin.top + margin.bottom)
      .append("g")
      .attr("transform", "translate(" + margin.left + "," +
      margin.top + ")");

    bars.selectAll(".bar")
      .data(data)
    .enter()
      .append("rect")
      .attr("class", "bar")
      .attr("x", function(d, i) { return x(i); })
      .attr("width", x.bandwidth())
      .attr("y", function(d) {return y(d); })
      .attr("height", function(d) {   return height - y(+d); });

    bars.append("g")
    .attr("class", "x axis")
    .attr("transform", "translate(0," + height + ")")
    .call(d3.axisBottom(x));
    bars.append("g")
    .attr("class", "y axis")
    .call(d3.axisLeft(y)
      .ticks(0));
```

```
        bars.append("text")
        .attr("transform",
              "translate(" + (width/2) + " ," +
                             (height + margin.top + 20) + ")")
        .style("text-anchor", "middle")
        .text("score");

      bars.append("text")
        .attr("transform", "rotate(-90)")
        .attr("y", 0 - margin.left)
        .attr("x",0 - (height / 2))
        .attr("dy", "1em")
        .style("text-anchor", "middle")
        .text("freqency");
    }

function updateBar(data){
        x.domain(d3.range(data.length));
        y.domain([0, d3.max(data)]);

        var test = d3.max(data);

        var rect = bars.selectAll(".bar")
            .data(data);

        rect.enter().append("rect");

          rect.attr("class", "bar")
          .transition()
          .duration(1000)
          .attr("x", function(d, i) { return x(i); })
          .attr("width", x.bandwidth())
          .attr("y", function(d) {return y(d); })
          .attr("height", function(d) {  return height - y(+d);
});
```

```
            bars.select(".x.axis")
                .transition()
                .duration(1000)
                .call(d3.axisBottom(x));

            bars.select(".y.axis")
                .transition()
                .duration(1000)
                .call(d3.axisLeft(y)
                    .ticks(test)
                    .tickFormat(d3.format("d")));
        }

    return{
        setup: setup,
        updateBar: updateBar
    }
})();
```

The Code Explained

The D3.js used in the application is similar to the example in Listing 7-1, but there is some new functionality. Table 7-3 explains the code in BarChart.js.

Table 7-3. *BarChart.js explained*

```var BarChart = (function(){ })();```	An anonymous function is created to hold the variables and functions for creating the visualization. It is held in a variable called BarChart. It calls itself when loaded.
```var margin = {top: 20, right: 20, bottom: 40, left: 40}; var width = 480 - margin. left - margin.right; var height = 500 - margin. top - margin.bottom; var x; var y; var bars;```	There are variables that will be used by different functions within BarChart, so they are added globally inside BarChart.js. They can only be seen within the scope of the function held in the variable BarChart.
```function setup(data){}```	The setup function has all the setup code for the visualization that was global in main.js and puts it in its own function.
```function updateBar(data){}```	The updateBar() function has all the update code for the visualization that was in main.js in the updateBar() function.

``return{
    setup: setup,
    updateBar: updateBar
}```
	You decide which functions and variables can be seen outside the function. To do this you need to return the functions. The name before ":" is how other functions will call the function and the name after ":" is the named function within the current function. You can return multiple functions and variables, and they are separated with a ",".

```
┌─────────────────────────────────────────────────────┐
│                  UPDATE MAIN.JS                      │
└─────────────────────────────────────────────────────┘
```

The main.js file has to be updated; first all the code connected to the Visualization needs to be removed, and then a call to the setup() and updateBar() function needs to be added. Open the main.js from Listing 7-2 and update it with the code in Listing 7-5.

Listing 7-5. Updated main.js code

```javascript
(function(){
    var socket = io();

    var accumulatorArrayA0 = [0,0,0,0,0,0,0,0,0,0,0,0];
    var accumulatorArrayA1 = [0,0,0,0,0,0,0,0,0,0,0,0];

    BarChart.setup(accumulatorArrayA0);

    socket.on("bar-data", function(data){
        var current = data.dataKey;
        var svgBar = document.getElementById(current);

        var newWidth = data.dataString * 40;

        svgBar.setAttribute("width", newWidth);

        currentInputValue(data);
        addRemoveClass("add");
    });

    socket.on("button-data", function(data){

        accumulatorArrayA0[data[0]] = accumulatorArray
        A0[data[0]] + 1;
        accumulatorArrayA1[data[1]] = accumulatorArray
        A1[data[1]] + 1;

        addRemoveClass("remove");
```

```
        BarChart.updateBar(accumulatorArrayA0);
    });

    function addRemoveClass(action){
        var buttonResponse = document.getElementById("bar-A0").
        getElementsByClassName("text-block-response")[0];

        buttonResponse.classList[action]("hidden");

        buttonResponse = document.getElementById("bar-A1").
        getElementsByClassName("text-block-response")[0];

        buttonResponse.classList[action]("hidden");
    }

    function currentInputValue(data){
        var targetP = document.getElementById("bar-" + data.
        dataKey).getElementsByClassName("text-block")[0].
        getElementsByTagName("p")[0];

        targetP.innerHTML = data.dataString;
    }
})();
```

You'll notice that in place of the code to create the visualization are two calls to the new functions. The format to call the function is shown in Figure 7-5.

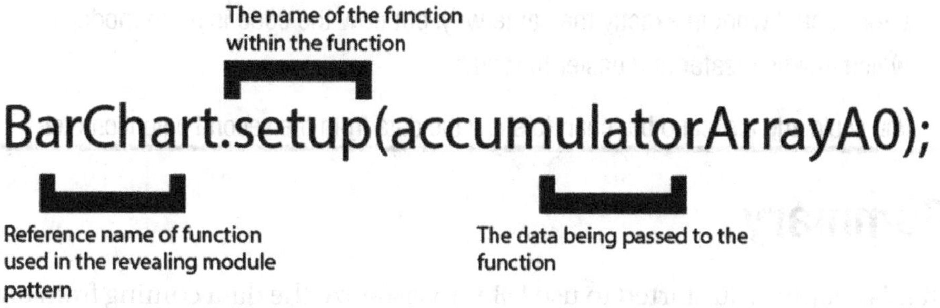

The name of the function
within the function

BarChart.setup(accumulatorArrayA0);

Reference name of function
used in the revealing module
pattern

The data being passed to the
function

Figure 7-5. Calling a function within a revealing module pattern

---

UPDATE INDEX.EJS

Finally, the index.ejs file needs to be updated to include the new JavaScript file. As main.js uses BarChart.js, BarChart.js needs to be called before main.js. Open the index.ejs from Listing 7-3 and add in the code in bold in Listing 7-6.

Listing 7-6. Adding BarChart.js to index.ejs

```
<!DOCTYPE html>
<html>
...
        <div id="bar-chart">
            <h2>Talk to someone new?</h2>
            <p>did people meet new people tonigt?</p>

        </div>

    </div>
    <script src="/socket.io/socket.io.js"></script>
    <script src="javascript/BarChart.js"></script>
    <script src="javascript/main.js"></script>

</body>
</html>
```

If you have localhost running, refresh the browser or restart the server. The page should work in exactly the same way, but now the code is more modular, which makes it safer and easier to read.

You could add a second bar chart to show the data from the second potentiometer.

Summary

In this chapter you started to use D3.js to visualize the data coming from an Arduino. You also tried out some new JavaScript concepts and now should have a better understanding of the structure of JavaScript. In the next chapter you will create a dashboard and use D3.js to create donut charts.

CHAPTER 8

Create a Web Dashboard

You can attach sensors to an Arduino and send that data to the front end to create an IoT dashboard. In this chapter you will use heat, light, and humidity sensors to gather data that will then be displayed on a web page. The visualizations on the dashboard will react to the live data and that data will be stored to give a daily high and low reading. By using data visualizations in this way, you can make the data easier to read, digest, and analyze.

The Dashboard

The dashboard in this chapter will take temperature, humidity, and light level data and display each in a donut graph. The data will be stored on the server, in a simple JavaScript object that will be reset every day. The object will be passed to the front end every time a value changes, so that the dashboard shows an accurate picture of the data. Figure 8-1 shows how the dashboard will look in the browser.

© Indira Knight 2018
I. Knight, *Connecting Arduino to the Web*, https://doi.org/10.1007/978-1-4842-3480-8_8

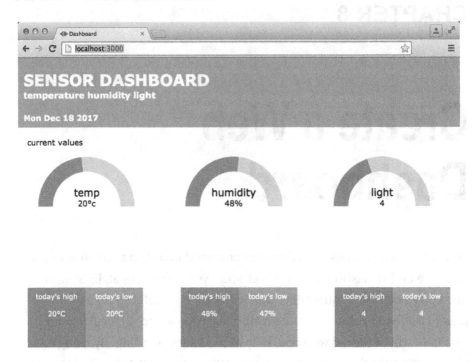

Figure 8-1. *The dashboard application for this chapter*

Principles of Data Visualization

We visualize data so we can understand it better, whether it's to explore the data, convey a message, or tell a story with the data. Data visualizations are made of points, lines, areas, surfaces, or volumes. These can be modified into what Jacques Bertin described as visual variables. He defined seven visual variables: position, size, value, texture, color, orientation, and shape. Figure 8-2 show the seven visual variables.

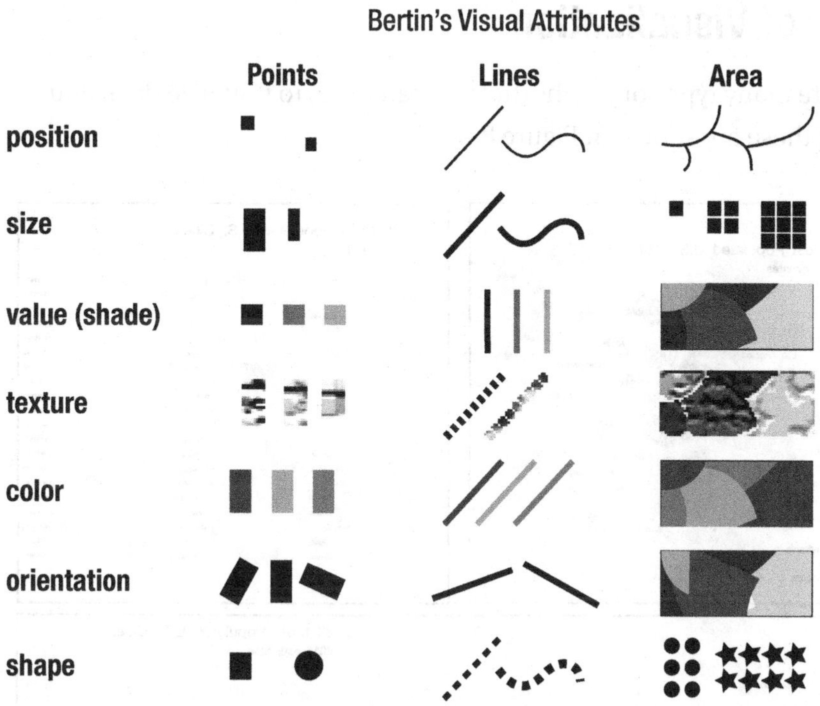

Bertin's Visual Attributes

Figure 8-2. *The seven visual variables and how they are related to points, lines, and area*

Over time these visual variables were added to by other researchers. Which visual variables you use to represent the data will depend on the type of data it is. Quantitative, ordinal, and categorical data works well with certain variables.

Quantitative data is data that has a quantity, for example, the number of apples in a bag. Ordinal data is data that has an order that we have given it, for example, your top 10 films. Categorical data is used for labeling and doesn't have a number associated with it, for example, a list of countries.

There are lots of different types of graphs you can use to represent data, and the type you choose will depend on the type of data you have and what you are trying to say. When picking which type of visualization you want to create, think about who will be looking at it, what level of complexity it needs to have, and does the visualization make it easy to understand the data.

Types of Visualization

There are many types of graphs that you can make to visualize data, and some of these are shown in Figure 8-3.

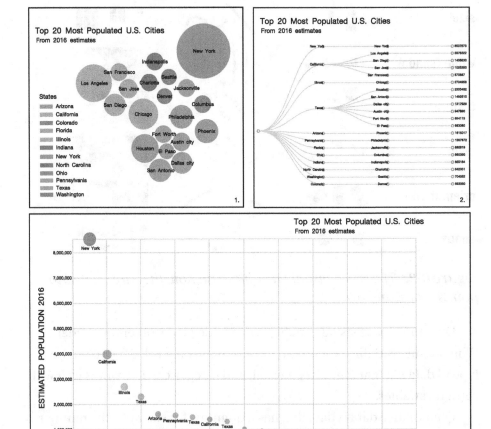

Figure 8-3. *1. Clustered force layout, 2. Cluster dendrogram, 3. Scatter plot. Visualizations of data from https://census.gov/data/ tables/2016/demo/popest/total-cities-and-towns.html showing population estimates for 2016 for the 20 highest populated cites in the United States*

Labeling a Visualization

It is very important to have the right labels on a visualization. You can start with a good title that matches what will be shown on the visualization. It is also important to have a key for the data

Color

The colors you use could obscure the meaning of the data. There are a couple of things to think about with color. First is that colors have different meanings to different people, and you shouldn't assume that because you associate a color with a certain meaning that others will also. You should consider this when thinking about your viewer.

If you are using color to represent a range of values, make sure that values that are similar don't have very different colors. The viewer will think that you are trying to highlight very different values.

There is a very useful online tool called ColorBrewer http://colorbrewer2.org/, and it was made to help choose colors for cartography. It will give you good color values for your visualization, and it also has a colorblind safe mode.

In Appendix B, I have listed some good resources for data visualizations.

The Sensors

This chapter will use a temperature and humidity sensor and photoresistor. There are many companies that produce these types of sensors; I have used the ones produced by Elegoo.

DHT11 Temperature and Humidity Sensor

This is a digital sensor that measures temperature and relative humidity. Relative humidity is the amount of water that is in the air compared to how much it could hold at a particular temperature. The temperature is measured in Celsius.

Photoresistor

A photoresistor reacts to light level. The resistance decreases as the intensity of light in an environment increases. It is connected to an Analog pin so will have a value between 0 and 1023. The higher the light levels, the closer to 0 the output will be.

Importing Libraries

Whichever make of temperature and humidity sensor you decide to use, you will probably need to install a library into the Arduino IDE for the temperature and humidity sensor. The Elegoo sensors have downloadable ZIP files that need to be installed. These next steps go through how to do this for Elegoo; but you may find different steps for another make of sensors.

1. Open the Arduino IDE.

2. In the menu go to Sketch/Include Library/Add .ZIP Library, and a window will open.

3. Navigate to ZIP file and double-click the file to import it.

4. You should now be able to see the imported library, so check by looking in menu Sketch/Include Library, and you should see the name of the library in the library list.

Note Different types of temperature and humidity sensors have different downloadable libraries. If you have used a different make of sensor, you will use its library and so the ino code will be slightly different. Refer to your sensor guide to find the right code.

SET UP THE TEMPERATURE AND HEAT SENSORS

To set up the temperature and humidity you will need a temperature and humidity sensor, an Arduino Uno, a USB cable, and female to male wires. Figure 8-4 shows the components.

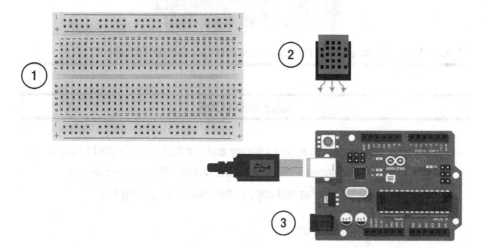

Figure 8-4. *The components needed to set up the temperature and humidity sensor: 1. Breadboard, 2. DHT11 temperature and humidity sensor, 3. Arduino Uno*

Figure 8-5 shows how the components should be connected.

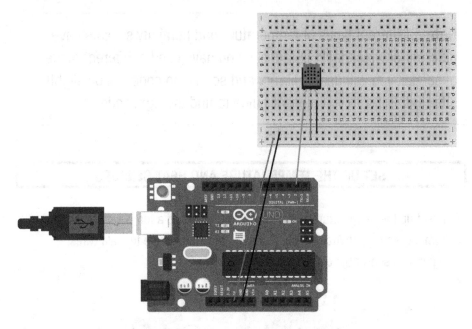

Figure 8-5. *Connecting the components to the Arduino*

ARDUINO CODE

The ino code will import the sensors library and use that library's dht11.read ()
function to import the sensors data. Open the Arduino IDE and create a new
sketch called chapter_08.ino and copy in the code from Listing 8-1.

Listing 8-1. chapter_08.ino

```
#include <SimpleDHT.h>
int pinTempHumidity = 2;
SimpleDHT11 dht11;
byte temperature = 0;
byte humidity = 0;
byte data[40] = {0};
void setup() {
```

```
  Serial.begin(9600);
}
void loop() {
  Serial.println("Current Reading");
  dht11.read(pinTempHumidity, &temperature, &humidity, data);
  Serial.print((int)temperature); Serial.print(" *C, ");
  Serial.print((int)humidity); Serial.println(" %");
  delay(10000);
}
```

The Code Explained

Table 8-1 explains the code in chapter_08.ino.

Table 8-1. *chapter_08.ino explained*

`#include <SimpleDHT.h>`	This includes the imported SimpleDHT library that is needed to work with the sensor.
`int pinTempHumidity = 2;`	A variable is created for the pin number used for the sensor.
`SimpleDHT11 dht11;`	A variable is created to hold the data from the sensor with a type of SimpleDHT11.

`byte temperature = 0;`
`byte humidity = 0;`
`byte data[40] = {0};`
	Three variables are created to hold the byte data returned from the sensor.

`dht11.read(pinTempHumidity,` `&temperature, &humidity, data);`	The dht11.read() function takes the pin number the sensor is connected to and returns the temperature, humidity, and the byte data from the sensor.

`Serial.print((int)temperature);`
`Serial.print(" *C, ");`
`Serial.print((int)humidity);`
`Serial.println(" %");`
	The Serial.print() function prints the values from the sensor, the (int) before temperature and humidity convert the byte data into integers.

241

Verify the code and then with the Arduino attached to a port via a USB, upload the sketch to the Arduino. Make sure you have the right port for the Arduino selected in the Tools menu: Tools/Port.

Now open the Serial Monitor for your sketch and you should see the data coming through every 10 seconds.

ADDING A PHOTORESISTOR

Unplug the Arduino from your computer to set up the photoresistor. The updated setup is shown in Figure 8-6.

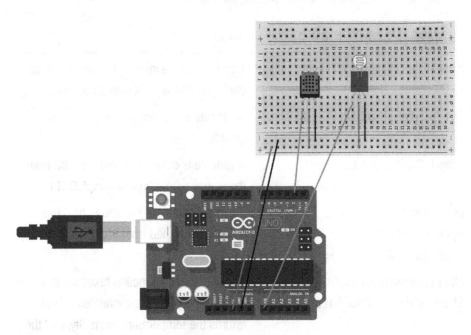

Figure 8-6. The setup for the photoresitor

Open up the .ino file from Listing 8-1 and update it with the code in bold in Listing 8-2.

Listing 8-2. Updated chapter_08.ino

```
#include <SimpleDHT.h>
int pinTempHumidity = 2;
SimpleDHT11 dht11;
byte temperature = 0;
byte humidity = 0;
byte data[40] = {0};
int pinLight = A0;
int valueLight = 0;
void setup() {
  Serial.begin(9600);
}
void loop() {
  Serial.println("Current Reading");
  dht11.read(pinTempHumidity, &temperature, &humidity, data);
  valueLight = analogRead(pinLight);

  Serial.print((int)temperature); Serial.print(" *C, ");
  Serial.print((int)humidity); Serial.println(" %");
  Serial.print(valueLight, DEC);
  delay(10000);
}
```

The Code Explained

Table 8-2 explains the updated code in chapter_08.ino.

Table 8-2. *chapter_08.ino updated*

`int  pinLight  = A0;` `int  valueLight = 0;`	Two new variables are created to hold the pin number and the value, which will come from the photoresistor.
`valueLight =` `analogRead(pinLight);`	The value from the resistor is stored in the variable valueLight.
`Serial.print(valueLight,` `DEC);`	The value is printed, and DEC is an optional argument of the Serial.print() function that makes sure the value printed is decimal.

Upload the updated sketch to the Arduino and open the Serial Monitor in the Arduino IDE; you should see the value from the photoresistor.

UPDATE THE ARDUINO SKETCH

If you can see the data from the temperature and humidity sensor and the photoresistor in the Serial Monitor, the sensors are set up correctly. Now you can write a sketch to format the data for the Node.js server. There are two main changes to the sketch; first, the serial.print function needs to send all the data separated by a comma. Second, the data from the photoresistor will be mapped so the values will go from 0 for low light to 10 for high light. Create a new sketch and copy the code from Listing 8-3.

Listing 8-3. chapter_08_final.ino

```
#include <SimpleDHT.h>
int pinTempHumidity = 2;
SimpleDHT11 dht11;
byte temperature = 0;
byte humidity = 0;
byte data[40] = {0};
```

```
int  pinLight  =  A0;
int  valueLight = 0;

void setup() {
  Serial.begin(9600);
}
void loop() {
  dht11.read(pinTempHumidity, &temperature, &humidity, data);
  valueLight =  analogRead(pinLight);
  valueLight = map(valueLight, 0, 1023, 10, 0);

  Serial.println((String)temperature + "," + (String)humidity +
  "," + (String)valueLight);
  delay(500);
}
```

The Code Explained

Table 8-3 explains the code in chapter_08_final.ino.

Table 8-3. chapter_08_final.ino explained

`valueLight = map(valueLight, 0, 1023, 10, 0);`	Once the value of the photoresistor is read into the variable valueLight, it is mapped into a new value. As it's reading from the analog pin, it will be a value between 0 and 1023, and the higher the number the lower the light. The mapping will take this number and convert it to a number between 0 and 10, with 0 for lower light.
`Serial.println((String) temperature + "," + (String) humidity + "," + (String) valueLight);`	Each of the values is turned into a string so that it can be concatenated with the other values using a comma. The comma is used in the Node.js server to work out where each new bit of data starts.

THE DASHBOARD APPLICATION

Now that the sensors are set up, you can create the dashboard application
for the data. First build the skeleton application, and the structure will be the
following:

```
/chapter_08
    /node_modules
    /public
        /css
            main.css
        /javascript
            main.js
            donut.js
    /views
        index.ejs
    index.js
```

The setup for creating the server is the same as in previous chapters:

1. Create a new folder to hold the application. I called mine
    chapter_08.

2. Open the command prompt (Windows operating system) or
    a terminal window (Mac) and navigate to the newly created
    folder.

3. When you are in the right directory, type npm init to create
    a new application; you can press return through each of the
    questions or make changes to them.

4. You can now start adding the necessary libraries; to
    download Express.js at the command line, type npm install
    express@4.15.3 --save.

5. Then install ejs, type npm install ejs@2.5.6 --save.

6. When that's downloaded, install serial port. On a Mac, type npm install serialport@4.0.7 –save; and on a Windows PC, type npm install serialport@4.0.7 --build-from-source.

7. Then finally install socket.io, type npm install socket.io@1.7.3 --save.

SET UP THE NODE.JS SERVER

There are three pieces of data coming from the Arduino: temperature, humidity, and light level. They will come as a single string separated by a comma. The string contents will be put into an array, which can then be passed to the front end. The string will contain a newline character at the end, which will need to be deleted. Open the index.js file for the application and copy in the code in Listing 8-4.

Listing 8-4. index.js

```
var http = require('http');
var express = require('express');
var app = express();
var server = http.createServer(app);
var io = require('socket.io')(server);
var SerialPort = require('serialport');
var serialport = new SerialPort('<add in the serial port for
your Arduino>', {
    parser: SerialPort.parsers.readline('\n')
});
app.engine('ejs', require('ejs').__express);
app.set('view engine', 'ejs');
app.use(express.static(__dirname + '/public'));
```

```
app.get('/', function (req, res){
    res.render('index');
});
io.on('connection', function(socket){
    console.log('socket.io connection');
    serialport.on('data', function(data){
        data = data.replace(/(\r\n|\n|\r)/gm,"");
        var dataArray = data.split(',');
        socket.emit("data", dataArray);
    });
    socket.on('disconnect', function(){
        console.log('disconnected');
    });
});
server.listen(3000, function(){
    console.log('listening on port 3000...');
});
```

Make sure you change the code to include the serial port that your Arduino is connected to.

The Code Explained

Table 8-4 explains the code in index.js.

Table 8-4. *index.js explained*

`data = data.replace(/(\r\n|` `\n|\r)/gm,"");`	The regular expression will remove any newline character by using the replace() function.
`var dataArray = data.` `split(',');`	The split function takes the data string and splits it every time it comes across a comma and creates an array of each word.

CREATE THE WEB PAGE

For now you will create the basic page that will hold the dashboard. It will
have a socket so you can test that the data is coming through to the front end.
Open or create the index.ejs file in the views folder and copy in the code in
Listing 8-5.

Listing 8-5. index.ejs

```
<!DOCTYPE html>
<head>
    <title>Dashboard</title>
</head>
<body>
    <div class="wrapper">
        <h1>Dashboard</h1>
        <p>This page will contain a dashboard of data</p>
    </div>
    <script src="https://cdn.socket.io/socket.io-1.2.0.js">
    </script>
    <script>
        var socket = io();
        socket.on("data", function(data){
            console.log(data);
        });
    </script>
</body>
</html>
```

Make sure the Arduino is connected to your computer but with the serial monitor closed. Go to the root of the application in the console and type either nodemon index.js or node index.js to start the server. Go to http://localhost:3000 and open the page. You should see the holding page and then start to see the data coming into the console. If you open the developer tools for the browser (Option + Command + i on a mac, CTRL + Shift + i on a Windows PC), you should also see the data in the console tab.

CREATE THE DONUT CHARTS

There are two main elements of this dashboard, the donut charts and the high/low data for the day. The donut charts will be created with D3.js and will be 180° instead of 360°. There are three charts, one for each type of data. The code to create the charts will be in a separate JavaScript file called donut.js; it uses the revealing module pattern. The donut charts themselves are created in the main.js file, calling methods from donut.js. This keeps the code separate and means you can use the same code for creating all charts. The donut.js file contains a number of methods to create and update the donuts.

Update index.js

The data coming into the Node.js server will be saved in an object. This object will be passed to the front end. Open up the code in Listing 8-4 and update it with the code in bold in Listing 8-6.

Listing 8-6. Updated index.js

```
var http = require('http');
var express = require('express');
var app = express();
var server = http.createServer(app);
```

```
var io = require('socket.io')(server);
var SerialPort = require('serialport');
var serialport = new SerialPort('<add in the serial port for
your Arduino>', {
    parser: SerialPort.parsers.readline('\n')
});
var sensors = {
    temp: {current: 0 , high:0, low:100 },
    humidity: {current: 0, high:0, low: 100},
    light: {current: 0, high:0, low: 10}
}
app.engine('ejs', require('ejs').__express);
app.set('view engine', 'ejs');
app.use(express.static(__dirname + '/public'));
app.get('/', function (req, res){
    res.render('index');
});
io.on('connection', function(socket){
    console.log('socket.io connection');
    socket.emit("initial-data", sensors);
    serialport.on('data', function(data){
        data = data.replace(/(\r\n|\n|\r)/gm,"");
        var dataArray = data.split(',');
        var hasChanged = updateValues(dataArray);
        if (hasChanged > 0){
            socket.emit("data", sensors);
        }
    });
});
```

```
    socket.on('disconnect', function(){
        console.log('disconnected');
    });
});
server.listen(3000, function(){
    console.log('listening on port 3000...');
});
function updateValues(data){
    var changed = 0;
    var keyArray = ["temp", "humidity", "light"];
    keyArray.forEach(function(key, index){
        var tempSensor = sensors[key];
        var newData = data[index];
        if(tempSensor.current !== newData){
            sensors[key].current = data[index];
            changed = 1;
        }
        if(tempSensor.high < newData){
            sensors[key].high = data[index];
            changed = 1;
        }
        if(tempSensor.low > newData ){
            sensors[key].low = data[index];
        }
    });
    return changed;
}
```

The Code Explained

Table 8-5 explains the code in index.js.

Table 8-5. *index.js explained*

```var sensors = {```
```   temp: {current: 0 , high:0,```
```   low:100 },```
```   humidity: {current: 0,```
```   high:0, low: 100},```
```   light: {current: 0, high:0,```
```   low: 10}```
```}```
	The variable sensor holds an object that contains the current value as well as the highest and lowest value for a sensor. As the object is stored on the server, it will store the values until the server is restarted. This object is updated when new data comes in from the sensors.

```socket.emit("initial-data",``` ```sensors);```	When a browser connects to the server the current sensor data is sent to it.
```var hasChanged =``` ```updateValues(dataArray);```	The variable hasChanged will hold the returned value from the function updateValues(). The variable hasChanged will be 0 if the data hasn't changed and will be 1 if it has.

```if (hasChanged > 0){```
```   socket.emit("data",```
```   sensors);```
```}```
	If hasChanged is greater than 0 the data has changed and a socket.emit is called, with an id of "data," passing the updated sensor data to the front end.

```function updateValues(data){}```	The updateValues() function is passed to the new data, and it checks it against the sensor object to see if any of the values have changed.
```var changed = 0;```	It initializes a variable called changed to 0; this is the variable that will be returned at the end of the function.

(continued)

Table 8-5. (*continued*)

```var keyArray = ["temp", "humidity", "light"];```	An array of the sensors to be tested is created.
```keyArray.forEach(function(key, index){ });```	The JavaScript forEach() function is called to be iterated through the array, and it will use the data of the array item for the key and use the position of the array item for the index.
```var tempSensor = sensors[key]; var newData = data[index];```	Two variables are created to hold the value of the key and the index.
```if(tempSensor.current !== newData){ sensors[key].current = data [index]; changed = 1; }```	An if statement checks if the current value of the data is not equal to the new data. If the data has changed the current value for that particular sensor in the sensors object, the sensor object is updated and the variable changed is set to 1. There are if statements to check if the high and low values have changed as well.
```return changed;```	The variable changed is then returned. If none of the values have changed, then the code won't have entered any of the if statements and changed returns 0. If any of the values have changed, then changed will return 1.

CREATE THE DONUT JAVASCRIPT

The code to create the donut chart will have its own JavaScript file. In the public/javascript folder create a file called donut.js and copy in the code in Listing 8-7.

Listing 8-7. donut.js

```
var DonutChart = function(){
    var pi = Math.PI;
    var sensorDomainArray;
    var divIdName;
    var sensorAmount;
    var sensorText = "";

    var sensorScale;
    var foreground;
    var arc;
    var svg;
    var g;
    var textValue;
    function setSensorDomain(domainArray){
        sensorDomainArray = domainArray;
    }
    function setSvgDiv(name){
        divIdName = name;
    }
    function createChart(sensorTextNew, sensorType){
        sensorText = sensorTextNew;
        var margin = {top: 10, right: 10, bottom: 10, left: 10};
        var width = 240 - margin.left - margin.right;
        var height = 200;
        sensorScale = d3.scaleLinear()
            .range([0, 180]);
```

```
arc = d3.arc()
    .innerRadius(70)
    .outerRadius(100)
    .startAngle(0);
svg = d3.select(divIdName).append("svg")
    .attr("width", width + margin.left + margin.right)
    .attr("height", height + margin.top + margin.
    bottom);
g = svg.append("g").attr("transform", "translate(" +
width / 2 + "," + height / 2 + ")");
g.append("text")
    .attr("text-anchor", "middle")
    .attr("font-size", "1.3em")
    .attr("y", -20)
    .text(sensorType);
textValue = g.append("text")
 .attr("text-anchor", "middle")
 .attr('font-size', '1em')
 .attr('y', 0)
 .text(sensorAmount + "" +  sensorText);
var background = g.append("path")
    .datum({endAngle: pi})
    .style("fill", "#ddd")
    .attr("d", arc)
    .attr("transform", "rotate(-90)")
foreground = g.append("path")
    .datum({endAngle: 0.5 * pi})
    .style("fill", "#FE8402")
    .attr("d", arc)
    .attr("transform", "rotate(-90)");
}
```

```
function updateChart(newSensorValue){
    sensorScale.domain(sensorDomainArray);
    var sensorValue = sensorScale(newSensorValue);
    sensorValue = sensorValue/180;
    textValue.text(newSensorValue + "" +  sensorText);
    foreground.transition()
      .duration(750)
      .attrTween("d", arcAnimation(sensorValue * pi));
}
function arcAnimation(newAngle)
  return function(d) {
    var interpolate = d3.interpolate(d.endAngle, newAngle);

    return function(t) {
      d.endAngle = interpolate(t);
      return arc(d);
    };
  };
}
return{
    setSensorDomain: setSensorDomain,
    setSvgDiv: setSvgDiv,
    createChart:createChart,
    updateChart: updateChart
}
};
```

The Code Explained

The code uses the D3.js arc function to create a donut chart. Usually these would be 360° but in this case it will be 180°. When new data is sent from the Arduino the updateChart() method is called, which calls a function arcAnimation() that works out the animation between the old and new angles. Table 8-6 goes into more detail about donut.js.

Table 8-6. *donut.js explained*

```var DonutChart = function(){ };```	All the code is wrapped in a function; this is part of the revealing module pattern. New donuts can be created by calling a new donutChart().
```function setSensorDomain (domainArray){ sensorDomainArray = domainArray; }```	This function sets the domain for the donut chart. The domain is a set of values for the highest and lowest possible value of the data.
```function setSvgDiv(name){ divIdName = name; }```	A function that puts the name of the HTML div into the variable divIdName.
```function createChart(sensorTextNew, sensorType){}```	The initial setup of the donut chart is contained in this method. It is passed two arguments: the symbol that is used with the data type, for example, %; then the type of data it will be representing, either temp, humidity, or light
```sensorScale = d3.scaleLinear() .range([0, 180]);```	sensorScale holds the range and domain for the visualization. The range is 0 to 180 as the donut can go from 0 to 180°.

(continued)

Table 8-6. (*continued*)

```arc = d3.arc()```
```   .innerRadius(70)```
```   .outerRadius(100)```
```   .startAngle(0);```
	The d3.js arc() function is stored in the variable arc, which was declared at the top of the code. You can set its inner and outer radii, and this will define its size and the donut hole.

```var background = g.append("path")```
```   .datum({endAngle: pi})```
```   .style("fill", "#ddd")```
```   .attr("d", arc)```
```   .attr("transform",```
```   "rotate(-90)")```
	The background arc is created that will always be 180° and will be gray; it is rotated to a horizontal position.

```foreground = g.append("path")```
```   .datum({endAngle: 0.5```
```   * pi})```
```   .style("fill",```
```   "#FE8402")```
```   .attr("d", arc)```
```   .attr("transform",```
```   "rotate(-90)");```
	The foreground arc is created, which has an orange fill.

```function``` ```updateChart(newSensorValue){}```	This function is called when there is new data and the donut chart needs to be updated. It has one argument, the new value.
```sensorScale.``` ```domain(sensorDomainArray);```	The domain for the scale is set.

(*continued*)

Table 8-6. (*continued*)

`var sensorValue = sensorScale(newSensorValue);`	Takes the new value and maps it to the donut charts scale.
`sensorValue = sensorValue/180;`	Fits the value to 180°.
`textValue.text(newSensorValue + "" + sensorText);`	Updates the text value.

`foreground.transition()`
`        .duration(750)`
`        .attrTween("d",`
`        arcAnimation(sensorValue *`
`        pi));`
	Creates a transition with a duration of 750 milliseconds for the donut chart. The arcAnimation() function is called, which works out the transition for the arc.

`function arcAnimation(newAngle) {`
`    return function(d) {`
`      var interpolate =`
`      d3.interpolate(d.endAngle,`
`      newAngle);`
`      return function(t) {`
`        d.endAngle =`
`        interpolate(t);`
`        return arc(d);`
`      };`
`    };`
`}`
	The function is passed the new angle for the new data, and the animation between the old and new angles is returned.

`return{`
`    setSensorDomain:`
`    setSensorDomain,`
`    setSvgDiv: setSvgDiv,`
`    createChart:createChart,`
`    updateChart: updateChart`
`}`
	A set of methods that can be called outside of donut.js are returned, and these will be used in main.js.

CREATE THE MAIN.JS FILE

Create or open the main.js file in the public/javascript folder and copy in the code in Listing 8-8.

Listing 8-8. main.js

```
(function(){
    var socket = io();
    var temperature = new DonutChart();
    temperature.setSensorDomain([-6,50]);
    temperature.setSvgDiv('#donut1');
    temperature.createChart('\u00B0'+"c", "temp");

    var humidity = new DonutChart();

    humidity.setSensorDomain([0,90]);
    humidity.setSvgDiv('#donut2');
    humidity.createChart('\u0025', "humidity");
    var light = new DonutChart();
    light.setSensorDomain([0,10]);
    light.setSvgDiv('#donut3');
    light.createChart('', "light");

    socket.on("initial-data", function(data){
        temperature.updateChart(data.temp.current);
        humidity.updateChart(data.humidity.current);
        light.updateChart(data.light.current);
});

    socket.on('data', function(data){
        temperature.updateChart(data.temp.current);
        humidity.updateChart(data.humidity.current);
        light.updateChart(data.light.current);
    });
})();
```

The Code Explained

This code will create three donut charts and will update them when new data comes to it. See Table 8-7 for more details about main.js.

Table 8-7. *main.js explained*

`var temperature = new DonutChart();`	Create a new donut chart held in a variable called temperature.
`temperature.setSensorDomain([-6,50]);`	Set the domain of the temperature; the donut.js setSensorDomain() method is called and passed the lowest and highest possible temperatures. This is the range of possible temperatures.
`temperature.setSvgDiv('#donut1');`	The donut.js setSvgDiv() method is passed the id of the HTML div that will hold the temperature donut chart.
`temperature.createChart ('\u00B0'+"c", "temp");`	The donut.js createChart() method is called, and it is passed the Unicode for the degree symbol along with the letter c for Celsius as well as the type of chart it is. The same methods are used to create the humidity and light donut charts.
`socket.on("initial-data", function(data){ temperature.updateChart (data.temp.current); humidity.updateChart (data.humidity.current); light.updateChart (data.light.current); });`	The initial-data is passed to the front end through the socket.on() method, and this calls the updateChart() method and passes in the current temperature, humidity, or light data.

(continued)

Table 8-7. (*continued*)

```socket.on('data', function(data){ temperature.updateChart (data.temp.current); humidity.updateChart (data.humidity.current); light.updateChart (data.light.current); });```	New data is passed to the front end via a socket.on() with an id of 'data'. This calls the updateChart() method and passes in the current temperature, humidity, or light data.

UPDATE THE FRONT END

Open the index.ejs code from Listing 8-5 and delete it; copy in the code from Listing 8-9.

Listing 8-9. index.ejs

```
<!DOCTYPE html>
<head>
    <meta charset="UTF-8">
    <title>Dashboard</title>
    <link href="/css/main.css" rel="stylesheet" type="text/css">
</head>
<body>
    <header>
        <h1>SENSOR DASHBOARD</h1>
        <h2>temperature humidity light</h2>
    </header>
```

```
    <main>
        <h3>current values</h3>
        <div class="container">
            <div id="donut1" class="donut flex-child"></div>
            <div id="donut2" class="donut flex-child"></div>
            <div id="donut3" class="donut flex-child"></div>
        </div>
    </main>
    <script src="https://cdn.socket.io/socket.io-1.2.0.js">
    </script>
    <script src="https://d3js.org/d3.v4.js"></script>

    <script src="javascript/donut.js"></script>
    <script src="javascript/main.js"></script>
</body>
</html>
```

The Code Explained

This code will create the divs for three donut charts that will update when new data comes in. It also includes the donut.js script and the main.js script. See Table 8-8 for more details about index.ejs.

Table 8-8. *index.ejs explained*

`<div id="donut1" class="donut flex-child"></div>` `<div id="donut2" class="donut flex-child"></div>` `<div id="donut3" class="donut flex-child"></div>`	There are three HTML div tags, one for each of the donut graphs.
`<script src="javascript/donut.js"> </script>` `<script src="javascript/main.js"> </script>`	The two scripts from the public folder are included. The donut.js script needs to be called first as it is used by main.js.

ADD THE CSS

Open or create the main.css in the public/css folder and add in the CSS in Listing 8-10.

Listing 8-10. main.css

```css
*{
  margin: 0;
  padding: 0;
}
body{
  font-family: Verdana, Arial, sans-serif;
}
h2{
  font-size: 18px;
}
h3{
  font-size: 16px;
}
p{
  font-size: 14px;
}
header{
  background: #6BCAE2;
  color: white;
}
header h1{
  padding-top: 25px;
}
header h2{
  padding-bottom: 25px;
}
```

```
header h3{
  padding-bottom: 10px;
}
header h1,header h2, header h3, header p{
    padding-left: 12px;
}
main h3{
  font-weight: normal;
  margin: 20px;
}
.container{
    display: flex;
    flex-direction: row;
    flex-wrap: wrap;
    margin-top: 20px;
    justify-content: space-between;
}
.flex-child{
  margin: auto;
}
```

You can check out how the page looks so far by navigating to the application in a console window and typing nodemon index.js or node index.js to start the application. Make sure the Arduino is connected to your computer and open a browser and go to http://localhost:3000/ to see the application running.

Adding in Daily Values

The live data now displays on the dashboard, but the data object also stores the highest and lowest values of the sensors, which could also be displayed. At the moment these values will be over the time the server has been running, but with a few changes you could make these into daily high and low values by resetting them at midnight. These values can then be added to the dashboard. You could also add a date to the dashboard, which will update at midnight.

To do this you will be using a new library called node-schedule. This library helps you schedule events to happen as specific times in Node.js. It's based on the idea of cron, a time scheduler for unix type operating systems. To use it in a Node.js server you need to require it, then use it as shown in Figure 8-7.

```
var schedule = require('node-schedule');
var x = schedule.scheduleJob('10 * * * * *', function(){
  console.log('This is a scheduled job');
});
```

Figure 8-7. *Basic code for the node-schedule library*

The system consists of a series of stars that from left to right represent the seconds (optional), minutes, hours, days of the month, the month, and days of the week. The code in Figure 8-7 will console log the text at 10 seconds past each minute. Figure 8-8 shows the format for the call

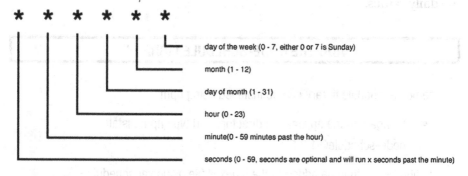

Figure 8-8. *node-schedule format*

This means that:

```
schedule.scheduleJob('10 * * * * *),
```

Will schedule a function to run at 10 seconds past each minute

```
schedule.scheduleJob('*/10 * * * * *),
```

Will schedule a function to run every 10 seconds

```
schedule.scheduleJob('10 * * * *),
```

Will schedule a function to run every 10 minutes past the hour. Notice that there are only 5 entries, not 6; the seconds * are optional, as it is not used here it has been omitted.

```
schedule.scheduleJob('*/10 * * * *),
```

Will schedule a function to run every 10 minutes

```
schedule.scheduleJob('* 0 * * *),
```

Will schedule a function to run at midnight every day, and this is what you will be using to update the day on the web page every day and reset the daily values.

ADD THE NODE-SCHEDULE LIBRARY

The node-schedule library can be installed using npm.

- Navigate to the application directory and type npm install node-schedule@1.2.5

The library can then be added to the index.js file using var schedule = require('node-schedule');

UPDATE INDEX.JS

Open the updated index.js file from Listing 8-4 and add in the code in bold:

```
var http = require('http');
var express = require('express');
var app = express();
var server = http.createServer(app);
var io = require('socket.io')(server);
var SerialPort = require('serialport');
var serialport = new SerialPort('<add in the serial port for
your Arduino>', {
    parser: SerialPort.parsers.readline('\n')
});
var schedule = require('node-schedule');
var sensors = {
    temp: {current: 0 , high:0, low:100 },
    humidity: {current: 0, high:0, low: 100},
    light: {current: 0, high:0, low: 10}
}
var changeDay = 0;

var j = schedule.scheduleJob('*/40 * * * * *', function(){
    for (key in sensors) {
        if (sensors.hasOwnProperty(key)) {
            sensors[key].current = 0;
            sensors[key].high = 0;
            sensors[key].low = 100;
        }
    }
    changeDay = 1;
});
```

```
app.engine('ejs', require('ejs').__express);
app.set('view engine', 'ejs');
app.use(express.static(__dirname + '/public'));
app.get('/', function (req, res){
    res.render('index');
});
io.on('connection', function(socket){
    console.log('socket.io connection');
    socket.emit("initial-data", sensors);
    serialport.on('data', function(data){
        data = data.replace(/(\r\n|\n|\r)/gm,"");
        var dataArray = data.split(',');
        var hasChanged = updateValues(dataArray);
        if (hasChanged > 0){
            socket.emit("data", sensors);
        }
        if(changeDay === 1){
            changeDay = 0;
            socket.emit('change-day', "true");
        }
});
    socket.on('disconnect', function(){
        console.log('disconnected');
    });
});
server.listen(3000, function(){
    console.log('listening on port 3000...');
});
```

You need to keep the updateValues() function, I haven't included it in this update as it hasn't changed.

The Code Explained

Table 8-9 explains the code in index.js.

Table 8-9. index.js update explained

```var schedule = require('node-schedule');```	Create a variable to hold node-schedule.
```var j = schedule.scheduleJob('* 0 * * * *', function(){});```	Create a schedule that calls a function at midnight.
```for (key in sensors) { if (sensors.hasOwn Property(key)) { sensors[key].current = 0; sensors[key].high = 0; sensors[key].low = 100; } }```	Loop through the sensors object with the JavaScript for key in function; and for each sensor reset the current, high, and low values.
```changeDay = 1;```	Set changeDay to 1 so the rest of the code knows there is a new day.
```if(changeDay === 1){ changeDay = 0; socket.emit ('change-day', "true"); }```	When new data is received from the sensors, there is a check to see if it is a new day by checking if the variable changeDay is 1. If it is, then the variable changeDay is reset to 0 and a socket.emit is sent to let the front end know the day has changed.

UPDATE MAIN.JS

The main.js file needs to be updated to process the new day data. There is also a function to add the day to the web page, open up the main.js file from Listing 8-8, and add in the code in bold.

```
(function(){
    var socket = io();
    var temperature = new DonutChart();
    temperature.setSensorDomain([-6,50]);
    temperature.setSvgDiv('#donut1');
    temperature.createChart('\u00B0'+"c", "temp");
    ...
    socket.on("initial-data", function(data){
        temperature.updateChart(data.temp.current);
        humidity.updateChart(data.humidity.current);
        light.updateChart(data.light.current);
        changeHighLow(data);
    });
    socket.on('data', function(data){
        temperature.updateChart(data.temp.current);
        humidity.updateChart(data.humidity.current);
        light.updateChart(data.light.current);
        changeHighLow(data);
    });
    socket.on('change-day', function(data){
        changeDate();
    }) ;
```

```
function changeHighLow(data){
    for (key in data) {
        if (data.hasOwnProperty(key)) {
            var className = key + "-high";
            document.getElementById(className).innerHTML =
            data[key].high;
            className = key + "-low";
            document.getElementById(className).innerHTML =
            data[key].low;
        }
    }
}
function changeDate(){
    var date = new Date();
    var displayDate = document.getElementById('date');
    displayDate.innerHTML = date.toDateString();
}
changeDate();
})();
```

The Code Explained

Table 8-10 explains the code in main.js.

Table 8-10. *main.js update explained*

`changeHighLow(data);`	A function is called that will update the web page with the last high and low values of the data.

`socket.on('change-day',`
`function(data){`
`    changeDate();`
`});`
	When the socket.emit with the id of 'change-day' is called, it means that it is midnight and the web pages date needs to be updated. The changeDate() function is called that will do this.

`function changeHighLow(data){}`	The changeHighLow() function will update the web page. It is passed to the data object as an argument; this object has the key and the value of the data.
`for (key in data) {}`	The for in JavaScript function will let you go through each item in the object.

`var className = key + "-high";`
`document.getElementById`
`(className).innerHTML =`
`data[key].high;`
	When new data is received, the key will be the string "temp," "humidity," or "light." This will be concatenated with the string "-high" to make the class name of the HTML tag that is holding the high value for the sensor. The innerHTML of that tag is then updated with the new value. The same is then done with the low value.

(continued)

Table 8-10. (*continued*)

```function changeDate(){ var date = new Date(); var displayDate = document. getElementById('date'); displayDate.innerHTML = date.toDateString(); }```	The function changeDate() uses the JavaScript Date() object. This gives you access to a number of JavaScript functions that can be applied to the Date() object, including the toDateString() method. This writes the date out as a string. The inner HTML of the tag that will hold the date is updated with the latest date.

UPDATE INDEX.EJS FILE

The index.ejs file needs to be updated to display the new data. Open up the index.ejs file from Listing 8-9 and add in the HTML in bold.

```
<!DOCTYPE html>
<head>
    ...
</head>
<body>
    <header>
        <h1>SENSOR DASHBOARD</h1>
        <h2>temperature humidity light</h2>
        <h3><time id="date"></time></h3>
    </header>
    <main>
        <h3>current values</h3>
        <div class="container">
            ...
        </div>
```

```
<div class="container">
    <div id="temp" class="high-low">
        <div class="high">
            <p>today's high</p>
            <p><span id="temp-high">27
            </span>&deg;C</p>
        </div>
        <div class="low">
            <p>today's low</p>
            <p><span id="temp-low">27
            </span>&deg;C</p>
        </div>
    </div>
    <div id="humidity" class="high-low">
        <div class="high">
            <p>today's high</p>
            <p><span id="humidity-high">27
            </span>%</p>
        </div>
        <div class="low">
            <p>today's low</p>
            <p><span id="humidity-low">27
            </span>%</p>
        </div>
    </div>
    <div id="light" class="high-low">
        <div class="high">
            <p>today's high</p>
            <p><span id="light-high">27</span></p>
        </div>
```

```
            <div class="low">
                <p>today's low</p>
                <p><span id="light-low">27</span></p>
            </div>
        </div>
    </div>
</main>
...
</body>
</html>
```

The Code Explained

Table 8-11 explains the code in index.ejs.

Table 8-11. index.ejs update explained

`<h3><time id="date"></time></h3>`	HTML has a time tag, and this is used by machine readers so they can interpret the time properly.
`<span id="temp-high">27</span>`	Spans are used to hold the data that updates.
`&deg;`	This puts the degree symbol on the page.

Update the CSS

Open up the main.css file from Listing 8-10 and add the following CSS to the bottom of the file.

```
.high-low{
    display: flex;
    flex-direction: row;
    justify-content: space-between;
```

```
      margin: 20px;
}
.high, .low{
  background-color: #FE8402;
  width: 120px;
  height: 120px;
  color: white;
  text-align: center;
  line-height: 2.5;
  display: inline-block;
  vertical-align: middle;
}
.low{
  background-color: #6BCAE2;
}
```

The application should now be complete; you can see how the page looks by navigating to the application in a console window and type nodemon index.js or node index.js to start the application. Make sure the Arduino is connected to your computer and open a browser and go to http://localhost:3000/ to see the application running.

Summary

You have used data to create a dashboard. You should now have a better understanding of how you can take the raw data, visualize it, and use it to get insights. The stored data could be analyzed and visualized in many different ways. This chapter should just be your starting point of what you could do with a dashboard.

CHAPTER 9

Physical Data Visualization with Live Data

In Chapter 7 and Chapter 8 you used the Arduino to send data to the web so it could be visualized on a web page. This chapter will turn that around. You will be getting data from an online source and using it to drive a piezo buzzer, an LED, and an LCD attached to an Arduino. You will create a Node.js server that will link to an external web site and request data from that website. This data will be cleaned and passed from your Node.js server to the Arduino via the serial port. The data is earthquake data from the United States geological Survey web site (USGS). The USGS earthquake data is updated regularly. USGS has created an API, a way to access that data, which you will use to request the data you want.

API

API stands for Application Programming Interface. It is the way that your application can talk to other external applications. Imagine it like a restaurant menu. The menu lists the items a kitchen is prepared to make for you; you ask a waiter for an item and they go to the kitchen, request

© Indira Knight 2018
I. Knight, *Connecting Arduino to the Web*, https://doi.org/10.1007/978-1-4842-3480-8_9

that item, and bring it back to you. In the same way your server can make a request to an external server, and if you request it in the right way your request will be fulfilled. By using the API's methods you can send to and receive data from an external web application.

Most sites that have an API will have a page with instructions on how to use it. It will list the methods available to you and the parameters they will need for those methods.

When you make a request to an API you are making a call to the API. There can be a limit to how many times you make an API call to a server. This is so the server doesn't get overloaded with requests.

A number of web applications have API's you can use. Twitter has an API that lets you search and download tweets. Microsoft has an Emotion API that lets you send it an image of a person and it will return an emotion score for that image.

An API can return a number of different types of documents depending on how it has been set up. You might receive the data in different formats. There will be a limit to how much data is returned to you. The applications API page should let you know that limit.

To access some servers' API's you will need to sign up with that application and be given an API key. They key is used each time you make a request, and it allows the external application to monitor your requests.

In this chapter you will be using the USGS API to get data about earthquakes. You don't need to register with the service or use an API key; there is a 20,000 limit of returned queries.

USGS API

The United States Geological Survey is a government agency that studies the geology of the United States. Their website includes a lot of information including information on water, volcanoes, and earthquakes. They have a number of API's including one on global earthquakes. The data can be returned in different data formats including CSV, XML, and GeoJSON. The data has a number of different fields including the time of the earthquake, its magnitude, the latitude and longitude coordinates, and the name of the place it happened.

The request to the API is a URL in which you pass a method; what action you want performed; and parameters, key/value pairs that ask for specific elements of that data. These parameters could be to return data from particular time periods, location and magnitude.

If a time zone isn't specified in the URL parameter for time, it is assumed it's a UTC. For example, the string 2017-12-26T12:47:47 can be the implicit UTC time zone, and 2017-12-26T12:47:47 +00:00 would be explicit. Figure 9-1 shows an example of a request URL to USGS.

Figure 9-1. *An API call URL to the USGS server*

The URL has a path to the server, a method, and parameters. There are a number of methods available for the USGS API, including a query method, which is a request for data. The type of data you want returned is also specified, in this case GeoJSON. There are also a number of parameters you can use to ask for specific parts of the data. Each parameter is a key value pair, and the "&" character separates each parameter. You can see a full list of methods and parameters available on the USGS website on their API documentation page at `https://earthquake.usgs.gov/fdsnws/event/1/`.

Getting Data from an External Server

In this chapter you will be making a request to an external server for data, and when you get this data you will take the parts you want and send that data to an Arduino via the serial port. To get the data from an external server, you need to make a client request from the Node.js server to the USGS server. Your server is called the client. To do this you will use an HTTP GET request. HTTP was looked at in Chapter 2 in the section "What Is A Web Server?"

You can use the http library that comes with Node.js to make your HTTP requests, but a lot of applications use third-party libraries that make requests simpler to implement. In this chapter you will be using a library called axios to make HTTP requests. One of the advantages of axios is that it uses promises while the Node.js native HTTP requests use callbacks.

Callbacks and Promises

Code can be synchronous or asynchronous. Synchronous code runs one line after other so the code

```
console.log("Tuesday");
console.log("Wednesday");
```

will print out the string Tuesday followed by Wednesday, and the code waits for the first console log to execute before he second one does.

Asynchronous code will start to run but the code after it will not wait until it has finished running before running. An HTTP request is asynchronous; this means that while the request is being made to an external server, your code will continue running; it doesn't wait for the external server to respond. The advantage of this is that your application keeps working while waiting for the external server's response. It also means that functions after the request won't have access to the response data, so you can't guarantee that the data has been returned before the other functions run.

You will need the response data from the HTTP request in other functions, so you need a way for the other functions that need the data to wait until the HTTP request has returned with the data. Callbacks or promises are a way to do this.

Callback Functions

Callback functions are functions passed as an argument to a function. This means that the second function can be passed data that the first function gets. Figure 9-2 shows an example of a simple callback function. The way to print a number is passed as an argument to the function that is creating the number.

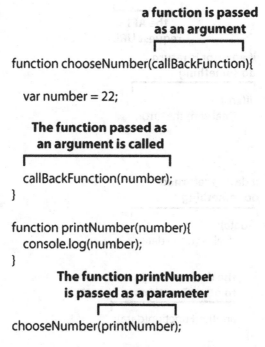

a function is passed as an argument

```
function chooseNumber(callBackFunction){

  var number = 22;
```

The function passed as an argument is called

```
  callBackFunction(number);
}

function printNumber(number){
  console.log(number);
}
```

The function printNumber is passed as a parameter

```
chooseNumber(printNumber);
```

Figure 9-2. *An example of a synchronous callback function*

This is a simple synchronous example of a callback function. They become very useful with asynchronous functions as the function that is passed as an argument is only called when the asynchronous function has done something. When you call an external server, you need to wait for it to return something to you before running a function; this can be done with a callback function. Figure 9-3 shows a pseudocode example of an asynchronous callback that makes a request to an external server. Pseudocode is a way to explain how code works without using a specific programming language; it won't run as a piece of code.

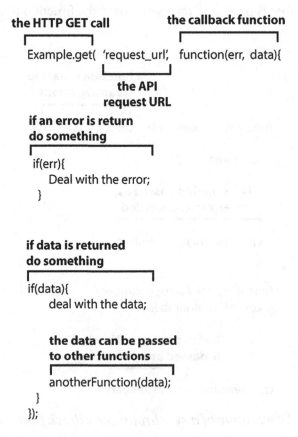

Figure 9-3. Pseudocode of an asynchronous callback

A disadvantage to using callbacks is you can end up with nested callbacks; if your application needed data from one server and then another, these calls would be nested inside each other; this can get messy and it can be difficult to work out what is calling what.

Promises

A promise is an alternative method to callbacks. It is an object created before a request is made. It is a promise that something will happen, which could be a success or a failure. It is a promise that there will be a value that the function will understand. It means that a promise returns a value immediately, just like a synchronous function. That value is a promise it will return a value in the future, which could be a success object or a failure object. Promises flatten out asynchronous code so you lower the number of nested callbacks.

In this chapter you will be using a library called axios to make requests to external servers. It is a promise-based library.

Request Response Status Codes

When you make an HTTP request to a server, the calling function will receive a response code from that server. This can be used to check if the response was successful, and if it wasn't why it wasn't. The responses fall into number categories of 100s, 200s, 300s, 400s, and 500s:

- 100s – Informational responses, they let you know that your request was received and understood; for example, 102 is the response for processing.

- 200s – Success response, your request has successfully been received and processed: for example, 200 OK is the response when an HTTP request has been successfully processed.

- 300s – Redirection responses.

285

- 400s – Client error responses, when the client calling the server made an error in the request: for example, 402 payment required.

- 500s – Server errors, when the server has an error: for example, 503 service unavailable; this is used if the server you are calling isn't currently running.

The Node.JS Application

The application in this chapter will be contacting the USGS server to request data. If there is new data, this will be processed and reformatted so it can be sent to the Arduino.

The API request to the USGS server is a URL that tells the USGS server the data you want back. In this chapter you will be requesting data every 15 minutes. Your server will want to ask the USGS server if there has been an earthquake since the last time your server asked. This will be done with a query string at the end of the URL. The query string contains the format of data you want returned, a start time for the query, an end time for the query, what magnitudes of earthquake you are interested in, and a limit to how many responses the USGS server will send you.

If you look at the USGS API you will see that the format for the data and time must be in the ISO8601 Date/Time format. This format is an international standard for sharing time. JavaScript has functions for turning its Date object into the ISO8601 format.

The axios request is inside a function called makeCall(). The makeCall() function is called every 15 minutes using a setTimeout() function. Before the function is called, a variable with a start time is created. You can set any time, but around 2 hours before you start running the application should be enough to make sure you get earthquake data returned. The startTime variable is used the first time, and makeCall() is called for the start time of your GET request. The end time is created using the JavaScript new Date() function. The Date() function takes the date and time from your server, which is your computer.

The axios GET request is then made, and a GeoJSON object is returned from the USGS server. This object will contain a lot of information about the latest earthquake including its magnitude, its latitude and longitude coordinates, and the alert type. Only parts of this data will be passed to the Arduino, partly because the LCD screen can only process 64 characters. The relevant data is retrieved from the GeoJSON and a string is created that can be passed to the Arduino.

The startTime variable then takes the value of the endTime variable; the function waits to be called again in 15 minutes. From this point on the startTime and the endTime will be 15 minutes apart.

Note   The JavaScript new Date function creates an object with the current time. This current time is taken from your computer's clock. If the time on your computer is incorrect, you will not get the latest earthquake data. You may also want to explicitly set the UTC in the API request.

---

setTimeout vs. setInterval

There are two scheduling functions in JavaScript: setTimeout and setInterval. Both will start something running after a certain number of milliseconds. Figure 9-4 shows how they work.

```
function makeCall(){
    console.log("make call");
}
setTimeout(makeCall, 1000);
setInterval(makeCall, 1000);
```

Figure 9-4. *A setTimeout() and a setInterval() function*

Both the setTimeout() and the setInterval() in Figure 9-4 will call the makeCall() function after 1000 milliseconds (1 second). The setTimeout() function will call it once and the setInterval() will keep calling it every second.

The Node.js application in this chapter uses the setTimout function to call the makeCall() function, even though it has to be called every 15 minutes. This is because setInterval will call its function repeatedly even if the function hasn't finished running from the last call. The setTimeout() function lets the function it calls run completely. It does run only once so setTimeout() has to be called again at the end of the function it is calling.

The GeoJSON Object

There are a number of different data types that can be returned by the USGS server and GeoJSON is one of them. It has a similar structure to JSON and is a standard for geographic data. The GeoJSON returned from USGS has a lot of fields including a status code, headers, and the data you want to parse. You parse the data as you would a JSON object. In the Node.js server, you will be using a line of code "var data = response.data. features;" that uses dot notation to dig down into the GeoJSON to get the features, an array of the data you want to send to the Arduino. An example of the GeoJSON features returned from USGS is shown in Figure 9-5.

```
[ { type: 'Feature',
    properties:
      { mag: 5,
        place: 'Central Mid-Atlantic Ridge',
        time: 1514460043540,
        updated: 1514460991040,
        tz: -120,
        url:
'https://earthquake.usgs.gov/earthquakes/eventpage/us1000bx4a',
        detail:
'https://earthquake.usgs.gov/fdsnws/event/1/query?eventid=us100
0bx4a&format=geojson',
        felt: null,
        cdi: null,
        mmi: null,
        alert: null,
        status: 'reviewed',
        tsunami: 0,
        sig: 385,
        net: 'us',
        code: '1000bx4a',
        ids: ',us1000bx4a,',
        sources: ',us,',
        types: ',geoserve,origin,phase-data,',
        nst: null,
        dmin: 12.99,
        rms: 0.55,
        gap: 57,
        magType: 'mb',
        type: 'earthquake',
        title: 'M 5.0 - Central Mid-Atlantic Ridge' },
     geometry: { type: 'Point', coordinates: [Object] },
     id: 'us1000bx4a' } ]
```

Figure 9-5. *An example of the GeoJSON from a GET request to the USGS server*

SET UP THE NODE.JS SERVER

In this chapter you will be sending data from the Node.js server to an Arduino so you don't need a web front end for the application. The directory structure for the application will be this:

```
/chapter_09
    /node_modules
    index.js
```

As there is not a front end to the application you do not need to install, express, ejs, or socket.io. There is a new library to install called Axios; it is the library that will be making the HTTP request to the USGS server:

1. Create a new folder to hold the application. I called mine chapter_09.

2. Open the command prompt (Windows operating system) or a terminal window (Mac) and navigate to the newly created folder.

3. When you are in the right directory type npm init to create a new application; you can press return through each of the questions or make changes to them.

4. When that's downloaded, install serial port. On a Mac type npm install serialport@4.0.7 --save; and on a Windows PC, type npm install serialport@4.0.7 --build-from-source.

5. Download the axios library; at the command line type npm install axios@0.17.1 --save.

Open or create an index.js file in the root of your chapter_09 application and copy the code from Listing 9-1.

Listing 9-1. index.js

```
var http = require('http');
var axios = require('axios');

var startTime = '2017-12-26T12:47:47'
var makeCall = function(){
    var endTime = new Date();
    endTime = endTime.toISOString();
    endTime = endTime.split('.')[0];
    var url =
  'https://earthquake.usgs.gov/fdsnws/event/1/query?format=
  geojson&starttime=' + startTime + '&endtime=' + endTime +
  '&minmagnitude=4&limit=1';
    var request = axios({
        method:'get',
        url:url,
        responseType:'json'
    });

    request.then(function(response) {
        console.log(response);
        var data = response.data.features;
        console.log(data);

        if(data.length > 0){
            var date = new Date(data[0].properties.time);
            var formatDay = (date.getMonth() + 1) + '/' + date.
            getDate() + '/' + date.getFullYear().toString().
            substr(2,2);
            var formatClock = date.getHours() + ":" + date.
            getMinutes();
```

```
        var quakeString = data[0].properties.mag + " "
        + formatDay + " " + formatClock + " " + data[0].
        properties.place;
        startTime = endTime;
      }
    })
      .catch(function(error){
        console.log('request error: ' + error);
    });
    setTimeout(makeCall, 600000);
  }
makeCall();
```

Go to the root of the application in the console and type either nodemon index.
js or node index.js to start the server. You should start to see data from the
console.log functions in your console window.

The Code Explained

Table 9-1 explains the code in index.js.

Table 9-1. *index.js explained*

`var axios = require('axios');`	Include the axios library into the Node.js server.
`var startTime = '2017-12-26T12:47:47'`	Create a variable to hold the start time for your request in the ISO8601 Date/Time format. You should reset this close to the time you are starting the server. To specify UTC, add the string "+00:00" to the end of the startTime string.

(continued)

Table 9-1. *(continued)*

```var endTime = new Date();``` ```endTime = endTime.``` ```toISOString();```	The variable endTime holds the time and date you want your request to the USGS server to end, and it is converted into an ISO string with the JavaScript toISOString() function. To specify UTC, add the string "+00:00" to the end of the endTime string.
```endTime = endTime.``` ```split('.')[0];```	The toISOString() function returns a string that also includes the timezone after a "."; the USGS URL doesn't understand this so it is removed along with the data after it with the JavaScript split() function, splitting on the "."
```var url =``` ```'https://earthquake.usgs.``` ```gov/fdsnws/event/1/que``` ```ry?format=geojson&star``` ```ttime=' + startTime +``` ```'&endtime=' + endTime +``` ```'&minmagnitude=4&limit=1';```	The variable url contains the URL that will be sent as the HTTP GET request to the USGS server. It contains the format, the start and end time of your request, and a limit of one earthquake returned. It also contains the minmagnitude parameter, which returns magnitude larger than the specified minimum.
```var request = axios({``` ``` method:'get',``` ``` url:url,``` ``` responseType:'json'``` ```});```	The variable request holds the axios HTTP request object, which specifies the HTTP method used: in this case GET, the URL it will call and the data type it expects as a response.
```request.``` ```then(function(response) {```	The request.then is a promise. When the request object returns data, a function is called with the response data as its parameter.

(continued)

Table 9-1. *(continued)*

`console.log(response);`	It is worth having a look in the console at the response data returned from USGS. You will dig into the response data to find the data about the earthquake.

`var data = response.data.`
`features;`
`console.log(data);`
	You parse the GeoJSON with dot notation, so you can drill down to the data you want; if you look at the response in the console you will see that the data you want is in data, features. If you console log this data you will see it is an array with an object inside.

`if(data.length > 0){`	Check if there has been an earthquake in the time period of your call to USGS. If there hasn't been, then the length of the array data will be 0 and you don't need to update the Arduino. If it's greater than zero, the code inside the if statement runs.

`var date = new`
`Date(data[0].properties.`
`time);`
	The date and time of the earthquake are stored in the variable data. data[0] is used as the object with the data in an array. As there is only one element in the array, it will always be data[0] to get it. You can then drill into the data going to properties and then time,

`var formatDay = (date.`
`getMonth() + 1) + '/'`
`+ date.getDate() + '/'`
`+ date.getFullYear().`
`toString().substr(2,2);`
	The variable formatDay holds the reformatted date; it will be in the form month/day/year. The substr(2,2) changes the four-digit-year string to a two-digit-year string.

(continued)

Table 9-1. *(continued)*

`var quakeString = data[0].`
`properties.mag + " "`
`        + formatDay + " " +`
`      formatClock + " " +`
`data[0].properties.place;`
	The variable quakeString will be the string that is sent to the Arduino, and it includes the magnitude, data and time, and place of the earthquake.

`startTime = endTime;`	The variable startTime takes the value of endTime, so the next time it loops around it will be 15 minutes before the endTime.

`.catch(function(error){`
`    console.log('request`
`    error: ' + error);`
`});`
	The catch function is part of the axios library, and it catches any errors from the external server and you can decide what to do next.

`setTimeout(makeCall,` `600000);`	Once the makeCall function has run, the setTimeout function is called to call it again in 600000 milliseconds (15 minutes).
`makeCall();`	Call the makeCall() function.

The Arduino Components

This application will use an LED, an LCD, and a piezo buzzer; the LED and piezo will be set up first.

A Piezo Buzzer

A Piezo buzzer produces sound. It contains a material that is Piezo electric. Piezo electric materials change shape when electricity is applied to them and that creates a sound. The faster you bend the material, the higher the frequency and the higher the sound. There is a function for Arduino called tone and this controls the piezo; and it has two arguments. The first argument is the pin number the piezo is attached to and the second is the frequency for the piezo.

SET UP THE LED AND PIEZO

First you will just set up the piezo and the LED and get them working. Figure 9-6 shows the components that you will need:

- 220 ohm resistor

- 1 LED

- 220 ohm resistor

- 1 Piezo

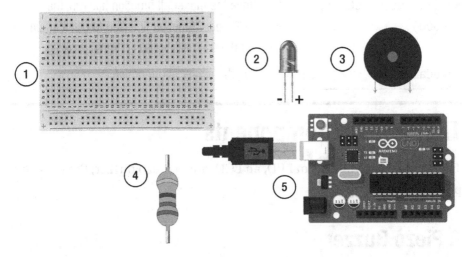

Figure 9-6. *The Arduino Components: 1. Breadboard, 2. LED, 3. Piezo, 4 220 ohm resistor, 5. Arduino Uno*

Set up the Arduino and the compoents as shown in Figure 9-7.

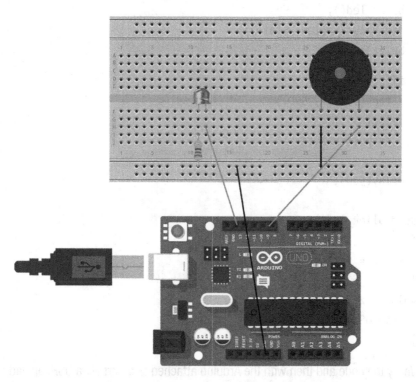

Figure 9-7. *Setup for the Arduino with Peizo and LED*

Open the Arduino IDE and create a new sketch called chapter_09_01.ino and copy in the code from Listing 9-2.

Listing 9-2. chapter_09_01.ino

```
const int buzzer = 9;
const int led = 13;
int state = LOW;
boolean piezoState = false;

void setup(){
  pinMode(buzzer, OUTPUT);
  pinMode(led, OUTPUT);
}
```

```
void loop(){
  blink_led();
  digitalWrite(led, state);
  buzz();

  if(piezoState){
    tone(buzzer, 500);
  }else{
    noTone(buzzer);
  }
  delay(500);
}
void blink_led()
{
  state = !state;
}
void buzz(){
    piezoState = !piezoState;
}
```

Verify the code and then with the Arduino attached to a port via a USB, upload the sketch to the Arduino. Make sure you have the right port for the Arduino selected in the Tools menu: Tools/Port. The light and piezo buzzer should go on and off every 500 milliseconds.

The Code Explained

Table 9-2 explains the code in chapter_09_01.ino.

Table 9-2. *chapter_09_01.ino explained*

```const int buzzer = 9;``` ```const int led = 13;```	Constant variables are created for the pin numbers of the piezo and LED.
```int state = LOW;``` ```boolean piezoState = false;```	The initial states are stored in variables for the piezo and the LED.
```pinMode(buzzer, OUTPUT);``` ```pinMode(led, OUTPUT);```	Both the piezo and the LED have their pin numbers set and are set to output.
```blink_led();```	A function called blink_led is called, and this will switch the state of the LED to high and low.

```void blink_led()```
```{```
```state = !state;```
```}```
	The function blink_led has no return value so it is declared as void. It makes state into the state it is not, either high or low (on or off).

```digitalWrite(led, state);```	Tell the LED what its state is.
```buzz();```	Call a function called buzz that will work out the current state of the piezo, buzzing or not buzzing, and do the opposite.

```void buzz(){```
```   piezoState = !piezoState;```
```}```
	The function buzz has no return value so it is declared as void. It makes piezoState into the state it is not, either true or false.

```if(piezoState){```
```   tone(buzzer, 500);```
```   }else{```
```   noTone(buzzer);```
```}```
	Check if the piezoState variable contains the value true; if it does, then call the function tone(). It takes two arguments, the pin number of the piezo and the frequency of the buzzer.

```
UPDATE THE NODE.JS SERVER
```

The Node.js Server needs to be updated to include the serialport library and send the data to the Arduino. Open up the code from Listing 9-1 and update it with the code in bold from Listing 9-3.

Listing 9-3. updated index.js

```javascript
var http = require('http');
var axios = require('axios');
var SerialPort = require('serialport');
var serialport = new SerialPort('<add in the serial port for
your Arduino>', {
    baudRate: 9600
});

serialport.on("open", function () {
    console.log('open');
    makeCall();
});

var startTime = '2017-12-26T12:47:47'

var makeCall = function(){

    var endTime = new Date();
      endTime = endTime.toISOString();
      endTime = endTime.split('.')[0];

    var url = 'https://earthquake.usgs.gov/fdsnws/event/1/query?
    format=geojson&starttime=' + startTime + '&endtime=' +
    endTime + '&minmagnitude=4&limit=1';

    var request = axios({
        method:'get',
        url:url,
```

```javascript
    responseType:'json'
});

request.then(function(response) {
    var data = response.data.features;
    console.log(data);

    if(data.length > 0){
        var date = new Date(data[0].properties.time);
            var formatDay = (date.getMonth() + 1) + '/' +
            date.getDate() + '/' + date.getFullYear().
            toString().substr(2,2);
        var formatClock = date.getHours() + ":" + date.
        getMinutes();

            var quakeString = data[0].properties.mag + " "
            + formatDay + " " + formatClock + " " + data[0].
            properties.place;

        console.log(quakeString);

        setTimeout(function() {
            serialport.write(quakeString, function() {
                console.log('written to serialport');
            });
        }, 2000);
        startTime = endTime;
    }
})
    .catch(function(error){
        console.log('request error: ' + error);
    });
    setTimeout(makeCall, 600000);
}
```

Delete <add in the serial port for your Arduino> and add in your own serial port into the new SerialPort() function. Notice that the makeCall() function call has been removed from the bottom of the script and added into the serialport. on() function.

The Code Explained

Table 9-3 explains the code in the updated index.js file.

Table 9-3. updated index.js explained

```serialport.on("open", function () { console.log('open'); makeCall(); });```	Once the serial port is opened the makeCall() function is called, you don't want to call it before the serialPort has opened as the makeCall() function passes data via the serial port.
```setTimeout(function() { }, 2000);```	This setTimeout function gives a two-second delay before sending the data to the Arduino; this is to make sure that the serial port is really ready to receive the data.
```serialport. write(quakeString, function() { console.log('written to serialport'); });```	The serialport.write() function sends the quakeString, which contains the data you want to send to the Arduino, to the serial port, and once the data has been received, it console logs that the data has been written to the serialport.

ADD AN LCD TO THE ARDUINO

When the Arduino receives new earthquake data, the LCD will start to display
the data, the LED will flash, and the buzzer will buzz. After a few seconds, the
flashing and buzzing will stop. The setup of the LCD is the same as in Chapter 5.
This also means the LCD has a character limit of 64 characters. This should be
fine for most of the data that is passed to it, but longer strings will be cut off. The
components are shown in Figure 9-8 and are the following:

- 220 ohm resistor

- Potentiometer

- LCD

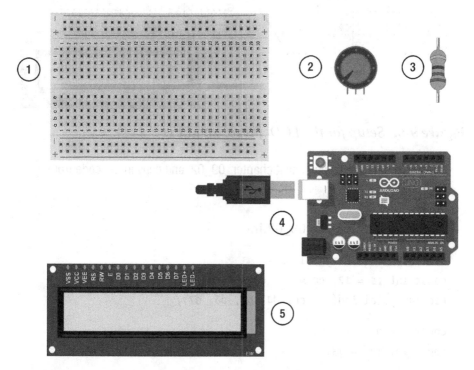

Figure 9-8. *The components for the LCD: 1. Breadboard,*
2. potentiometer, 3. 220 ohm resistor, 4. Arduino Uno, 5. LCD

You need to set up the LCD so it works with the piezo and the LED. I used two small breadboards.

Follow the setup in Figure 9-9 to link the LCD, Piezo, and LED to the Arduino.

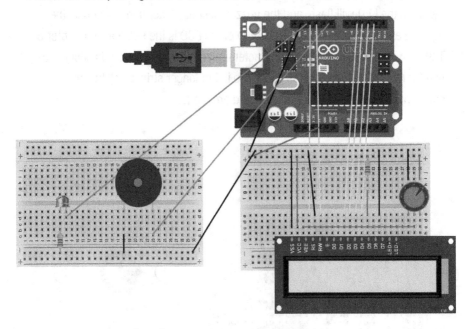

Figure 9-9. *Setup for the LCD, Piezo, and LED*

Open up a new sketch and call it chapter_09_02, and copy in the code from Listing 9-4.

Listing 9-4. chapter_09_02.ino

```
#include <LiquidCrystal.h>
const int rs = 12, en = 11, d4 = 5, d5 = 4, d6 = 3, d7 = 2;
LiquidCrystal lcd(rs, en, d4, d5, d6, d7);

const int buzzer = 9;
const int led = 13;

int state = LOW;
boolean piezoState = false;
```

```
int newData = 14;

void setup() {
  lcd.begin(16, 1);
  pinMode(buzzer, OUTPUT);
  pinMode(led, OUTPUT);
  Serial.begin(9600);
}

void loop() {
  if(Serial.available()){
    newData = 0;
    lcd.home();
    while(Serial.available() > 0){
      lcd.write(Serial.read());
    }
  }
  lcd.scrollDisplayLeft();
  if(newData < 12){
    newData = newData + 1;
    blink_led();
    digitalWrite(led, state);
    buzz();
    if(piezoState){
      tone(buzzer, 500);
    }else{
      noTone(buzzer);
    }
  }
  delay(500);
}

void blink_led(){
  state = !state;
}
```

```
void buzz(){
    piezoState = !piezoState;

}
```

Verify the script and then upload it to the Arduino. Make sure that the Node.js application is turned off. If it is still running, the code will not be uploaded to the Arduino as the serial port is already being used by the Node.js application.

The setup for the LCD is the same as in Chapter 5, and the variables for the pins and states of the LED and piezo are the same as Listing 9-2.

The Code Explained

Table 9-4 explains the code in the chapter_09_02.ino.

Table 9-4. chapter_09_02.ino explained

`int newData = 14;`	The variable newData holds a value that will stop the piezo buzzing and the LED flashing.
`lcd.begin(16, 1);`	The lcd.begin() function set up the number of rows and columns used by the LCD. For this application you want 1 row and 16 columns.
`if(Serial.available()){`	Check to see if data is coming from the serial port.
`newData = 0;`	If there is new data coming, set the newData variable to 0 so that the LED and buzzer will be activated.
`lcd.home();`	Place the LCD cursor in the upper left-hand corner of the screen.
`while(Serial.available() > 0){ lcd.write(Serial.read()); }`	While there is serial data coming through, read the serial data and write it to the LCD.

When the sketch has uploaded to the Arduino, make sure your Arduino
is still attached to your computer by USB. In the console navigate to the
Chapter 9 application. Type in node index.js, or nodemon index.js, to start the
application. The initial call to the USGS server should return earthquake data,
so the piezo should buzz and the LED flash and the text should appear on the
LCD. Remember that you might have to turn the potentiometer to see the text
on the LCD.

Summary

This chapter has used a Node.js server to get data from another server
rather than serve its own web pages. This gives you the ability to get data
from many different sources to drive components on an Arduino. You
could extend the project in Chapter 9 by adding different LED's for the
different magnitudes of earthquake, or change the sound the piezo makes.

The next chapter will be a look at 3D in the browser, and how we can
manipulate 3D objects with Arduino components.

CHAPTER 10

Creating a Game Controller

With animation you can create anything you can think of: real or the surreal, simple or complex. It can tell a story or be completely abstract, or anywhere in between. When HTML5 was released it contained a canvas element that can be used for 2D and 3D animation.

In this chapter you will be creating a game, with a Joystick attached to an Arduino, which is used as the game controller. The 3D graphics in this chapter are created and manipulated using a JavaScript library called Three.js, and data from an Arduino is used to manipulate the graphics.

Animation

The smoothness of an animation depends on two things: the frames per second (FPS), the frame rate an animation runs at; and how different one frame is to the next.

When you produce an animation for a web browser you can't guarantee its frame rate. Each frame has to be rendered by the viewer's computer, so it will depend on how fast their computer can render a frame. The more complex the scene, the more work the computer's processor has to do, so this can slow down the frame rate.

© Indira Knight 2018
I. Knight, *Connecting Arduino to the Web*, https://doi.org/10.1007/978-1-4842-3480-8_10

The HTML5 Canvas Element

When HTML5 was released in 2014 it supported new multimedia and graphic formats that previous version of HTML couldn't support. It included new elements such as video, audio, and canvas.

The canvas element creates a region on the web page for graphical elements. It has the same structure as other HTML elements and like other elements can have attributes such as width and height. <canvas></canvas> creates a canvas element.

It is in the DOM and can be selected by JavaScript and used to display and animate scripted shapes and scenes. A number of JavaScript libraries were developed to make it easier to create animation in the canvas; these include processing.js, PixiJS, Paper.js, BabylonJS, and the one used in this chapter, Three.js.

CSS Animation

There is an alternative to animating with JavaScript and that is animating with CSS. It has advantages in that it uses less processing power. It has become a popular way to create 2D animations on web pages, and a number of CSS animation frameworks have been published that make it easier to produce CSS animations. These include Animate.css, Animatic, and Loader CSS.

3D on the Web

Three-dimensional graphics on modern web browsers use WebGL. It allows you to create animations that can be displayed in the HTML canvas element.

WebGL

WebGL (Web Graphics Library) is a JavaScript API that lets you create and animate 3D objects in a web browser. It is based on OpenGL and works on most modern web browsers. It uses the computer's Graphic Processing Unit (GPU) to process 3D scenes, rather than the browser. WebGL uses two programming languages to process and render a scene, JavaScript and GLSL (OpenGL Shading Language). GLSL translates the JavaScript so it can run the code through the GPU. There are two shader programs that run through the GPU, a vertex shader and a fragment shader. You need to implement both of these to render a scene.

Coding in WebGL can become quite complex; it does not come with a renderer so you have to write all the shading functions. A number of JavaScript libraries have been built on top of WebGL; to make using it easier, one of these is Three.js.

3D Space

Three-dimensional graphics use three dimensions to create a world. Objects (meshes) exist in the 3D world and animate and interact with other objects in the world. A 3D scene can be made up of meshes, lights, and cameras as well as colors and textures.

There are three axes, one for each dimension: an x-, y-, and z-axis. In Three.js the x-axis is the horizontal axis, the y-axis is the vertical axis, and the z-axis is depth. Figure 10-1 shows the 3D axis in WebGL and Three.js.

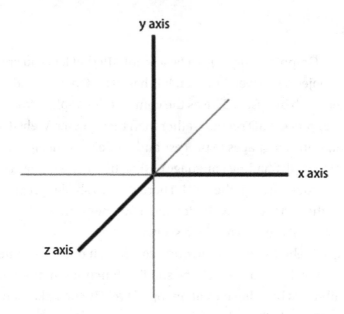

Figure 10-1. *The x-, y-, and z-axes*

The coordinate system inside a Three.js scene is different from the coordinate system for a browser. The browser's coordinate system is normally made up of a unit called a pixel. It starts at 0,0 at the top left of the browser window. The position 1,1 will be 1 pixel to the right and 1 pixel down. The WebGL coordinate system starts at 0,0 in the center of the WebGL scene. 1 unit in WebGL isn't 1 pixel. So moving a WebGL object 1,1 will move it more than 1 pixel.

The browser is also two-dimensional, so 3D scenes need to be converted to fit onto a 2D canvas.

3D Meshes

Three-dimensional (3D) objects are made of vertices (points) in 3D space, connected by edges, which form faces. The objects exist in a 3D space that has x, y, and z coordinates. Figure 10-2 shows 3D objects points, lines, and faces.

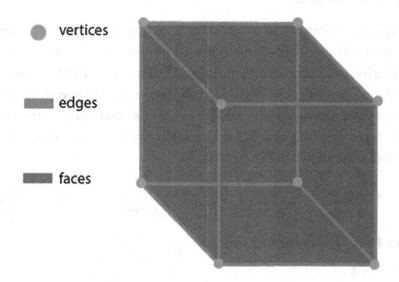

Figure 10-2. *A 3D object*

Shaders

Shaders calculate how an object is rendered in the 3D space. The shaders work out the position and color of the object as it animates. They also work out how light and dark that each part of the object should be in relation to its position and other elements in the scene such as lighting. WebGL uses the GPU's vertex shader and fragment shader to render a scene.

Vertex Shader

Objects in 3D are made up of vertices. A vertex shader processes each of these vertices and gives it a position on screen. It converts a 3D position of a vertex into a 2D point on a screen.

Fragment Shader

The fragment shader works out the color of an object when it is rendered. There can be a number of elements that determine the color of an object including its material color and the lighting in the scene. WebGL makes up the faces of an object by creating triangles between three vertices. The fragment shader works out the value of each vertex and interpolates the values at the vertices to work out the overall color. The basic steps involved in rendering are shown in Figure 10-3.

Figure 10-3. *The rendering process*

An array of vertices is sent to the GPU vertex shader function, and once processed they are assembled into triangles and rasterized. Rasterization converts the triangles that are represented as vectors into a pixel representation. These are then sent through the fragment shader function on the GPU and once processed are sent to a frame buffer ready to be rendered on the web page.

Cameras and Lights

Cameras and lights can be added to the space. Three.js has a number of different cameras available, including an orthographic camera and a perspective camera.

314

There are different types of light available in Three.js. They are ambient, directional, point, and spot. Ambient light will light the entire scene equally. Its position, rotation, and scale have no effect, but its color and intensity do. Directional lights are similar to the sun; they have a direction but are infinitely far away. This means the distance from the object doesn't matter, but the position and rotation do. Point lights are similar to light bulbs; they light a space in all directions and their position matters. Spotlights are similar to point lights as their position matters but they generate light in one direction.

Three.js

Three.js is one of a number of JavaScript libraries built on top of WebGL. Its functions let you create a scene in a few steps and add in the shaders, lights, camera, and meshes.

Three Vectors

A Three.js Vector3 is a class that represents a vector with three elements, used to represent the x-, y-, and z-axes. The main things a Vector3 represent are a point in 3D space, a direction and length in 3D space, or an arbiter ordered triplet of numbers. In this chapter a Vector3 is used in the camera setup.

CREATE A THREE.JS SCENE

The basic components needed to view anything in Three.js are a scene, a camera, and a renderer. Elements such as 3D objects and lights are attached to the scene object. The scene object and the camera object are attached to the renderer object in order to be rendered.

Create a file called basic_scene.html and copy the code in Listing 10-1 into it.

Listing 10-1. Basic_scene.html

```html
<html>
    <head>
        <title>three.js </title>
        <style>
            body { margin: 0; }
            canvas { width: 100%; height: 100% }
        </style>
    </head>
    <body>
        <script src="https://cdnjs.cloudflare.com/ajax/libs/three.
        js/r71/three.js"></script>
<script>
        var scene = new THREE.Scene();
        var camera = new THREE.PerspectiveCamera( 75, window.
        innerWidth/window.innerHeight, 0.1, 1000 );
        var renderer = new THREE.WebGLRenderer();
        renderer.setSize( window.innerWidth, window.innerHeight );
        document.body.appendChild( renderer.domElement );
        var geometry = new THREE.BoxGeometry( 1, 1, 1 );
        var material = new THREE.MeshBasicMaterial( { color:
        0x00ff00 } );
        var cube = new THREE.Mesh( geometry, material );
        scene.add( cube );
        cube.rotation.y = 40;
        camera.position.z = 5;

        renderer.render(scene, camera);
    </script>
    </body>
</html>
```

Open up the file in a web browser and you should see a green cube in the browser. The Three.js code in Listing 10-1 first creates a Three scene, then a camera, and then a renderer. The renderer is attached to the body of the HTML. A cube is created that is added to the scene. The cube has a position and rotation. The renderer is called at the end of the code, with the scene and camera attached.

The Code Explained

Table 10-1 goes into the basic_scene.html in code in more detail.

Table 10-1. basic_scene.html explained

`var scene = new THREE.` `Scene();`	The Three.js function Three.Scene() is used to create a new scene object that is stored in the variable scene.

`var camera = new THREE.`
`PerspectiveCamera( 75,`
`window.innerWidth/window.`
`innerHeight, 0.1, 1000 );`
	A new camera object is stored in the variable camera. It is a Three.js perspective camera. 0.1 is the field of view and 1000 is the aspect ratio.

`var renderer = new THREE.` `WebGLRenderer();`	A Three.js renderer object is stored in the variable renderer.

`renderer.setSize( window.`
`innerWidth, window.`
`innerHeight );`
	The setSize function will resize the canvas; in this example the canvas is the size of the browser window so it uses the current width and height of the browser window.

`document.body.appendChild` `( renderer.domElement );`	The renderer is attached to a DOM element so it can be placed on the web page.
`var geometry = new THREE.` `BoxGeometry( 1, 1, 1 );`	Three.js has a number of geometry objects; these are objects that contain the points (vertices) and fill (faces) for an object.

(continued)

Table 10-1. (*continued*)

`var material = new THREE.`
`MeshBasicMaterial( { color:`
`0x00ff00 } );`
	MeshBasicMaterial is one of the materials available in Three.js. They all take an object of properties, and this one has been given the color green using a hexadecimal number. The 0x before the hexadecimal number tells JavaScript that the following digits are a hexadecimal number. It is a syntax used in JavaScript and other programming languages.

`var cube = new THREE.Mesh` `( geometry, material );`	The Three.js mesh object adds the material to the geometry.
`scene.add( cube );`	The cube is added to the scene.
`cube.rotation.y = 40;` `camera.position.z = 5;`	The cube is rotated in the y-axis and is given a position in the z-axis.
`renderer.render(scene,` `camera);`	The renderer is rendered on the web page, with the scene and camera being the render functions parameters.

ANIMATING THE CUBE

At the moment the cube is static. There needs to be an animation loop to create an animation. The JavaScript requestAnimationFrame (callback) function is used. It is called when you want the browser to redraw the web page. A callback function is passed to the function and it normally runs at a rate of 60 frames per second. Open up the basic_scene.html from Listing 10-1 and update it with the code in bold in Listing 10-2.

Listing 10-2. basic_scene.html updated

```html
<html>
    <head>
        <title>three.js basics</title>
        <style>
            body { margin: 0; }
            canvas { width: 100%; height: 100% }
        </style>
    </head>
    <body>
    <script src="https://cdnjs.cloudflare.com/ajax/libs/three.
    js/r71/three.js"></script>
    <script>
        var scene = new THREE.Scene();
        var camera = new THREE.PerspectiveCamera( 75, window.
        innerWidth/window.innerHeight, 0.1, 1000 );
        var renderer = new THREE.WebGLRenderer();
        renderer.setSize( window.innerWidth, window.innerHeight );
        document.body.appendChild( renderer.domElement );
        var geometry = new THREE.BoxGeometry( 1, 1, 1 );
        var material = new THREE.MeshBasicMaterial( { color:
        0x00ff00 } );
        var cube = new THREE.Mesh( geometry, material );
        scene.add( cube );
        cube.rotation.y = 40;
        camera.position.z = 5;
        var animate = function () {
            cube.rotation.x += 0.05;
            cube.rotation.y += 0.01;
            cube.rotation.z += 0.007;
            renderer.render(scene, camera);
```

```
            requestAnimationFrame( animate );
    };
    animate();
    </script>
    </body>
</html>
```

Notice that the renderer is now inside the animate function. Reload the page in the web browser; you should now see the cube animating. It is rotating in the x-, y-, and z-axes, at a slightly different rate in each axis.

The Code Explained

Table 10-2 explains the code in basic_scene.html in more detail.

Table 10-2. basic_scene.html updated explained

`var animate = function () {}`	A function is created that will contain the code to animate the scene objects.

`cube.rotation.x += 0.05;`
`cube.rotation.y += 0.01;`
`cube.rotation.z += 0.007;`
	The cubes rotation is changed slightly in the x-, y-, and z-axes.

`renderer.render(scene, camera);`	The scene and camera are rendered to the browser.
`requestAnimationFrame( animate );`	The JavaScript requestAnimationFrame() function is called once the changes to the cube have been made. The animate function is passed as the callback function so it will keep running the animate function.

The Game

The game you will create in this chapter will use Three.js for the browser and a Node.js server to get the data from the Arduino via the serial port. It is a simple game where the player tries to catch a ball on a paddle. A joystick attached to an Arduino controls the paddle. The paddles movement speeds up on the x-axis the farther the joystick is from the center position. The ball can either be blue, green, or red. The player needs to change the color of the paddle to the color of the ball with the button on the joystick; if they do they get a point, and if not, they lose a point. They also lose a point if they miss the ball. The game is timed, and when the time runs out the score is given and there is an option to play again. A screenshot of the game is shown in Figure 10-4.

Figure 10-4. *A screenshot of the game*

The joystick allows you to control movement in two directions; it also has a button that can be pressed. The paddle can move in the x- and y-axes. The movement in the y-axis is small, but it is enough for the player to move up a bit to catch a ball early or move down a bit if they need a bit more time. The movement of the paddle on the x-axis is limited to be within the width of the browser window.

The ball uses animation to move. Its initial position in the y-axis is just above the browser window height. Its initial position in the x-axis is a random position within the browser window's width. It drops at a constant rate.

321

The ball and paddle need to interact, so a collision object is added to both so they can detect when they make contact with each other.

The last three elements of the game are a scoreboard, a timer, and a way to start the game. The user clicking on the message "Start Game" starts the game. The timer then starts counting down to 0. Points are gained and lost as the player tries to catch the ball. When the timer reaches 0 a new message appears on the browser with the player's final score and the option to play again.

SET UP THE JOYSTICK

There are a lot of makes of joysticks available for the Arduino. I used one made by Elegoo; it has 5 pins, GND (ground), +5V, VRx (controls movement on the x-axis), VRy (controls movement on the y-axis), and SW (for the switch, the press button). Depending on the make or the joystick, the pins may be the opposite way around. To set up the Arduino you will need the following:

- 5 male to female jumper wires

- An Arduino joystick

- An Arduino

The components are shown in Figure 10-5, and the setup of the joystick is shown in Figure 10-6.

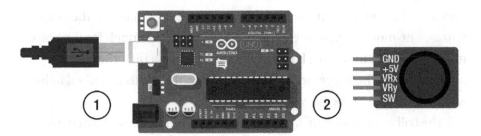

Figure 10-5. *1. An Arduino Uno; 2. A Joystick*

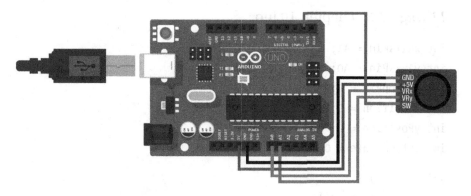

Figure 10-6. *The setup*

THE ARDUINO CODE

The pins that capture the x and y movement on the joystick are analog, and the switch(button) is digital. These values are captured in individual variables and then concatenated together in the Serial.println() function. A letter is also added in front of each value so that the web application can differentiate the values if needed. Each value is separated by a "," character, and this is so the incoming string can be split in the Node.js server into an array of strings at the "," character. The connections are the following:

- GND on the joystick attached to GND on the Arduino

- +5V on the joystick attached to 5V on the Arduino

- VRx attached to pin A01

- VRy attached to pin A02

- SW attached to pin 2 (a digital pin)

The joystick is not connected to a breadboard so male to female wires are needed. Create a new sketch in the Arduino IDE and call it chapter_10; copy the code from Listing 10-3.

Listing 10-3. chapter_10.ino

```
int xAxisPin = A1;
int yAxisPin = A0;
int buttonPin = 2;
int xPosition = 0;
int yPosition = 0;
int buttonState = 0;

void setup() {
  Serial.begin(9600);
  pinMode(xAxisPin, INPUT);
  pinMode(yAxisPin, INPUT);
  pinMode(buttonPin, INPUT_PULLUP);
}

void loop() {
  xPosition = analogRead(xAxisPin);
  yPosition = analogRead(yAxisPin);
  buttonState = digitalRead(buttonPin);
  xPosition=map(xPosition,0,1023,1,10);
  yPosition=map(yPosition,0,1023,1,10);
Serial.println("x" + (String)xPosition + ",y" + (String)
yPosition + ",b" + (String)buttonState);
delay(100);
}
```

Verify the code, then upload it to the Arduino, if you open the serial monitor in the Arduino IDE you should see the data from the joystick.

The Code Explained

Table 10-3 explains the code in chapter_10.ino in more detail.

Table 10-3. *chapter_10.ino explained*

`pinMode(buttonPin, INPUT_PULLUP);`	As the button is a switch it has to be set to INPUT_PULLUP so that the Arduino knows what value to give it when the switch is up.
`xPosition = analogRead(xAxisPin); yPosition = analogRead(yAxisPin); buttonState = digitalRead(buttonPin);`	On each loop the value is recorded for the x- and y-axes and the button.
`xPosition=map(xPosition,0,1023,1,10); yPosition=map(yPosition,0,1023,1,10);`	The analog data can be between 0 and 1023; these values are mapped to values between 1 and 10. This makes them easier to work with in the web application.
`Serial.println("x" + (String)xPosition + ",y" + (String)yPosition + ",b" + (String)buttonState);`	The data is concatenated together and the numbers from the x- and y- axes and the button are converted to strings so they can be sent to the Node.js server.

The Web Application

The game will be written using the Three.js JavaScript library. The Node. js server will be similar to other applications in this book. The client-side code will be broken up into a number of JavaScript files: one for the game play, one for the timer and one for the score with a main.js file getting the data from the Node.js server. The structure for the application will be:

```
/chapter_10
    /node_modules
    /public
        /css
            main.css
        /javascript
            Countdown.js
            Game.js
            main.js
            Points.js
    /views
        index.ejs
    index.js
```

SET UP THE NODE.JS SERVER

This chapter will be using Express, ejs, and socket.io again. To set up the skeleton application:

1. Create a new folder to hold the application. I called mine chapter_10.

2. Open the command prompt (Windows operating system) or a terminal window (Mac) and navigate to the newly created folder.

3. When you are in the right directory type npm init to create a new application; you can press return through each of the questions or make changes to them.

4. You can now start adding the necessary libraries, so to download Express.js at the command line, type npm install express@4.15.3 --save.

5. Then install ejs, type npm install ejs@2.5.6 --save.

6. When that's downloaded install serial port. On a Mac type npm install serialport@4.0.7 –save, and on a Windows PC type npm install serialport@4.0.7 --build-from-source.

7. Then finally install socket.io, type npm install socket.io@1.7.3 --save.

Open or create an index.js file at the root of the application, and copy in the code in Listing 10-4, making sure to update the serial port with the serial port your Arduino is attached to.

Listing 10-4. index.js

```
var http = require('http');
var express = require('express');
var app = express();
var server = http.createServer(app);
var io = require('socket.io')(server);
var SerialPort = require('serialport');
var serialport = new SerialPort('<add in the serial port for
your Arduino>', {
    parser: SerialPort.parsers.readline('\n')
});
app.engine('ejs', require('ejs').__express);
app.set('view engine', 'ejs');
app.use(express.static(__dirname + '/public'));
app.get('/', function (req, res){
    res.render('index');
});
serialport.on('open', function(){
    console.log('serial port opened');
});
io.on('connection', function(socket){
```

```
console.log('socket.io connection');
serialport.on('data', function(data){
    data = data.replace(/(\r\n|\n|\r)/gm,"");
    var dataArray = data.split(',');
    console.log(dataArray);
    socket.emit("data", dataArray);
});

socket.on('disconnect', function(){
    console.log('disconnected');
});
});

server.listen(3000, function(){
    console.log('listening on port 3000...');
});
```

When the data is received via the serial port from the Arduino, any extra characters such as newline characters are removed, and then the data is split into an array and emitted using socket io with an id of "data."

As the serial port function only checks for data when there is a socket io connection, you won't see the data coming through if you start the server, as the socket io connection will be made in the main.js file that hasn't been created yet.

Building Up the Game

There are a number of distinct elements to the game, and these will be the steps that build up the game. They are the following:

1. Creating the main index.ejs page that contains the HTML.

2. Creating the main.js file that will have a socket to get the data from the server.

3. Creating a scene with a paddle that moves in the x- and y-axes with constraints.

4. Updating the scene by adding an animated ball that can collide with the paddle.

5. Creating a JavaScript file that holds the code for scoring the game.

6. Creating a JavaScript file that will be the timer.

7. Adding functions to start and restart the game.

CREATE THE WEB PAGE

The index.ejs page will contain a number of div elements that will hold the score, timer, and start and restart text. The Three.js scene will be attached to the body of the HTML. Open or create the index.ejs file in the views folder and copy in the code from Listing 10-5.

Listing 10-5. index.ejs

```
<html>
    <head>
        <title>three.js basics</title>
        <style>
            body { margin: 0; }
            canvas { width: 100%; height: 100% }
        </style>
    </head>
    <body>
    <script src="/socket.io/socket.io.js"></script>
    <script src="https://cdnjs.cloudflare.com/ajax/libs/
    three.js/r71/three.js"></script>
```

```
<script src="javascript/Game.js"></script>
<script src="javascript/main.js"></script>
</body>
</html>
```

If you have created the Game.js and main.js files, even if they are empty, you should be able to run the code. In the console go to the root of the application and type nodemon index.js or node index.js. This should start the server; you can open the page on a web browser by typing in http://localhost:3000.

CREATE MAIN.JS

Open or create the main.js file in the public/javascript folder and copy in the code from Listing 10-6.

Listing 10-6. main.js

```
(function(){
    var socket = io();
    socket.on('data', function(data){
        Game.newData(data);
    });
})();
```

A variable is created to hold the socket. When the socket.emit() function with the id of "data" runs on the server, the socket.on() function in main.js with the id of "data" receives the data. This data is then passed to the Game.js file using its newData() function.

CREATE GAME.JS

The Game.js file contains all the code to create the Three.js scene and meshes as well as the animation. It needs the data from the server to know where to move the paddle. It contains a function called newData(), which receives the data from the joystick and updates the paddle accordingly.

The paddle needs to stay within the browser window so there needs to be a check that the new position of the paddle won't take it off the screen. The position of the paddle in Three.js uses different coordinates to the position of the paddle on the screen. For example, if the screen width were 625, the maximum position you would want the paddle to go would be 625 – the paddle width. Three.js doesn't understand 625; it has its own coordinate system. For a browser width of 625 the maximum position of the paddle on the x-axis would be around 4 and the minimum position -4. In the code there is a function that makes this conversion so you can work out where the paddle is in relation to the browsers coordinate system.

The paddle also speeds up in the x-axis depending on how far the joystick is from its center position. To do this, the data for the axis from the Arduino has to be mapped into a new value that will be used to tell the cube how much to move by and in which direction. This has to be implemented for the positive and negative direction so moveObjectAmount() is called. The first thing it does is call a function called scaleInput() that takes the number from the Arduino data and maps to a new number. This number is returned to the moveObjectAmount() function where it is divided by 10 to make it small enough so the increase or decrease in the paddles position doesn't move too far.

Open or create the Game.js file in the public/javascript folder and copy in the code from Listing 10-7.

Listing 10-7. Game.js

```
var Game = (function(){
    var windowWidth = window.innerWidth;
    var windowHeight = window.innerHeight;
    console.log(windowWidth);
    var scene = new THREE.Scene();
    var camera = new THREE.PerspectiveCamera( 75, windowWidth/
    windowHeight, 0.1, 1000 );
    var renderer = new THREE.WebGLRenderer();
    renderer.setSize( windowWidth, windowHeight );
    document.body.appendChild( renderer.domElement );
    var geometry = new THREE.BoxGeometry( 2, 0.2, 0.8 );
    var material = new THREE.MeshLambertMaterial( { color:
    0x00ff00 } );
    var paddle = new THREE.Mesh( geometry, material );
    scene.add( paddle );

    paddle.position.y = -2;
    camera.position.z = 5;
    var light = new THREE.DirectionalLight(0xe0e0e0);
    light.position.set(5,2,5).normalize();
    scene.add(light);
    renderer.render(scene, camera);
    var newData = function(data){
        updateScene(data);
    }
    var updateScene = function(data){
        var screenCoordinates = getCoordinates();
        var moveObjectBy;
        var x = data[0];
        var y = data[1];
```

```
var button = data[2];
x = x.substr(1);
y = y.substr(1);
button = button.substr(1);
if(x > 5){
    if(screenCoordinates[0] < windowWidth - 80){
        moveObjectBy = moveObjectAmount(x);
        paddle.position.x = paddle.position.x +
        moveObjectBy;
    }

} else if (x < 5){
    if(screenCoordinates[0] > 0 + 80){
        moveObjectBy = moveObjectAmount(x);
        paddle.position.x = paddle.position.x +
        moveObjectBy;
    }
}
if(y > 5){
    if(screenCoordinates[1] < windowHeight - 100){
        paddle.position.y = paddle.position.y - 0.2;
    }

} else if (y < 5){
    if(screenCoordinates[1] > 0 + 300){
        paddle.position.y = paddle.position.y + 0.2;
    }
}
renderer.render(scene, camera);
}
var moveObjectAmount = function(x){
    var  output = scaleInput(x);
```

```
            output =  utput/10;
            output = Math.round( utput * 10) / 10;
        return  output;
    }
    var scaleInput=function(input){
        var xPositionMin = -4;
        var xPositionMax = 4;
        var inputMin = 1;
        var inputMax = 10;
        var percent = (input - inputMin) / (inputMax - inputMin);
        var  output = percent * (xPositionMax - xPositionMin) +
        xPositionMin;
        return  output;
    }
    var getCoordinates = function() {
            var screenVector = new THREE.Vector3();
            paddle.localToWorld( screenVector );
            screenVector.project( camera );
            var posx = Math.round(( screenVector.x + 1 ) *
            renderer.domElement.offsetWidth / 2 );
            var posy = Math.round(( 1 - screenVector.y ) *
            renderer.domElement.offsetHeight / 2 );
            return [posx, posy];
    }
    return{
        newData: newData
    }
})();
```

The Code Explained

Table 10-4 explains the code in Game.js in more detail.

Table 10-4. Game.js explained

```var windowWidth = window.innerWidth;``` ```var windowHeight = window.innerHeight;```	The window width and height of the browser are used multiple times in the code so it makes sense to put them in their own variables. It means you only need to make two calls to the window function in your code.
```var material = new THREE.MeshLambertMaterial``` ```({ color: 0x00ff00 });```	In Listing 10-1 the material on the paddle used a THREE.MeshBasicMaterial. This scene uses a MeshLamabertMaterial as the basic material doesn't respond to lights, while the lambert material does.

```var light = new THREE.DirectionalLight(0xe0e0e0);```
```light.position.set(5,2,5).normalize();```
```scene.add(light);```
	A new directional light is created, and its position is set and is added to the scene. Normalize makes sure that the new position is in the right direction.

```var newData = function(data){```
```updateScene(data);```
```}```
	The function newData is called by main.js when new data comes from the Arduino. When it is called it passes the data to the Game.js function updateScene(), which will then process the data and update the scene.

```var updateScene =```
```function(data){```
```...```
```}```
	The updateScene data has one argument, the data from the Arduino.

(continued)

Table 10-4. (*continued*)

`var screenCoordinates = getCoordinates();`	The getCoordintes() function is called; this is the function that works out the screen coordinates in relation to the browser windows coordinate system rather than the Three.js coordinate system. The coordinates are returned by the function and stored in a variable.
`var moveObjectBy;`	This variable will hold the amount the paddle should move by in the x-axis.

`var x = data[0];`
`var y = data[1];`
`var b = data[2];`
	The data from the Arduino contains information for the x-axis, y-axis. and the button; the variables hold the data from the relevant position in the array.

`x = x.substr(1);`
`y = y.substr(1);`
`b = b.substr(1);`
	The data from the Arduino contains an identifying character at the start, which is removed with the JavaScript substr() function.

`if(x > 5){`
`...`
`}`
	There are a series of if statements that check if the x and y data is greater or less than 5. If it is greater than 5 the position of the paddle will be updated in a positive direction; less than 5 will be updated in a negative direction.

`if(screenCoordinates[0] < windowWidth - 80){`
`...`
`}`
	Each of the if statements has another if statement inside it. It checks if the screen coordinates of the paddle are within the limits of the browser window; if it is the paddle can be moved.

(continued)

Table 10-4. (*continued*)

`moveObjectBy =` `moveObjectAmount(x);`	If the movement is for the x-axis the data from the Arduino is mapped to get a value for how much the paddle moves. The moveObjectAmount() function is passed to the Arduino value for x. The moveObjectBy variable holds the return value from that function.
`paddle.position.x = paddle.` `position.x + moveObjectBy;`	The paddle position is updated with the new value, adding it to the current position of the paddle.

`if(screenCoordinates[1] <`
`windowHeight  - 100){`
`   paddle.position.y =`
`   paddle.position.y - 0.2;`
`}`
	The change in the y position of the paddle is constant, so it will be either +0.2 or -0.2 depending on the position of the joystick. The new value is added to the current position of the paddle in the y-axis.

`renderer.render(scene, camera);`	When all the if statements have been resolved, the renderer is called to update the scene.

`var moveObjectAmount =`
`function(x){`
`...`
`}`
	The moveObjectAmount() function takes one argument, the value of x from the Arduino.

`var output = scaleInput(x);`	The scaledInput() function is called, passing the x value, and the return value from this call is put into a variable.
`output = output/10;`	10 divides the return value. This makes it small enough to increment the x value of the paddle.

(*continued*)

Table 10-4. (*continued*)

`output = Math.round(output * 10) / 10;`	The value is then rounded to 1 decimal place.
`return output;`	The value is returned to the calling function.

`var scaleInput=function(input)`
`{`
`...`
`}`
	The scaleInput() function has one argument, a number that needs to be mapped.

`var xPositionMin = -4;` `var xPositionMax = 4;`	Two variables hold the minimum and maximum number the input number can be mapped to.
`var inputMin = 1;` `var inputMax = 10;`	Two variables hold the minimum and maximum number the input could be.

`var percent = (input -`
`inputMin) / (inputMax -`
`inputMin);`
`var output = percent *`
`(xPositionMax - xPositionMin)`
`+ xPositionMin;`
	The mapped value is calculated.

`var getCoordinates =`
`function() {`
`....`
`}`
	The getCoordinates() function will find the current position of the paddle in Three.js coordinate space and convert the position to browser coordinates.

`var screenVector = new THREE.` `Vector3();`	A variable is created that holds a Three. js vector.

Make sure the Arduino is connected to your computer but with the serial monitor closed. Go to the root of the application in the console and type either nodemon index.js or node index.js to start the server. Go to http://localhost:3000 and open the page.

ADD AN INTERACTIVE BALL

The ball needs to drop from the top of the browser window. It can either be caught by the paddle or miss the paddle. After either of those events, it needs to be moved to its initial y position and a random x position that is within the browser window and drop again. The paddle needs to change color to match the ball before the ball hits the paddle.

Open your Game.js file from Listing 10-7 and make the changes that are in bold in Listing 10-8.

Listing 10-8. Game.js first update

```
var Game = (function(){
    var windowWidth = window.innerWidth;
    var windowHeight = window.innerHeight;
    var colorArray = [0xff0000, 0x00ff00, 0x0000ff];
    var ballColor = Math.floor(Math.random() * 3);
    var colorChoice = 0;
    var collisionTimer = 15;
    var minMaxX = xMinMax(windowWidth);
    minMaxX = (parseFloat((minMaxX/10))-3.0.toFixed(1));

    var scene = new THREE.Scene();
    var camera = new THREE.PerspectiveCamera( 75, windowWidth/
    windowHeight, 0.1, 1000 );
    var renderer = new THREE.WebGLRenderer();
```

```
renderer.setSize( windowWidth, windowHeight );
document.body.appendChild( renderer.domElement );
var geometry = new THREE.BoxGeometry( 2, 0.2, 0.8 );
var material = new THREE.MeshLambertMaterial( { color: 0x00ff00 } );

var geometrySphere = new THREE.SphereGeometry( 0.3, 32, 32 );
    var materialSphere = new THREE.MeshLambertMaterial(
    {color: colorArray[ballColor]} );

var paddle = new THREE.Mesh( geometry, material );

var ball = new THREE.Mesh( geometrySphere, materialSphere );
updateBallPosition();

paddle.position.y = -2;
camera.position.z = 5;
var light = new THREE.DirectionalLight(0xe0e0e0);
light.position.set(5,2,5).normalize();

scene.add(light);
scene.add(new THREE.AmbientLight(0x656565));
scene.add( paddle );
scene.add( ball );
// renderer.render(scene, camera);
var newData = function(data){
    updateScene(data);
}
var updateScene = function(data){
    var screenCoordinates = getCoordinates();
    var moveObjectBy;
    var x = data[0];
    var y = data[1];
    var button = data[2];
    x = x.substr(1);
    y = y.substr(1);
    button = button.substr(1);
```

```
if(button ==="0"){
    updatePaddleColor();
}
if(x > 5){
    if(screenCoordinates[0] < windowWidth - 150){
        moveObjectBy = moveObjectAmount(x);
        paddle.position.x = paddle.position.x +
        moveObjectBy;
    }
} else if (x < 5){
    if(screenCoordinates[0] > 0 + 150){
        moveObjectBy = moveObjectAmount(x);
        paddle.position.x = paddle.position.x +
        moveObjectBy;
    }
}
if(y > 5){
    if(screenCoordinates[1] < windowHeight  - 100){
        paddle.position.y = paddle.position.y - 0.2;
    }
} else if (y < 5){
    if(screenCoordinates[1] > 0 + 300){
        paddle.position.y = paddle.position.y + 0.2;
    }

}
renderer.render(scene, camera);
}

var moveObjectAmount = function(x){
    var scaledX = scaleInput(x);
    scaledX = scaledX/10;
    scaledX = Math.round(scaledX * 10) / 10;
    return scaledX;
}
```

```
var scaleInput=function(input){
    var xPositionMin = -4;
    var xPositionMax = 4;
    var inputMin = 1;
    var inputMax = 10;
    var percent = (input - inputMin) / (inputMax - inputMin);
    var outputX = percent * (xPositionMax - xPositionMin) +
    xPositionMin;
    return outputX;
}
var getCoordinates = function() {
        var screenVector = new THREE.Vector3();
        paddle.localToWorld( screenVector );
        screenVector.project( camera );
        var posx = Math.round(( screenVector.x + 1 ) *
        renderer.domElement.offsetWidth / 2 );
        var posy = Math.round(( 1 - screenVector.y ) *
        renderer.domElement.offsetHeight / 2 );
        return [posx, posy];
}

var updatePaddleColor = function(){
    colorChoice++;
    if(colorChoice === 3){
        colorChoice = 0;
    }
     paddle.material.color.setHex( colorArray[colorChoice]);
}
function randomPosition(num){
    var newPostion = (Math.random() * (0 - num) + num).toFixed(1);
    newPostion *= Math.floor(Math.random()*2) == 1 ? 1 : -1;

    return newPostion;
}
```

```
function xMinMax(input){
    xPositionMin = 4;
    xPositionMax = 184;

        xWindowMin = 200;
        xWindowMax = 2000;

        var percent = (input - xWindowMin) / (xWindowMax -
        xWindowMin);
        var outputX = percent * (xPositionMax - xPositionMin) +
        xPositionMin;
        return outputX;
    }
    function updateBallPosition(){
            xPos = randomPosition(minMaxX);
            ball.position.y = 5;
            ball.position.x = xPos;
            ballColor = Math.floor(Math.random() * 3);
            ball.material.color.setHex( colorArray[ballColor]);
    }
    var animate = function () {
        var firstBB = new THREE.Box3().setFromObject(ball);
        var secondBB = new THREE.Box3().setFromObject(paddle);
        var collision = firstBB.isIntersectionBox(secondBB);
        if(!collision){
        collisionTimer = 15;
        if(ball.position.y > (paddle.position.y - 0.5)){
            ball.position.y -= 0.08;
        } else {
            updateBallPosition();
        }
    }
        if(collision){
            if(collisionTimer > 0){
                collisionTimer = collisionTimer -1;
            } else {
```

```
            updateBallPosition();
            }
        }
        renderer.render(scene, camera);
        requestAnimationFrame( animate );
    };
    animate();
    return{
        newData: newData
    }
})();
```

The Code Explained

Table 10-5 explains the code in Game.js first update in more detail.

Table 10-5. Game.js *first update explained*

`var colorArray = [0xff0000,`
`0x00ff00, 0x0000ff];`
`var ballColor = Math.floor`
`(Math.random() * 3);`
`var colorChoice = 0;`
	An array containing three color values is held in a variable. This array is cycled through to change the color of the paddle each time the joystick button is pressed. The colorChoice variable holds the array position for the paddle color. The color of the ball is a random choice from the array. The JavaScript Math.random() function is used to choose a number between 0 and 3.

`var collisionTimer = 15;`	When there is a collision between the ball and the paddle, the ball will be moved to its initial y position and then fall again. So it doesn't disappear as soon because they touch a timer that is set and counts down when there is a collision.

(continued)

Table 10-5. (*continued*)

`var minMaxX =` `xMinMax(windowWidth);`	When calculating the ball's new x position, it needs to be within the width of the current browser window. The function xMinMax is called and passed to the current browser window width. This window width will be mapped to a number that will keep the ball inside the browser window. The return value is stored in a variable.

`minMaxX =`
`(parseFloat((minMaxX/10))-`
`3.0.toFixed(1));`
	The return value is divided by 10 so it fits within the Three.js coordinate system. The toFixed() function sets it to one decimal place. The toFixed() function returns a string.

`updateBallPosition();`	The ball's starting position needs to be reset throughout the game, and the updateBallPosition() function does this.
`// renderer.render(scene,` `camera);`	This line has been commented out as it can be removed, and the call to render the scene now happens when the ball animates or the paddle moves.

`if(button ==="0"){`
`updatePaddleColor();`
`}`
	There is a check to see if the data from the joystick button is "0"; if it is the paddle color is changed by calling the updatePaddleColor() function.

(*continued*)

Table 10-5. (*continued*)

```var updatePaddleColor = function(){ colorChoice++; if(colorChoice === 3){ colorChoice = 0; } paddle.material.color.setHex (colorArray[colorChoice]); }```	The colorChoice variable is used as the index for the array of colors. As the paddle loops around the array, the variable is incremented by 1. This is so if colorChoice becomes 3 (outside the array index), it is changed to 0. The material color on the paddle is then changed.
```function randomPosition(num){ var newPostion = (Math. random() * (0 - num) + num). toFixed(1); newPostion *= Math.floor (Math.random()*2) == 1 ? 1 : -1; return newPostion; }```	The function takes a number and works out a new random number between 0 and the number it was passed. It then makes it randomly either positive or negative. The function is used to find a new y position for the ball.
```function updateBallPosition(){ xPos = randomPosition (minMaxX); ball.position.y = 5; ball.position.x = xPos; ballColor = Math.floor(Math. random() * 3); ball.material.color.setHex (colorArray[ballColor]); }```	The function sets the initial position of the ball before it animates down. A random x position is found by calling the randomPosition() function. The initial position on the y stays the same; it is outside the top of the browser window. A random color for the ball is also selected.

(*continued*)

Table 10-5. (*continued*)

`var firstBB = new THREE.`
`Box3().setFromObject(ball);`
`var secondBB = new THREE.`
`Box3().setFromObject(paddle);`
	A box is created around the ball and the paddle. They are bounding boxes that fit around the objects and are used to check for a collision.

`var collision = firstBB.` `isIntersectionBox(secondBB);`	The isIntersectionBox() function checks if the first bounding box (the ball) is touching the second bound box (the paddle). The variable collision holds the return value: true if it is touching, false if it isn't.

`if(!collision){`
`  collisionTimer = 15;`
`  if(ball.position.y >`
`  (paddle.position.y - 0.5)){`
`  ball.position.y -= 0.08;`
`  } else {`
`updateBallPosition();`
`}`
`}`
	If the collision variable is false the collisionTimer stays at 15. There is then a check to see if the ball position is below the paddle position; if it is the ball resets to its initial y position and starts animating down again. If it's not then the ball keeps falling down.

`if(collision){`
`        if(collision`
`        Timer > 0){`
`        collisionTimer =`
`        collisionTimer -1;`
`        } else {`
`        updateBall`
`        Position();`
`        }`
`        }`
	If there is a collision there is a check to see if the collisionTimer is greater than 0, and 1 depreciates the collisionTimer. When it has reached 0 the ball is reset to its initial y position and starts animating down again.

(*continued*)

If you restart the server, you should now be able to catch the falling ball with the paddle. When you catch it, it should wait a split second and then start falling again. You should also be able to change the color of the paddle.

UPDATE INDEX.EJS

The final steps are to score the game, create a countdown clock, and have a way to start and restart the game. The first thing is to update the index.ejs with elements and scripts for the score and clock and create the main.css file. Open up the index.ejs file from Listing 10-5, and update it with the code in bold in Listing 10-9.

Listing 10-9. Upated index.ejs

```
<html>
    <head>
        <title>three.js game</title>
        <link href="/css/main.css" rel="stylesheet" type="text/css">
    </head>
    <body>

    <div id = "again" class="hidden">
        <h1>you scored <span id="current-score"></span></h1>
        <h2 id="replay">PLAY AGAIN</h2>
    </div>
    <div id="start">
        <h1>start game</h1>
    </div>

    <div id="score">
        <h1>points: <span id="points"></span></h1>
        <div id="timer">
            <h1 id="countdown"><time></time></h1>
        </timer>
    </div>
```

```
        <script src="/socket.io/socket.io.js"></script>
        <script src="https://cdnjs.cloudflare.com/ajax/libs/three.
        js/r71/three.js"></script>
        <script src="javascript/Points.js"></script>
        <script src="javascript/Countdown.js"></script>
        <script src="javascript/Game.js"></script>
        <script src="javascript/main.js"></script>
        </body>
</html>
```

You'll notice that the CSS has gone and there is now a link to a CSS file. There are a number of new div elements; these show the points and score as well as start and play again button.

The order the scripts are in is important. A function in Countdown.js won't be recognized by Game.js if the script is added after Game.js.

The HTML Explained

Table 10-6 explains the code for the updated index.ejs file in more detail.

Table 10-6. *updated index.ejs explained*

`<div id = "again"` `class="hidden">`	This div will appear when the game is over; it has a class of "hidden" which is removed when the game is over. The implementation of this is in the CSS.
`<h1>you scored <span id=` `"current-score"></span></h1>`	Using JavaScript the final score will be displayed in this element.
`<h2 id="replay">` `PLAY AGAIN</h2>`	By pressing "PLAY AGAIN" a new game starts; this is implemented in JavaScript.
`<h1>points: <span id=` `"points"></span></h1>`	This element will update when the points get updated.
`<h1 id="countdown"><time>` `</time></h1>`	This element holds the countdown clock. It is updated using JavaScript.

CREATE MAIN.CSS

Open or create a file called main.css in public/css and copy the CSS from
Listing 10-10.

Listing 10-10. main.css

```
*{
    margin: 0;
    padding: 0;
}
body {
    margin: 0;
}
body {
    font-family: Verdana, Arial, sans-serif;
}
canvas {
    width: 100%; height: 100%
    z-index: -1;
}
#start{
    position: absolute;
    left: 30;
    top: 40;
    color: white;
    cursor: pointer;
    background: red;
    z-index: 10;
}
#start h1{
    padding: 6px;
}
```

```
#score{
    position: absolute;
    left: 30;
    top: 10;
    color: white;
    width: 200px;
    height: 120px;
}
#score h1{
    font-size: 16px;
}
#again{
    position: absolute;
    left: 30;
    top: 40;
    color: white;
    cursor: pointer;
    z-index: 10;
}
#again h2{
    margin-top: 4px;
}
#replay{
    cursor: pointer;
    z-index: 11;
    background: red;
}
.hidden{
    visibility: hidden;
}
```

The CSS Explained

You want the score and countdown clock to be within the game. Because of this, they have to be positioned absolutely on the page. These elements also have to have a higher z-index than the canvas. The z-index specifies the order the elements are stacked on top of each other. Elements with a lower z-index are placed below those with a higher z-index. Table 10-7 explains the CSS in main.css in more detail.

Table 10-7. main.css explained

`canvas {`
`    width: 100%; height: 100%`
`    z-index: -1;`
`}`
	The canvas is set to the width and height of the web browser. The canvas is given a z-index of -1, and it needs to be behind the elements that need to be clicked on.

`position: absolute;`
`left: 30;`
`top: 40;`
	The elements with an id of "start," "score," "again," and "replay" all are positioned absolutely on the browser page with the CSS command position: absolute. They then need to be given the position on the page using the left or right command, and the top or bottom command.

`cursor: pointer;`	An element with this command changes the cursor to a pointer whenever it goes over it.
`z-index: 11;`	Specify the z-index for an element.

CREATE POINTS.JS

You need to write the JavaScript to work out and display the points. Open or
create a file called Points.js in public/javascript and copy the code in
Listing 10-11 into it.

Listing 10-11. Points.js

```javascript
var Points = (function(){
    var points = 0;
    var pointDisplay = document.getElementById("points");
    var resetPoints = function(){
        points = 0;
    }
    var updatePoints = function(num){
        points = points + num;
        pointDisplay.innerHTML = points;
    }
    var getPoints = function(){
        return points;
    }
    return{
        resetPoints: resetPoints,
        updatePoints: updatePoints,
        getPoints: getPoints
    }
})();
```

The Code Explained

Table 10-8 explains the code in Points.js in more detail.

Table 10-8. Points.js explained

```var updatePoints = function(num){ points = points + num; pointDisplay.innerHTML = points; }```	When this function is called it is passed a positive or negative number, the points variable is updated, and the innerHTML of the element with the id of "points" is updated.
```var getPoints = function(){ return points; }```	This function returns the current points.

CREATE A COUNTDOWN CLOCK

You need to have a countdown clock to time the game. A Boolean variable controls when the countdown clock starts and stops. When the variable "stopGame" is false, the clock will run. The function that runs the clock checks each loop to see if the clock is at zero; if it is the variable "stopGame" is set to true. It has a function that returns the value of "stopGame" that can be used by other scripts to check if the game should be over.

If has a function called add, which lets other scripts start the clock. Within the function are checks on the current time as well as a ternary operator that checks where zeros should be for the display of the clock.

A ternary operator is a different form of an if/else statement. The if else statement

```
if(condition){
    do something
} else{
    do a different thing
}
```

can be written as

```
var statementResult = (condition) ? do something : do a
different thing;
```

The : separate the if and else results

You can set the hours, minutes, and seconds that you want the game to run with the countdown clock within the init() function.

Open or create the file Countdown.js in the public/javascript folder and copy in the code from Listing 10-12.

Listing 10-12. Countdown.js

```
var Countdown = (function(){
    var countdown = document.getElementById('countdown');
    var seconds;
    var minutes;
    var hours;
    var stopGame;
    var init = function(){
        hours = 0;
        seconds = 25;
        minutes = 1;
    }
    var add = function(stop){
        stopGame = stop;
        seconds--;
```

```
        if(seconds === 0 && minutes === 0){
            stopGame = true;
        }
        if(seconds < 0){
            seconds = 59;
            minutes--;
        }
        countdown.textContent = (hours ? (hours > 9 ? hours :
        "0" + hours) : "00") + ":" + (minutes ? (minutes > 9 ?
        minutes : "0" + minutes) : "00") + ":" + (seconds > 9 ?
        seconds : "0" + seconds);
        if(!stopGame){
            setTimeout(add, 1000);
        }
    }
    var getStopGame = function(){
        return stopGame;
    }

    return{
        init:init,
        add: add,
        getStopGame: getStopGame
    }
})();
```

The Code Explained

Table 10-9 explains the code in Countdown.js in more detail.

Table 10-9. *Countdown.js explained*

| ```
var add = function(stop){
...
}
``` | The function is passed one augment, a Boolean. The function is used by another script to start the clock. |
| ```
stopGame = stop;
``` | The variable stopGame is given the value passed to it. |
| ```
seconds--;
``` | The seconds are decremented. |
| ```
if(seconds === 0 &&
minutes === 0){
        stopGame = true;
}
``` | There is a check to see if seconds and minutes are at 0, and if they are it's the end of the game and the variable stopGame becomes true. |
| ```
if(seconds < 0){
seconds = 59;
minutes--;
}
``` | There is then a check if just seconds are 0; if they are it means that the minutes need to be decremented and seconds becomes 59. |
| ```
countdown.textContent =
(hours ? (hours > 9 ? hours :
"0" + hours) : "00") + ":" +
(minutes ? (minutes > 9 ?
minutes : "0" + minutes) : "00") +
":" + (seconds > 9 ? seconds :
"0" + seconds);
``` | A ternary operator is used to check what leading numbers should be in the output string: for example, there should be a 0 before the minute's variables if minutes are less than 9. The string that results updates the clock element on the browser page. |
| ```
if(!stopGame){
        setTimeout(add, 1000);
}
``` | If the game is still playing the countdown should keep running so the setTimeout calls the add function again after 1000 milliseconds (1 second). |
| ```
var getStopGame = function(){
    return stopGame;
}
``` | This function returns the current value of stopGame. |

UPDATE GAME.JS

The Game.js file has to be updated to include the clock and the score.
Open up the Game.js file from Listing 10-8 and copy in the code in bold from
Listing 10-13.

Listing 10-13. Game.js second update

```
var Game = (function(){
    var currentScore = document.getElementById('current-score');
    var playAgainElement = document.getElementById('again');

    var windowWidth = window.innerWidth;
    var windowHeight = window.innerHeight;

    var colorArray = [0xff0000, 0x00ff00, 0x0000ff];
    var ballColor = Math.floor(Math.random() * 3);
    var colorChoice = 0;

    var collisionTimer = 15;

    var stopGame;

    var minMaxX = xMinMax(windowWidth);
    minMaxX = (parseFloat((minMaxX/10))-3.0.toFixed(1));

    var scene = new THREE.Scene();
    var camera = new THREE.PerspectiveCamera( 75, windowWidth/
    windowHeight, 0.1, 1000 );
    var renderer = new THREE.WebGLRenderer();
    renderer.setSize( windowWidth, windowHeight );
    document.body.appendChild( renderer.domElement );
    var geometry = new THREE.BoxGeometry( 2, 0.2, 0.8 );
    var material = new THREE.MeshLambertMaterial( { color:
    0x00ff00 } );
    var geometrySphere = new THREE.SphereGeometry( 0.3, 32, 32 );
```

```
var materialSphere = new THREE.MeshLambertMaterial(
{color: colorArray[ballColor]} );
var paddle = new THREE.Mesh( geometry, material );
var ball = new THREE.Mesh( geometrySphere, materialSphere );
updateBallPosition();
paddle.position.y = -2;
camera.position.z = 5;
var light = new THREE.DirectionalLight(0xe0e0e0);
light.position.set(5,2,5).normalize();
scene.add(light);
scene.add(new THREE.AmbientLight(0x656565));
scene.add( paddle );
scene.add( ball );

var newData = function(data){
    updateScene(data);
}
var updateScene = function(data){
    var screenCoordinates = getCoordinates();
    var moveObjectBy;
    var x = data[0];
    var y = data[1];
    var button = data[2];
    x = x.substr(1);
    y = y.substr(1);
    button = button.substr(1);
    if(button ==="0"){
        updatePaddleColor();
    }
    if(x > 5){
        if(screenCoordinates[0] < windowWidth - 150){
            moveObjectBy = moveObjectAmount(x);
            paddle.position.x = paddle.position.x + moveObjectBy;
        }
```

```
    } else if (x < 5){
        if(screenCoordinates[0] > 0 + 150){
            moveObjectBy = moveObjectAmount(x);
            paddle.position.x = paddle.position.x + moveObjectBy;
        }
    }
    if(y > 5){
        if(screenCoordinates[1] < windowHeight  - 100){
            paddle.position.y = paddle.position.y - 0.2;
        }

    } else if (y < 5){
        if(screenCoordinates[1] > 0 + 300){
            paddle.position.y = paddle.position.y + 0.2;
        }

    }
    renderer.render(scene, camera);
}

var moveObjectAmount = function(x){
    var scaledX = scaleInput(x);
    scaledX = scaledX/10;
    scaledX = Math.round(scaledX * 10) / 10;
    return scaledX;
}

var scaleInput=function(input){
    var xPositionMin = -4;
    var xPositionMax = 4;

    var inputMin = 1;
    var inputMax = 10;

    var percent = (input - inputMin) / (inputMax - inputMin);
```

```
        var outputX = percent * (xPositionMax - xPositionMin) +
        xPositionMin;

        return outputX;
    }
    var getCoordinates = function() {
            var screenVector = new THREE.Vector3();
            paddle.localToWorld( screenVector );
            screenVector.project( camera );
            var posx = Math.round(( screenVector.x + 1 ) *
            renderer.domElement.offsetWidth / 2 );
            var posy = Math.round(( 1 - screenVector.y ) *
            renderer.domElement.offsetHeight / 2 );
            return [posx, posy];
    }

function randomPosition(num){
    var newPostion = (Math.random() * (0 - num) + num).toFixed(1);
    newPostion *= Math.floor(Math.random()*2) == 1 ? 1 : -1;

    return newPostion;
}

    function xMinMax(input){
        xPositionMin = 4;
        xPositionMax = 184;

        xWindowMin = 200;
        xWindowMax = 2000;

        var percent = (input - xWindowMin) / (xWindowMax -
        xWindowMin);
        var outputX = percent * (xPositionMax - xPositionMin) +
        xPositionMin;
        return outputX;
    }
```

```javascript
function updateBallPosition(){
        xPos = randomPosition(minMaxX);
        ball.position.y = 5;
        ball.position.x = xPos;
        ballColor = Math.floor(Math.random() * 3);
        ball.material.color.setHex( colorArray[ballColor]);
}

var updatePaddleColor = function(){
    colorChoice++;
    if(colorChoice === 3){
        colorChoice = 0;
    }

     paddle.material.color.setHex( colorArray[colorChoice]);
}

var animate = function () {
    var firstBB = new THREE.Box3().setFromObject(ball);
    var secondBB = new THREE.Box3().setFromObject(paddle);

    var collision = firstBB.isIntersectionBox(secondBB);

    if(!collision){
        collisionTimer = 15;
        if(ball.position.y > (paddle.position.y - 0.5)){
            ball.position.y -= 0.08;
        } else {
            Points.updatePoints(-1);
            updateBallPosition();
        }
    }

    if(collision){
        if(collisionTimer > 0){
            collisionTimer = collisionTimer -1;
        } else {
```

```
        var tempPaddleColor = paddle.material.color;
        var tempBallColor = ball.material.color;

            if((tempBallColor.r === tempPaddleColor.r)&&
            (tempBallColor.g === tempPaddleColor.g) &&
            (tempBallColor.b === tempPaddleColor.b) ){

        Points.updatePoints(1);
        } else {

        .   Points.updatePoints(-1);
        }
        updateBallPosition();
        }
    }
    renderer.render(scene, camera);
//  requestAnimationFrame( animate );

        stopGame = Countdown.getStopGame();

        if(!stopGame){
            requestAnimationFrame( animate );
        } else {
            updateBallPosition();
            var gamePoints = Points.getPoints();
            currentScore.innerHTML = gamePoints;
            playAgainElement.classList.remove("hidden");
        }
    };
//  animate();
    return{
        newData: newData,
        animate: animate
    }
})();
```

The Code Explained

Most of the changes are around the animate function. Now you only want the game to play when the player presses start. The animate function is now returned so it can be called by main.js, which has access to the start button. There is now a call to check the value of stopGame from the countdown script and only if it is false is the requestAnimateFrame() function called. If it is true the game is over. The ball position and points have to be reset, and the play again element has to be seen. Table 10-10 explains the code in the second update of Game.js in more detail.

Table 10-10. *Game.js second update explained*

```stopGame = Countdown.getStopGame();```	On each loop of the requestAnimateFrame, the current state of the countdown clock is needed; this is done by calling its getStopGame() function, and the result of the call is a Boolean placed in the stopGame variable.
```if(!stopGame){ requestAnimation Frame(animate); }```	If the variable stopGame is false, the game is still being played so requestAnimateFrame(animate) is called to run the animation loop again.
```else { updateBallPosition(); var gamePoints = Points.getPoints(); currentScore.innerHTML = gamePoints; playAgainElement.classList.remove("hidden"); }```	If the variable stopGame is true, the game is over and the else statement is called. This calls the function updateBallPosition() to reset the ball. It also gets the current gamePoints and sets the innerHTML on the HTML element with an id of "current-score." The HTML element with the id "again" has the class hidden removed so it can be seen on the web browser.
```// animate();```	The animate function is no longer called at this position; the animation is started in main.js.

UPDATE MAIN.JS

Finally, you need to update the main.js file from Listing 10-6, open it, and copy in the code in bold from Listing 10-14.

Listing 10-14. main.js updated

```
(function(){
    var socket = io();
    var stopGame = false;
    var startElement = document.getElementById('start');
    var playAgainElement = document.getElementById('again');

    socket.on('data', function(data){
        Game.newData(data);
    });

    startElement.addEventListener("click", function(){
        Countdown.init();
        Countdown.add(stopGame);
        Points.updatePoints(0);
        Game.animate();
        startElement.classList.add('hidden');
    });

    playAgainElement.addEventListener("click", function(){
        stopGame = false;
        Points.resetPoints();
        Points.updatePoints(0);
        Countdown.init();
        Countdown.add(stopGame);
        Game.animate();
        playAgainElement.classList.add("hidden");
    })
})();
```

The Code Explained

When a player clicks the start button, the game needs to begin. At the end of the game, the play again button appears, and when the player clicks on it the game needs to play again. Both of these actions happen from the main.js file.

Variables hold references to HTML elements with the id of "start" and "again." They have click event listeners attached to them that call functions to start the game and update the front end. Table 10-11 explains the code in the updated main.js file in more detail.

Table 10-11. main.js update explained

`var stopGame = false;`	A variable holds the Boolean value false; this will be passed to the countdown clock to start it.
`startElement.addEventListener ("click", function(){` `...` `});`	When the HTML start element is clicked, a number of functions are called.
`Countdown.init();`	The countdown clocks init method is called that sets the clock to its initial value.
`Points.updatePoints(0);`	The updatePoints method is called to reset the points to 0.
`Game.animate();`	The animate function is called in the Game.js file to start the ball animating.
`startElement.classList. add('hidden');`	The element holding the text Start is hidden on the browser page.
`playAgainElement. addEventListener ("click", function(){` `})`	When the HTML play again element is clicked, a number of functions are called to restart the game.

Now if you restart the server, the changes should be picked up. You should be able to play the game if you go to http://localhost:3000 on a web browser.

Summary

This chapter has given you the basics needed to create an application with Three.js and how you can use it with an Arduino. Being able to use complex animations on a web page really opens up the possibilities for interactions with an Arduino.

Throughout this book, new JavaScript and Arduino concepts have been introduced to give you a basic understanding of the technology and the code. These basic structures can be built upon to make evermore complex and interesting projects.

APPENDIX A

Arduino Community And Components

If you want to learn more about Arduino and build new projects, there is a lot of support on- and offline. Components are easy to source with a number of websites available as well as shops selling a range of Arduino boards, components, and peripherals.

Arduino Community

The maker community is very friendly and helpful and a good place to start if you want to keep learning about Arduino and produce projects with electronic components. There are maker spaces around the world that you can join; they often hold workshops and events for non-members. There is a good list of them on the hacker space website `https://wiki.hackerspaces.org/List_of_Hacker_Spaces`.

There are also Fab labs around the world. It started as a project at MIT and has grown. You can join a Fab lab and get access to its equipment. There is a list of Fab labs on their website `https://www.fablabs.io/labs`.

There is also a big online community that publishes their projects on different sites. These include Instructables `http://www.instructables.com/`, hackster.io `https://www.hackster.io/arduino`, and the Arduino website `https://playground.arduino.cc/Projects/Ideas`.

© Indira Knight 2018
I. Knight, *Connecting Arduino to the Web*, https://doi.org/10.1007/978-1-4842-3480-8

There are a number of books by Apress on different areas of Arduino programming including *Arduino Music and Audio Projects* (2015), by Mike Cook, https://www.apress.com/us/book/9781484217207; *Building Arduino Projects for the Internet of Things* by Adeel Javed (2016), https://www.apress.com/us/book/9781484219393; and *Coding for Arduino* by Robert Dukish (2018), https://www.apress.com/us/book/9781484235096.

Arduino Components

There are a number of places you can buy components for an Arduino; most of them are online but others have stores as well. It's also worth checking out if there are stores in your area that sell electronic components.

The Arduino Store

https://store.arduino.cc/

The Arduino Store is online and sells Arduino boards as well as starter kits, books, and other components.

RS Components

https://uk.rs-online.com/web/

RS Components sells electrical and industrial components online and they also have a number of branches throughout the United Kingdom.

Cool Components

https://coolcomponents.co.uk/

You can buy Arduino boards and components as well as other products for electronic projects.

SparkFun

`https://www.sparkfun.com/`

On the SparkFun site you can shop for electrical components as well as view tutorials and blog posts. They also have a list of SparkFun distributors around the world.

Adafruit

`https://www.adafruit.com/`

Adafruit makes their own components and boards as well as sell other brands. They sell a number of kits and project packs. They also have tutorials and videos on their site.

Cooking hacks

`https://www.cooking-hacks.com/`

Cooking hacks sell Arduino boards, kits, and shields as well as a range of sensors.

Farnell

`http://www.farnell.com/`

Farnell sell a wide range of products including Arduino boards, sensors, and peripherals.

Amazon

`https://www.amazon.com`

You can find Arduino and electronic components on Amazon.

APPENDIX B

More Front End Development

If you want to continue learning JavaScript, there are a lot of good resources to help. Even when you are confident with coding in JavaScript, you will still have questions and need a reference to how the code works.

The Mozilla documents, MDN web docs `https://developer.mozilla.org/en-US/`, are great; they are written by developers and are continually updated. They explain different JavaScript concepts and syntax and give examples of how to use them.

Stackoverflow is also very useful; anyone can post a question about programming that the development community answers, `https://stackoverflow.com/`.

Also check out your local Meetups, `https://www.meetup.com/`. There are lots of coding and tech groups, and it's good to see what people are working on, show what you are working on, ask questions, and learn.

If you are interested in web development and design, A List Apart `http://alistapart.com/` is a good site; it has articles that really explore all aspects of web development.

JavaScript

This book will give you a foundation in the programming concepts and techniques of JavaScript; however, if you would like to know more there are a lot of resources including books, videos, and online tutorials that go deeper into the language and JavaScript Frameworks. One online resource I have found really useful is on GitHub and is called "You Don't Know JS" `https://github.com/getify/You-Dont-Know-JS`.

ES6 and Beyond

When the ES6 standard was released, it was a big change for web developers. It allowed developers to make really complex web applications. There were syntax changes and new functionality. JavaScript is still changing, and if you decide you want to learn more about JavaScript, newsletters such as *JavaScript Weekly* help you keep up with the changes; see `http://javascriptweekly.com/`.

Three of the major changes were block scope, constants, and arrow functions.

Block Scope

When you create a variable inside a function, that variable can be referred to inside the function and not outside it; its scope is within the function. This means the application won't get confused when there are variables with the same name in your code that are in different functions.

In JavaScript there are block statements; these are normally conditional statements such as the if statement or the while statement. Before ES6, variables in block statements didn't have scope just within the block statements. Variables in block statements could be accessed by other parts of the code. ES6 added a new keyword to create a variable called let, and let can be used in block statements to declare a variable with block scope. The code in Listing B-1 doesn't use let.

Listing B-1. A variable in a block statement without block scope

```
if(true){
    var number = 5;
    console.log("number inside if statement = " + number);
    //number will be 5
}
console.log("number outside if statement = " + number);
//number will be 5
```

The variable number does not have its own scope within the if statement so the console log outside the if statement will have access to the variable number. The code in Listing B-2 uses the let keyword to create a variable.

Listing B-2. A variable defined with the let keyword has block scope

```
if(true){
    let number = 5;
    console.log("number inside if statement = " + number);
    //number will be 5
}
console.log("number outside if statement = " + number); //
nothing is logged out
Uncaught ReferenceError: number is not defined
```

As the variable number inside the if statement is created using let, its scope is inside the if statement. There is an error when the console log outside the if statement is called. It does not have access to the variable number.

Constants

A number of programming languages allow you to create constants. These are values that can't be changed when the program is running. This is very useful as you can't make a mistake and change a value that you want to be constant. In ES6 the const keyword was introduced. Variables defined with this keyword can't be changed later in the code; if you try to you will get an error. Variables defined with const also have block scope. You can create a constant variable by using the const keyword rather than var. The code in Listing B-3 shows how a reassignment to a variable defined as const causes an error in the code.

Listing B-3. A example of creating a variable with the const keyword

```
const number = 10;
console.log(number);   //10

number = 11;
console.log(number); //10
Uncaught TypeError: Assignment to constant variable
```

If you ran that code you would get an error and the value of number would remain 10, as you can't change a constant.

Arrow Functions

ES6 introduced a new way to write functions, arrow functions. Arrow functions are a more concise way of writing functions, and also have a different functionality. Listing B-4 shows an arrow function.

Listing B-4. An arrow function

```
var subtract = (x,y) => x - y;
console.log(subtract(3,2));
```

Listing B-5 shows the same function written without an arrow.

Listing B-5. A function written without an arrow function

```
var subtract = function(x,y){
    return x - y;
}

console.log(subtract(3,2));
```

The arrow function has an implicit return, so you don't have to write return. If there is only one statement, you don't need parentheses around the statement.

JavaScript Frameworks

There are a number of Frameworks for JavaScript that can impose a structure on your code. A few of these are React, Angular, and Ember. If you are creating a complex JavaScript application it helps to use a framework as it can set a structure for the application and allow it to be built in modules with specific functions.

React

React was created at Facebook and released in 2013. With it you can create components on a web page that can be updated with data without reloading the whole page. The components are written in JSX, a syntax extension of JavaScript. It can speed up the running of a page as it uses a virtual DOM. The virtual DOM is a copy of the actual DOM, and any changes to the page are calculated on the virtual DOM first so that the actual page can then be updated more efficiently. There are some good online tutorials to get started with react; a couple are https://egghead.io/courses/start-learning-react and https://egghead.io/courses/getting-started-with-redux.

Angular

Angular.js is open source; it is mainly maintained by Google and was first released in 2010. It implements the MVC (Model, View, Controller) design pattern, which separates the data (the model), from the view (the page) with a controller that is in between the users' interactions with the page and the model. In 2016 a new version of Angular was released, and it is often called Angular 2. It isn't compatible with Angular.js, and it no longer uses the MVC pattern and has a different syntax and uses ES6.

Ember

Ember was released in 2011 and is maintained by the Ember core team. It is based on the Model-view-viewmodel pattern.

Databases

In this book data is stored in variables; variables are good ways to store small amounts of data that you don't want to keep long term. On a web page a variable will store data until the page is refreshed, and then it will reset to its initial value. On a web server a variable will store data until the server is restarted, and then the variable will reset to its initial value. Once you start collecting a lot of data that you want to keep, analyze, and display, you will need to store it on a database. With a database you can use queries to filter your data and return values with certain relationships. For example, if your database held information about tomatoes you could find the names of all medium-sized tomatoes that are yellow.

There are a number of different databases you can use with Node.js, which can be SQL or NoSQL. SQL (standard query language) is a language for managing relational databases, databases that have tables that have a relationship between each other. In NoSQL databases, the data is not stored in tabular form.

A common database used with Node.js is MongoDB. It is a NoSQL database, which stores the data in a JSON-like format. CouchDB is another NoSQL database that uses JSON to store the data.

You can also use SQL databases. MySQL is a common SQL database and there are a number of Node.js modules to implement it. PostgreSQL is another SQL database you can use. It is normally referred to as Postgres.

Node.js Template Engines

There are a number of different template engines apart from ejs that can be used with Node.js; some of them are the following:

Jade `http://jade-lang.com/`

Handlebars `http://handlebarsjs.com/`

Dust.js `http://www.dustjs.com/`

Pug `https://pugjs.org/api/getting-started.html`

It's worth trying a number of engines and finding one that you like and feel comfortable using.

Serial Port

The SerialPort library is used throughout this book to pass data between an Arduino and a Node.js server. If you want to find out more about it, the GitHub page has a lot of detail about how it can be set up and the different functions you can use with it. See `https://github.com/EmergingTechnologyAdvisors/node-serialport#module_serialport--SerialPort.parsers`

johnny-five is a JavaScript robotics programming framework that lets you pass data with the serial port. You can find out more about it on the npm page at `https://www.npmjs.com/package/johnny-five`.

CSS

There are a lot of good resources for finding out more about CSS. CSS-Tricks is a great site for learning CSS and finding out the latest developments; see `https://css-tricks.com/`. Sara Soueidan is a good person to follow on Twitter: @SaraSoueidan.

Flexbox

CSS-Tricks has a good tutorial on Flexbox, and other good tutorials are on interneting is hard at `https://internetingishard.com/html-and-css/flexbox/` and Tutorialzine at `https://tutorialzine.com/2017/03/css-grid-vs-flexbox`.

CSS Grid

The MDN web docs have a good explanation of the CSS grid layout at `https://developer.mozilla.org/en-US/docs/Web/CSS/CSS_Grid_Layout/Basic_Concepts_of_Grid_Layout` and Grid, by example, goes through grid basics and more advanced topics. See `https://gridbyexample.com/learn/`.

Data Visualization

Data visualization is a huge topic with a long history and a lot of research. There is a good website called bl.ocks `https://bl.ocks.org/`, which lists examples of D3.js visualizations, including the code. There are other libraries you can use other than D3.js to produce online data visualizations.

Data Visualization Libraries

There are a few JavaScript libraries developed on top of D3.js and other libraries you can use to create JavaScript data visualizations. Some libraries produce one type of chart, so it can be a lightweight way to produce a timeline or force-directed charts.

NVD3.js

> http://nvd3.org/
>
> A collection of reusable charts that were built with D3.js.

Processing.js

> http://processingjs.org/
>
> Processing.js is similar to processing but using JavaScript. Processing was developed to get artists and designers into programming. You can use it to create data visualizations, animations, and games, among other things.

Paper.js

> http://paperjs.org
>
> A library that lets you use code to create and animate vector graphics.

Arbor.js

> http://arborjs.org/
>
> A library for creating force-directed graphs.

Sigma.js

> http://sigmajs.org/
>
> A library for drawing network graphs.

Data Visualization Resources

If you are interested in learning more and developing data visualizations, there are a lot of resources that can help.

Flowing Data

> `https://flowingdata.com`

> A good collection of articles and tutorials.

Eagereyes

> `https://eagereyes.org/`

> Robert Kosara's website, it contains posts on developments in data visualization.

Visualizing Data

> `http://www.visualisingdata.com/`

> The site is regularly updated with examples of online data visualizations; it's a good place to get inspiration and to see the latest visualizations.

Data Stories

> `http://datastori.es/`

> Data Stories is a podcast with discussions on data visualization.

Makeover Monday

> `http://makeovermonday.co.uk/`

> Makeover Monday publishes a chart and data set each week to let other people create and share new visualizations from that data.

Maps

You can use maps to visualize data; you can do this with D3.js but I really recommend also having a look at Mapbox. They have good tutorials for getting started and are continually adding new features. See `https://www.mapbox.com/mapbox-gl-js/api/`.

Color

Color is an important part of data visualization and choosing colors can be difficult, but there are online resources that help you choose colors.

ColorBrewer

> `http://colorbrewer2.org/`

> It will create a palate of colors for your visualization depending on a number of filters including if you want multi or single hue and the number of data classes. It also lets you choose a color-blind safe palette.

Color Picker for Data

> `http://tristen.ca/hcl-picker/#/hlc/6/1/15534C/E2E062`

> An interactive web tool to pick colors.

Index

A

© Indira Knight 2018
I. Knight, *Connecting Arduino to the Web*, https://doi.org/10.1007/978-1-4842-3480-8

Printed in the United States
By Bookmasters

Printed in the United States
By Bookmasters